PRAISE FO

Start Where You Are, But D... There,
Second Edition

"Milner is one of the premier voices in urban education. In the second edition of *Start Where You Are, But Don't Stay There,* he once again demonstrates why. Through an exploration of case studies he has conducted across urban settings, he uses his research and experiences to inform, inspire, and reimagine a way forward for stakeholders in education. This work beautifully strikes the delicate balance between the theoretical and practical through the provision of an academic framework that concurrently serves as a charge and challenge. Milner's 'opportunity-centered teaching' and the ideas that generate from it are essential to teaching and learning. This is a must-have book."

—**Christopher Emdin**, associate professor of science education, Teachers College, Columbia University

"Milner's book has been my constant companion as a teacher educator. This new edition serves to do more than demonstrate that this work is still relevant. Milner extends his theoretical insights—including his work on *relational efficacy* and *instructional fidelity*—in ways that will guide educators on their journey to becoming the educators they want to be. Milner's new edition should serve as a central text for all teacher education programs."

—**Maisha T. Winn**, Chancellor's Leadership Professor, School of Education, University of California, Davis

"Milner has written an important and powerful book. When this text was originally written, Milner's brilliant insights changed the pedagogical practice of educators around the country. With this second edition, we are even better equipped to understand how the educational experiences of the vulnerable are not due to a lack of talent or initiative, but considerable gaps in resources and opportunities. Milner builds on his rigorous conceptual and structural analysis by offering concrete strategies and solutions to practitioners of all backgrounds. While this is an invaluable resource to educators, it should be read by policy makers, administrators, scholars, and parents alike."

—**Marc Lamont Hill**, professor and Steve Charles Chair in Media, Cities, and Solutions, Temple University, and author of *Nobody: Casualties of America's War on the Vulnerable, from Ferguson to Flint and Beyond*

"In *Start Where You Are, But Don't Stay There,* Milner leverages his deep knowledge of teachers and teaching to build a bold framework for transforming schools for youth of color. Grounded in an understanding of robust and equitable teaching, the book offers a vision for addressing diversity and opportunity gaps and imagining new futures for youth of color. An important read for teachers and teacher educators."

—**Kris D. Gutiérrez**, professor and Carol Liu Chair in Educational Policy, Graduate School of Education, University of California, Berkeley

"Milner, one of the most influential education scholars, has rewritten one of the most important books for educators. The brilliance and usefulness of the first edition are elevated in this second edition. Its groundbreaking focus on 'opportunity-centered teaching' makes this text a must-read for all in our field."

—**Shaun R. Harper**, provost professor and Clifford and Betty Allen Chair in Urban Leadership, University of Southern California, Rossier School of Education

"Milner never disappoints. His writing is always clear, powerful, and centered where it needs to be, giving teachers practical tools and strategies to support student success. This book is no different. His concept of the opportunity gap gave the entire field of education a new language to boldly speak back to the relic idea of the achievement gap. Now, he has revised his timeless book, *Start Where You Are, But Don't Stay There,* to include a teaching approach that every teacher needs—'opportunity-centered teaching'—which transforms learning by recognizing the power of student-teacher relationships, community knowledge, and families working together for equity and justice. This book is more than a resource, it is what we desperately need to create successful schools."

—**Bettina Love**, associate professor, College of Education, University of Georgia

"In this revised edition of an important book, Milner writes truth to power and declares that students will do better once teachers *know* and *act* better. *Start Where You Are, But Don't Stay There* compels readers to understand how opportunity gaps engender achievement disparities. To close those gaps, Milner articulates that only when students are exposed to 'opportunity-centered teaching'—which he highlights by featuring exemplary educators steeped in the awareness of the racial, political, and economic realities of historically underserved students of color—then schooling will truly do its wonder."

—**Prudence Carter**, dean and professor of the Graduate School of Education at the University of California, Berkeley

Start Where You Are, But Don't Stay There

SERIES | RACE AND EDUCATION

Series edited by H. Richard Milner IV

OTHER BOOKS IN THIS SERIES

Urban Preparation
Chezare A. Warren

Truth Without Tears
Carolyn R. Hodges and Olga M. Welch

Millennial Teachers of Color
Edited by Mary E. Dilworth

Justice on Both Sides
Maisha T. Winn

Culturally Responsive School Leadership
Muhammad Khalifa

Science in the City
Bryan A. Brown

Race, Sports, and Education
John N. Singer

Start Where You Are, But Don't Stay There

Understanding Diversity, Opportunity Gaps, and Teaching in Today's Classrooms

SECOND EDITION

H. Richard Milner IV

HARVARD EDUCATION PRESS
CAMBRIDGE, MASSACHUSETTS

Paperback ISBN 978-1-68253-439-7
Library Edition ISBN 978-1-68253-440-3

Library of Congress Cataloging-in-Publication Data
Names: Milner, H. Richard, IV, author.
Title: Start where you are, but don't stay there : understanding diversity, opportunity gaps, and teaching in today's classrooms / H. Richard Milner IV.
Other titles: Race and education series.
Description: Second. | Cambridge, Massachusetts : Harvard Education Press, [2020] | Series: Race and education series | Includes bibliographical references and index. | Summary: "In the thoroughly revised second edition of Start Where You Are, But Don't Stay There, H. Richard Milner IV addresses the knowledge and insights required on the part of teachers and school leaders to serve students of color"— Provided by publisher.
Identifiers: LCCN 2019045275 | ISBN 9781682534397 (paperback) | ISBN 9781682534403 (library binding)
Subjects: LCSH: Multicultural education—United States. | Minorities—Education—United States. | Educational equalization—United States. | Teaching—Social aspects—United States. | Teachers—Training of—United States. | Teacher-student relationships—United States. | Teachers and community—United States.
Classification: LCC LC1099.3 .M56 2020 | DDC 370.117—dc23
LC record available at https://lccn.loc.gov/2019045275

Published by Harvard Education Press,
an imprint of the Harvard Education Publishing Group

Harvard Education Press
8 Story Street
Cambridge, MA 02138

Cover Design: Wilcox Design
Cover Photo: Rolf Bruderer via Getty Images

The typefaces used in this book are Minion and Helvetica Neue.

This revised edition of my book
is dedicated to my twin daughters:
Anna Grace Milner and Elise Faith Milner
(born July 30, 2010)

You are my heartbeats . . .

Contents

Preface to the Second Edition of *Start Where You Are, But Don't Stay There*

THE FIRST EDITION of *Start Where You Are, But Don't Stay There: Understanding Diversity, Opportunity Gaps, and Teaching in Today's Classrooms* was written and published in 2010 for pre- and in-service educators. By outlining what I called opportunity gaps, the book aimed to advance instructional and other educational practices that (better) meet the needs of students who are too often placed on the margins of schools and classrooms across the United States and beyond: Black and Brown students, students whose first language is not English, Muslim students, immigrant students, students with ability differences, LGBTQIA+ (lesbian, gay, bi, trans*, queer/questioning, intersex, agender/asexual) students, and students who live below the poverty line. I wanted to produce a text that supported teachers in more deeply developing the knowledge, attitudes, dispositions, understandings, mind-sets, skills, and consequently practices necessary to meet the needs of all young people. As I have worked with teachers in different teacher education programs in the United States and Canada, and as I have studied educational contexts from prekindergarten through high school, I attempted to capture what is essential to help educators address opportunity gaps.

As a former high school English teacher, I aspired to write the text that I wish had been available to me when I was in my own teacher education program and when I subsequently taught high school years ago. Moreover, as a teacher educator, I wrote in *Start Where You Are* what I believed to be foundational to educator learning and development across grade levels and subject areas. Ways to address gaps in opportunity were anchored in real-world classroom examples intended to increase teachers' understandings of themselves, others, and the places in which they would inevitably work. Many White teachers I worked with reported, for example, that they planned to return to their hometown with mostly White students to teach in the same schools they attended as students. These teachers did not necessarily understand how quickly school demographic trends are shifting across the United States. In short, schools as they were experienced by many teachers as students will no longer exist, at least in terms of their racial, linguistic, religious, and ethnic demographics.

But mostly, I wrote *Start Where You Are* to foster an ethos of studying, listening, and learning among teachers. A central theme of this book is that teachers can and do improve when they allow students to help them examine, reflect on, and improve their teaching practices. I wanted teachers to vicariously witness and experience other teachers—those both similar to and different from them in terms of gender, race, religion, socioeconomic status, sexual identity, language, ethnicity, and cultural background—learning from their students, taking responsibility when conflicts and challenges emerge, and assertively addressing opportunity gaps. Indeed, even the most accomplished and successful teachers have challenges and struggles. But when they develop the capacity and the will to do better, our students have a fighting chance for an educational experience that (1) transforms instead of oppresses, (2) liberates instead of limits, (3) propels instead of stifles, and (4) accelerates rather than remediates.

While the book was designed to help newer educators build practices that better aligned with student needs and realities, as I have traveled throughout the United States and beyond, more experienced educators, too, have consistently expressed to me the power of the book. For some educators, the book provides a much-needed reminder of what is necessary to improve their practices. For others, the book serves as a wake-up call that, as their students, families, and communities change, they—the schools—must shift as well. But I am perhaps most proud of the feedback that I receive from educators writ large (not only teachers) who share their appreciation for a text that describes the complexities and nuances of teaching and simultaneously provides examples of educators addressing gaps in opportunity. Addressing opportunity gaps is difficult work, and I hope this book provides good examples of teachers refusing to give up on students too often placed on the margins of teaching and learning. However, rather than a set of predetermined practices or prescriptions, the first edition provided insights into how educators think and how their mindsets shaped their practices.

As I worked with educators over the years, I yearned for a text that captured the principles that I outline to address what I call opportunity gaps. The framework of the first edition and the new, second edition covers issues of (1) race and color blindness; (2) culture and conflict; (3) expectations and rigor; (4) meritocracy and socioeconomic status; and (5) context and place. I believe this book has been able to bring together in one volume essential features necessary to support teachers in closing opportunity gaps. Drawing from my own research and that of others, the framework has been adopted in courses, teacher education programs, and school districts inside and outside of the United States. Researchers and scholars, too, have adopted, adapted, and drawn from the framework to describe and make sense of their own empirical research.

While evidence would suggest that the first edition of the book has made an important contribution to the field of education, and particularly to professional development, I have been asked consistently by colleagues within and outside of higher education to revise the text. To be frank, I am hopeful that the book will be used to support the preparation and development of teachers for many years to come. Also, after ten years of assigning the text and studying aspects of it that seem to be the most transformative as well as those that could use improvement, I offer here a revised book that maintains the assets of the first edition but also updates certain aspects to further support the learning of educators for the benefit of a dynamic group of students across different contexts: urban, suburban, rural, public, private, and otherwise.

FROM OPPORTUNITY GAPS TO OPPORTUNITY-CENTERED TEACHING: THE NEW EDITION

This new edition of *Start Where You Are* is a fully revised and updated version of the book I wrote more than ten years ago. Most important, in this new edition, I endeavor to expand my discussion and examples of opportunity gaps to those of *opportunity-centered teaching*. In other words, I demonstrate how opportunity-centered teaching addresses gaps in opportunity in schools, districts, and classrooms across the nation. Opportunity-centered teaching counters and disrupts gaps in opportunity in ways that can have a lasting impact on students, their families, and communities. Four interrelated principles shape the framework, which is designed to help teachers and other educators reimagine how they think about their students and build practices that advance student learning and development. Opportunity-centered teaching begins with and is grounded in the premise that relationship building and cultivation are essential to co-constructing a classroom environment that fosters excellence. A second tenet of opportunity-centered teaching concerns the importance of community knowledge and learning as ways to build alignment outside of school. A third tenet stresses the importance of understanding outside-of-school practices as well as those inside of school. In short, this tenet focuses on educators' considering how student engagements and interests outside of school should be drawn on inside of school to address opportunity gaps. In addition, opportunity-centered teaching insists that educators understand the psychological, social, emotional, and mental health of both themselves and their students as necessary for teaching and learning success.

What do educators need to know to be able to more effectively meet the needs of students? Indeed, all communities—regardless of the zip code—are deeply rich in human capital. But educators in schools may struggle to understand how to build on the many talents and assets of a community—perhaps because in order to recognize and acknowledge expertise in the community, we (as educators) must see the brilliance of the students with whom we work. As an educator, I have heard teachers and administrators from different racial, ethnic, and linguistic backgrounds talk about what their students, parents, and communities lack. But every single student in our schools should be viewed as a vessel of knowledge, knowing, and potential.

Finally, when I wrote the first edition of this book, I believed it would help the educators with whom I worked. Several thousand people have read the first edition; my hope now is that others will read this new edition and commit to building and improving their practices for the sake of students whose educational experiences fall far from what they should be. Indeed, as educators in the fight for social justice, equity, inclusion, and transformation, it is necessary for us to START WHERE WE ARE BUT NOT STAY THERE. Our students are counting on us.

Acknowledgments

I HAVE BEEN THINKING about revising this book for several years. When I told my wife, Shelley, that I thought summer 2019 would be the time for the revision, she looked at me, paused for a moment, then smiled and said, "Let's do it." I was a bit concerned because we had just made a major move from Pittsburgh, Pennsylvania, to Nashville, Tennessee, not even a year earlier. She is my "ride or die" partner. She brings out the very best in me. I remain thankful for a partner who understands and believes in the work of equity, diversity, and justice. For being a stellar partner and outstanding mother to our children, I am eternally thankful to Shelley.

I am also grateful to my parents, Henry III and Barbara Milner, for teaching me what it means to live life on purpose. What I appreciate most is how they taught me to see the good and the worth in others, especially those too often placed on the fringes of the mainstream. I am also thankful to my sister, Tanya, and brother, Reginald. As I am the youngest of three, my siblings have played an important role in my development. In addition, special recognition and appreciation to my mother-in-law, Margaret Banks (Mother Banks), who has been an "other mother" to my children and me over the years.

I stand on the shoulders of my elders both inside and outside of education. I honor the memory of my grandparents, great-grandparents, aunts, uncles, and cousins who have transitioned from this earth. I know they are "with" me on this journey.

I honor the memory and life of my earthly brother, Matthew Davis. Matthew pushed me to live my best life. I count Matt as one of the most important mentors I have had in life. In addition, I honor the memory of my research partner and dear friend, Margaret Smithey, who became my first real Vanderbilt colleague in 2001.

Few words can express my gratitude, appreciation, and love for my father-in-law, Willie Banks, who fought a fearless battle with cancer of the pancreas. Although the physicians predicted that he would live three months after the diagnosis, he defied the odds and lived three years. Father Banks was my "other father."

Finally, Tyrone Howard, John Singer, Mark Gooden, and William Tate are my brothers from another mother. They remain a source of strength in this journey toward justice in education!

Introduction

Start where you are, but don't stay there.

—AFRICAN SAYING

THERE ARE MOMENTS in our lives that help define and shape them, times and experiences that we never forget. I recall such a moment during my first semester of doctoral studies at The Ohio State University. I was nervous. I wondered if I "belonged" in graduate school. I worried that I would not succeed. And then it happened. Associate Dean Charles Hancock began his comments to a group of us, all first-semester doctoral students, with the African saying above: "*Start where you are, but don't stay there,*" he stated. I was astonished—simply stunned. I cannot share much with readers about what else occurred or was said during that meeting. All I can recall is that moment when he uttered those words. I knew then—right in that moment—that Dean Hancock had shared some wisdom with us that would forever change how I thought about my personal and professional life. He had encouraged us to embrace a lifelong cognitive, social, and emotional journey that would allow us to do our best work, realizing that we are never really finished learning and contributing to education and society. I immediately started to transfer and apply what he had shared to a range of experiences and emotions I was working through. He had spoken directly to me on that day as I wrestled with my decision to leave my comfortable teaching position in Columbia, South Carolina, and move to Columbus, Ohio, for doctoral study.

As I have thought about the many roles I have assumed and continue to assume in education, such as student, former high school teacher, teacher, teacher educator, social scientist, and researcher, I have pondered how to improve and move forward in these various aspects of my professional life. Moreover, as a father of two daughters, watching them grow and develop, I find something particularly educative about embracing life as a never-ending journey. In a similar way, I am hopeful that readers of this book—teachers, administrators, principals, school counselors, school psychologists, staff, graduate students, teacher educators, and researchers from within and outside of education—will critique, embrace, and learn from the ideas presented here, with the ultimate goal of improving their work and progressing in their own journey. The work of preparing teachers, for me, is a deeply personal endeavor, one that requires us to engage inwardly as we work to support others. The work of teaching is deeply political, and rather than criticizing the practices of others for the sake of an intellectual exercise, my hope is that readers find transferable features that can improve practices with students.

Each of us, from those early in our careers to those more seasoned, has room to grow and to improve. Thus, I invite readers to think about the lessons and the moments captured in this book as sites from which to learn and to grow. My goal in this book is not to beat up on teachers. As a former public school teacher, I believe that teachers are sometimes blamed for situations and issues far beyond their control. However, I do believe that most teachers can and must put forth more energy and effort to become more effective in the classroom with their students. Thus, educators, particularly White teachers, must critically examine their own biases, privileges, assumptions, worldviews, inconsistencies, racism, xenophobia, homophobia, sexism, and other forms of oppression on their journey to teach better and to teach more effectively. I encourage readers to strive to improve the practices that are in their control and that have a real bearing on students' opportunities to learn.

I care deeply about what happens to students, all students, in schools. I have been perplexed and baffled for many years, though, about why some students—students of color (Black and Brown students), students whose first language is not English, Muslim students, immigrant students, students with ability differences, LGBTQIA+ (lesbian, gay, bi, trans*, queer/questioning, intersex, agender/asexual) students, and students who live below the poverty line—too often struggle to succeed in schools. To be sure, in teacher education, we must better support teachers in building the essential knowledge, skills, attitudes, dispositions, mind-sets, and practices they need to embark upon their teaching journeys and, hopefully, to teach all students effectively.

Among the many questions I have pondered over the years are: How do teachers design learning environments that build on the many talents and strengths that preK–12 students bring into the classroom? What is essential for teachers and students to build the kinds of relationships that allow both teachers and students the space to "not stay there" as everyone improves academically, socially, psychologically, emotionally, and physically? How do (and should) we build learning ecologies that teach from, to, and through diversity in a classroom? Throughout my work with teachers and schools, I have focused my attention on inputs—tools, strategies, and mechanisms to support student learning—over outputs that too often focus narrowly on test scores. As emphasis on standardized testing intensifies, it is not difficult to ponder whether we are focusing on too much testing and not enough teaching.

TOO MUCH TESTING, NOT ENOUGH TEACHING

Educational researcher and teacher educator Gloria Ladson-Billings has concluded that in US society there is not so much an achievement gap as an "education debt" that the educational system owes to the many students it has poorly served.[1] Ladson-Billings challenged educational researchers and the field of education to question and rethink our overemphasis on achievement gap discourse and related practices. Her deep analyses provided a solid foundation for the field to reimagine educational research beyond achievement gaps and test scores. Ladson-Billings's critique helped shape my own view on the overreliance and overfocus on achievement gaps in education. Moreover, educational researcher and teacher educator Jacqueline Irvine suggests that a perceived achievement gap is the result of other gaps that seduce people into believing that an achievement gap actually exists.[2] Rather than focus on a perceived achievement gap, Irvine recommends that we shift our attention to closing the other gaps that exist in education; these include "the teacher quality gap; the teacher training gap; the challenging curriculum gap; the school funding gap; the digital divide gap; the wealth and income gap; the employment opportunity gap; the affordable housing gap; the health care gap; the nutrition gap; the school integration gap; and the quality childcare gap."[3]

From an ecological perspective, many teachers design the learning milieu believing that their students of color are underachievers, poorly prepared, and lagging behind their White classmates. Such a position can lead teachers into mind-sets and practices that do not recognize the strengths and expertise (even genius) among entire groups of students. While the achievement gap discourse in education usually focuses on students' scores on standardized tests, it also concerns student graduation rates, patterns in gifted and advanced placement and talent programs, and other measurable outcomes that allow comparisons between White students and other racial groups of students. Standardization, in many ways, is antithetical to diversity because it suggests that all students live and operate in homogeneous environments and are afforded equality of opportunity. In this way, standardization is the opposite of diversity. While on the one hand it is necessary to hold educators accountable for providing optimal learning opportunities for students, on the other hand, our instructional practices need to be tailored for students in ways that honor them as diverse human beings by building their intellectual, social, psychological, and emotional muscles to succeed academically.

My analyses of empirical research and policy reports will not allow me to accept a "eugenics" explanation for an "achievement gap"—that there is a "biological basis for the superiority of Whites."[4] Put simply, White people *are not, are not, are not* biologically, genetically, or innately superior to other groups in terms of intelligence or any other indicators. If educators agree with this reality—that no group of people is intellectually superior to another—then they should be willing to delve into the complex social maze of rationales for what are perceived as achievement gaps. Even at a time in US and world history when formal sanctions of slavery and Jim Crow have long since ended, there are still deeply ingrained social factors that inhibit certain populations of students from reaching their full capacity to learn. The question is: why?

In this book, I argue that we need to refocus attention away from an achievement gap and toward an opportunity gap. I invite readers to engage in a *paradigm and mind-set shift*—to alter their thinking, ideologies, belief systems, and overall worldviews in terms of how we socially construct achievement and success. Consider four important, interrelated questions regarding this necessary mind shift: (1) To what extent is achievement synonymous with learning? (2) What does it mean to experience learning opportunities in one school community in comparison to another? (3) Who decides what it means to achieve and why? (4) How do (and should) we address the kind of learning that never shows up on achievement measures—including high-stakes tests?

Critical theorist Michael Apple stresses that those of us in education must continue to question what knowledge is, how it is constructed and validated, and who decides the worth, value, and meanings of knowledge and knowledge construction.[5] I believe similar questions should be posed about achievement. As with knowledge, certain areas of achievement are privileged over others. In this sense, there are societal high and low cultural ways of looking at achievement and knowledge. For instance, in literacy, knowledge about traditional canonical texts from authors such as William Shakespeare and Charles Dickens is considered "high culture," while African American literature written by authors such as Zora Neale Hurston and James Baldwin may be classified as "low culture" (from a White-dominated societal perspective).

Some sociologists would argue that it is ineffectual to spend extensive amounts of time comparing one group with another.[6] I agree, and focusing on an achievement gap inherently forces us to compare culturally diverse students with White students without always understanding the reasons that undergird disparities and differences.

I will not spend pages comparing the opportunity gaps between White students and culturally diverse students. Rather, I invite readers to think about opportunity in a broader sense, as all students and teachers deserve to be engaged in opportunities that improve their lives. For instance, students from different racial and ethnic backgrounds bring assets into the classroom that should be maximized. Students in predominantly White settings should have opportunities to engage in race- and diversity-related learning opportunities as well. However, this kind of learning, where students are actively involved with understanding issues of diversity in preK–12 schools, may never show up on a standardized test, although developing such knowledge and awareness is important.

I am asking readers of this book to rethink their conceptions of why many students of color do not fare well in a range of schools across US society, from urban to suburban to rural settings, and why we focus on the measures of success and achievement that we do. It is important to understand that I am not suggesting that educators should not be concerned about achievement gaps and test scores. I realize that educators operate in systems that require them to focus on these matters. I understand that we should work to prepare all students for success on these examinations because they operate in an educational system that is steeped in traditional, White, classed, gendered notions of achievement.

However, if we can cultivate lifelong learners—those who are inquisitive, who pose insightful questions and push beyond the obvious and the traditional, who are empathetic and committed to collective advancement—we have a better chance of student success. In short, in this book, I demonstrate the importance of educators' thinking very seriously and deliberately about the interrelated nature of diversity, opportunity, and teaching in a range of different classroom spaces. As they build knowledge and practices, I am hopeful that their relational efficacy and instructional agility intensify.

RELATIONAL EFFICACY AND INSTRUCTIONAL AGILITY

Based on my many years of studying teachers' practices and talking with teachers about their work, I have found that it is difficult for teachers to teach their particular subject-matter area if they do not understand the diversity-opportunity nexus. As students become increasingly diverse, it is becoming more difficult to teach them and for teacher education programs, whether traditional or nontraditional, to prepare teachers. These diversity aspects include but are not limited to race, ethnicity, gender, sexual orientation, language, religion, ability, socioeconomic background, and geography. These general, more traditional (yet still essential) categories are complicated by individual circumstances, such as whether students are supported and encouraged to complete homework, whether parents have the ability and skill to help children complete their homework, whether students live in two-family homes, whether adequate financial resources are available to families (e.g., could parents hire a tutor to assist their children with homework?), and whether there is social, emotional, and psychological safety and support for students. While the factors just described focus on students' realities outside of school, the general features of diversity such as race, class, and gender are also exacerbated based on in-school realities, such as the number of years teachers have been teaching, their preparedness to work with a diverse cadre of learners, their knowledge of and ability to teach their content, the types of professional learning teachers experience, and the types of support, coaching, and mentoring educators receive. Moreover, students' experiences are also influenced by the types of school counselors available to them, technological and other resources available, discipline/punishment referral practices embedded in a school, club and extracurricular opportunities available, and the training and availability of psychologists and social workers.

This book addresses two critical aspects of the diversity-opportunity nexus in the classroom: (1) focusing on diversity and opportunity to better understand social relationships between educators and students, and (2) focusing on diversity and opportunity to incorporate and infuse those dimensions into curriculum and instructional practices. The first emphasis is on what I call *relational efficacy*—on teachers' confidence in their ability to develop the knowledge, insights, understandings, mind-sets, skills, abilities, and ultimately practices necessary to connect with, care about, and empathize with students and co-create learning contexts where students feel safe, affirmed, whole, and loved. In other words, I attempt to demonstrate in this book that teaching and learning are not only about teaching a subject. Opportunity and diversity connections require teachers to build relational efficacy—particularly when students are placed on the margins of learning and are underserved in classrooms and schools.

Educators do tend to grasp that they need to understand themselves and how their own experiences shape who they are in relation to others. Similarly, educators seem to understand that they should design a learning environment that promotes respect and care between and among students. However, educators often struggle with how to co-develop social contexts where they are able to relate to their students and keep their students connected to the learning environment. Moreover, they can find it difficult to design and construct classroom settings where all their students feel safe to speak up and speak out, not only against oppressive, sexist, racist, or homophobic subject matter they are learning, but also against social structures—the sociology of the classroom—that can make them feel inferior or voiceless, or that is designed to control them (how they think and what they do). Teachers may wonder how to help students from different cultural backgrounds to feel that they possess valuable knowledge and skills that can and should contribute to classroom learning opportunities.

A second focus—how teachers build and enact *instructional agility*—is about adaptability of teachers' instructional practices and also essential because research demonstrates that all students become disengaged, disinterested, and disconnected from lessons and learning opportunities when they do not see themselves reflected in the curriculum and related opportunities to learn. Instructional agility ensures that educators consciously and deliberately co-construct learning environments that consistently and unwaveringly push normative ways of thinking about what gets taught (curriculum) and how (instruction). Instructional agility is about teachers' ability to be flexible and responsive to the students in front of them. Researchers and theoreticians agree that a race-centered,[7] culture- and diversity-focused,[8] and multicultural[9] curriculum is essential for student academic and social success. So this book is about the social as well as the cognitive. It showcases the possibilities of the relational and the instructional. Indeed, all students need and deserve to encounter a curriculum that highlights and reflects the life experiences and contributions of people of color, women, and other marginalized groups—not just those of the White, male mainstream.

In addition, students need to have opportunities to critique curriculum practices and instructional practices—even when teachers practice instructional agility. Students should be able to provide counterpositions to what they are reading, solving, thinking about, and addressing across subject matter, grade, and age. The very *nature* of content and *how* it is actually incorporated into learning opportunities are critical for students, especially those who are too often seen as consumers, not contributors, of knowledge construction.[10] Multicultural educator Geneva Gay stresses that students often feel "insulted, embarrassed, ashamed, and angered when reading and hearing negative portrayals of their ethnic groups or not hearing anything at all."[11] Thus, it is not enough to incorporate the historical, political, and social experiences, events, and challenges of various ethnic groups into curriculum practices. Educators must recognize that the essence of that curricular content (what is actually included, how, and why) is very important as students come to understand themselves and others in a pluralistic and ever-changing society. Students need to see themselves and their cultural group, viewpoint, ways of being, origins of existence, and other such factors from positions of strength and tenacity, not servitude or submission. These two necessities, relational efficacy and instructional agility, are essential elements of addressing diversity and opportunity as they are considered throughout this book. Indeed, relational efficacy requires educators to build necessary confidence in cultivating and sustaining relationships. Instructional agility encourages educators to coconstruct learning opportunities in a fluid, dynamic way that honors the diversity among all students.

I have intentionally parsed race from diversity in some discussions throughout this book, although I realize that race is a dimension of diversity. I have done this because too many educators gloss over race and racism as important areas of consideration in broader diversity discourses, for a variety of reasons: (1) they are uncomfortable talking about them, (2) they find race and racism irrelevant to teaching and learning, (3) race and racism are sometimes considered taboo subjects due to their horrific history in US society, (4) discussions of race and racism are deeply political and emotionally charged, (5) race is misunderstood by so many, and can be divisive both within and outside of education, and (6) some see race and racism as marginal to studying and advancing knowledge in a particular domain of teaching and learning. A much more nuanced and elaborate discussion of these and related issues will be explored in chapter 1, where I discuss an Opportunity Gap Framework, and in other parts of the text.

OPPORTUNITY GAPS

Opportunity gaps are input-related practices and policies that are process driven and can result in students' academic, cognitive, social, affective, emotional, behavioral, and psychological challenges. Opportunity gaps tend to result from educators' and policy makers' inability to deeply understand the mechanisms essential for all students to learn, develop, and improve over time. Opportunity gaps are exacerbated when educators and policy makers have a myopic view of excellence and success, seeing White performance as the gold standard to which all others should strive.

Moreover, opportunity gaps are intensified when educators and policy makers are unable or perhaps unwilling to question who decides what knowledge and knowing are and have a static view of both.

I believe that when we address opportunity gaps, achievement results improve. I am a product of opportunity. People in society, in institutions, and in education have given me many chances to demonstrate my capacity. Ultimately, it was up to me to embrace and to maximize those opportunities, but others first had to give me a chance to succeed within complex systems that were racist, classist, and patriarchal. Too many students in preK–12 institutions have not been provided ample opportunities to develop into successful students because our educational system has not been structurally designed to do so. Opportunity is at the core of success and failure in *society* as well as in *schools*.[12]

However, a dominant, oppressive, and repressive view is that the performances, experiences, and outcomes of White students are "the norm" by which others are compared, measured, assessed, and evaluated.[13] Static and exclusively Eurocentric views of normality are problematic.[14] In essence, it is difficult for many to embrace what multicultural educator and teacher educator Cynthia Dillard explains: people of color are not simply White people with colored or pigmented skin.[15] Their normality is shaped by (among other qualities) their racial, ethnic, and cultural heritage beliefs and values. So, who decides what is normal and acceptable? How can we broaden our mind-sets and our conceptions of difference so that our work in education benefits all students? Further, how do we co-create learning spaces where students feel safe and connected to the curriculum?

CURRICULUM PRACTICES

The curriculum can be defined as what students have the opportunity to learn. Curriculum practices are closely tied to instruction—they are the enactment of learning opportunities available to people. Of course, while students are exposed to learning opportunities inside the classroom, learning also occurs in other spaces: in students' homes and communities, on their bus rides and walks to and from school, on the playground, and in the corridors of their schools. Although the evidence is clear that learning occurs in and across multiple and varied sites, teachers are mostly taught to consider a "formal," explicit curriculum of the classroom. Curriculum practices can be constructed in ways that (1) attempt to strip students of their identity, culture, and cultural practices (their language, the way they dress, their reading and music preferences, and so forth); (2) build competition as students work to out-test (masked through the language of achievement) their classmates and others; and (3) do not attempt to help students heal and work through difficult situations that result in hurt, pain, and disappointment (even when schools are the places that breed these emotions and feelings).

Curriculum theorist Elliot Eisner conceptualized three essential forms of the curriculum. First, the *explicit curriculum* concerns learning opportunities that are overtly taught and stated or printed in documents that are typically drawn from standards, policies, and related guidelines. Second, the *implicit curriculum* may be intended or unintended but is not stated or written down; it can also be considered the hidden curriculum.[16] For instance, when students receive messages about gender stereotypes such as "hitting like a girl" or that boys are "stronger than girls," they are learning, but these learning opportunities are not explicit or written down, and the implicit messages may be intentional or unintentional. Third, the *null curriculum* refers to what students do not have the opportunity to learn. Learning opportunities that are not available for students are also forms of the curriculum. Students are learning something based on the absence of certain experiences, discourses, and overall learning opportunities. For example, if students are not taught to question or to critically examine power structures, they are learning something—that they are not intended to critique power structures or change them. In short, *what is absent or not included in the curriculum is actually present in what students are learning.*

CURRICULUM PRACTICES, RACE, AND THE NULL

After the terror attack by White supremacists in Charlottesville, Virginia, and the assassination of Heather Heyer, I learned that many students were left confused, frustrated, hurt, and uncertain about what they believed they knew and had come to believe about people and the United States of America (US). I found that too many educators went about their work just as they had in the past: not teaching the real history of the United States and not teaching the underlying realities of what Charlottesville meant for society writ large (locally and domestically). Most schools (from elementary to high) did not work to explicitly help students heal and think about social injustice. Educators taught the occurrences of Charlottesville and consequently their students' feelings of hurt through what can be described as a null curriculum. Yet one could argue that it is likely that these same educators will be disappointed and perhaps even surprised when the next Charlottesville occurs, and their students are involved. Thus, when we teach through the null, we can be complicit in the maintenance of the status quo and the consequences of White supremacy, hate, and patriarchy.

WE CAN AND MUST DO BETTER

Teachers work hard—their hearts tend to be in the right place. They want to be difference-makers in the lives of their students. But teachers need support in building the kinds of tools necessary for students to heal from the layers of abuse and punishment they have experienced. And perhaps most important, teachers need to experience emancipatory spaces that allow them to make professional judgments as they deeply learn about their students. The Charlottesville, Virginia, terror attack committed by a White supremacist who drove his car into a crowd serves as an excellent opportunity for school leaders and teachers across the United States and the world to reimagine the null curriculum and explicitly shepherd students into becoming social justice activists. Engaging these issues across the curriculum (not just during an abbreviated time period, such as homeroom or a social studies classroom) sends a real message to students that we must create the kind of world we want to live in—one that fights against bigotry in all forms.

Systemic, institutional shifts are ideal to build the kind of citizenry that enables us to take forward steps toward equity and healing. To build organizational and institutional shifts, educators must remember the following:

- Individuals (such as policy makers, school leaders, educators, parents, and students) make systems; teachers must feel supported to teach in ways that honor all students and that disrupt, challenge, name, and call out the perpetuation of racist, sexist, homophobic, and xenophobic thinking, mind-sets, practices, policies, and discourses.
- Administrators have to build a culture of love, anti-hate, and liberation and not expect teachers to engage in this work inside of their classroom without overt commitment and support from those in positions to make decisions on behalf of the broader citizenry. Focusing solely on individuals (such as teachers) to make real, long-term, systemic change is short-sighted and will not result in the systemic, institutional, and long-term shifts that are needed.

If Charlottesville, Virginia, is addressed once or perhaps over a few days in isolation and then curriculum practices shift back to learning sites as usual—spaces that teach fallacies of US history, fallacies that suggest that one group of people is inherently better than another, or that individuals merit their success based on their intellect, abilities, and hard work—I suspect we will continue to get nowhere fast. But if we allow Charlottesville, Virginia, to serve as a true anchor to reimagine the curriculum (and especially the null), we can move toward healing—healing that faces the reality of so many other issues that need addressing and that continue to keep particular groups of students feeling angry, hurt, frustrated, sad, and hopeless. If we reimagine what we teach and place social justice at the center of our work, we have an opportunity to help students think through issues of injustice and perhaps build tools to address and change them.

These are just a few examples of how curriculum practices can explicitly help students to heal and learn to disrupt injustice once such issues are explored:

- High-profile police-involved shootings in Baton Rouge, Louisiana; Dallas; and Falcon Heights, Minnesota (as well as those in their own communities) where unarmed Black bodies are shot and killed by police
- Colin Kaepernick's refusal to stand during the national anthem and the consequent backlash from the National Football League and fans
- Ongoing national immigration debates over children being taken from their parents and placed in fenced cages
- The Flint, Michigan, water crisis
- The brutal shooting of nine parishioners in a church in Charleston, South Carolina

In other words, if Charlottesville, or any of the above occurrences, is perceived and taught as an isolated incident or not taught at all, we stand to do more harm than good. But when we reimagine the very nature of the curriculum, we have a better chance of changing the world. Helping students embrace their identity, build transferable skills (such as thinking, analyzing, problem solving), and fall in love with learning in order to make the world better for the collective should be our central aims in education. Students' learning and development allow them to examine society and make decisions that benefit the masses—not just a selected few or not just decisions that benefit the individual. In this way, *society offers a real curriculum site* that must be taught if we have a fighting chance at helping all students deal with and counter the effects of racism and other manifestations of hate.

HOW TERMS AND CONSTRUCTS ARE USED

Throughout this book, I use *students of color* to represent non-White students. I do not use the term *minority* because the word carries a historically negative connotation and because White people and others in the mainstream of society are sometimes in the "minority" in particular places at particular times. Moreover, demographic trends suggest that White people will be the racial minority over the next several decades, particularly in public schools.

I also refer to *culture* and *cultural practices* at times. I attempt to honor the orientations, cultural histories, people's orientations, preferences, experiences, and practices (their language, their customs, and so forth). However, I try to avoid perpetuating stereotypes that lead people to believe that culture is "inside" of people and static. To the contrary, for instance, just because a person speaks Spanish does not mean that person is of Spanish descent or culture. Moreover, if someone participates in Shabbat, such a practice does not mean that person is part of the Jewish culture or community.

Also, when I use the term *we* throughout this book, I am referring to those in education and society, from parents to teachers to policy makers, who are interested in the educational experiences of all students. In some cases, I use *preservice teachers* to refer to those who are in traditional or nontraditional teacher education programs and may not yet be employed in school systems. When I use the term *in-service teachers,* I am referring to those who are already teaching in schools. I use the terms *teacher* and *educator* interchangeably, as I do *African American* and *Black*. To be clear, I believe the insights, findings, and recommendations in this book that are mostly focused on teachers are transferable to other educators. Thus, at times I use *teacher* and at other times I invoke a broader *educator* label in hopes that teachers as well as other educators build on the lessons in this book. Also, I consistently use *preK–12* to refer to prekindergarten through grade twelve. My point is that teachers across the grade span, teaching all subject matters (including band, art, science, social studies, English arts, chorus, mathematics, and so forth) should take the recommendations of this book seriously. I use the term *urban* to describe a place, not a person or group of people such as students, parents, or teachers.

AUDIENCE FOR THIS BOOK

Although the book has a clear teacher focus, there are important lessons and ideas that are also relevant for other educators, such as principals, school counselors, teachers' assistants, athletic and academic coaches, social workers, psychologists, and psychiatrists. While the narratives given in chapters 2 through 4 are from middle and high school teachers, the six White teachers showcased in chapter 5 demonstrate teacher learning challenges and successes in their teacher education courses that they encountered in grades preK–12. Practicing teachers in urban, rural, and suburban schools as well as students in teacher education programs should read this book, as should teacher educators and researchers interested in students' opportunities to learn.

ORGANIZATION OF THE BOOK

In chapter 1, I share what I call an Opportunity Gap Framework to ground and shape the narratives that follow. This framework includes five interrelated areas or tenets: (1) rejection of color blindness; (2) ability and skill to work through cultural conflicts; (3) ability to understand the myth of meritocracy; (4) ability to recognize and shift low expectations and deficit mind-sets; and (5) rejection of context-neutral mind-sets and practices.

In chapters 2, 3, and 4, I showcase narratives from real teachers in US public middle and high schools who capture the nexus of diversity, opportunity, and teaching in their practices. The teachers highlighted are not perfect, and the social contexts in which they work present very challenging realities. They live and function in complex and difficult circumstances. However, they persist despite difficulties as they work to address, embrace, and honor diversity and students' opportunities to learn. Among other important lessons, these chapters demonstrate that teachers from different racial and cultural backgrounds can be (and are) successful teachers of students who are very different from them. Moreover, the cases demonstrate teachers' astute, persistent, and necessary learning. These teachers build knowledge about their practices and improve. These teachers *start where they are, but they do not stay there!*

Mr. Hall is a White science teacher who learns from moments in his teaching practices and successfully teaches in an urban middle school, Bridge Middle School. Mr. Hall and his students are very different, and Mr. Hall builds knowledge and practices to better meet his students' needs as he listens to what they need from him to succeed. Mr. Jackson, an African American mathematics and science teacher, and Ms. Shaw, an African American social studies teacher, also teach at Bridge Middle School. Although they share the same racial background as their students, their cultural practices and consequently pedagogical practices are very different. Dr. Johnson is an African American language arts teacher who expands her notions of the opportunity-diversity connection by infusing her curriculum and instructional approaches with cultural and gender content in a mostly White, wealthy suburban high school, Stevenson High School. The collective cases in this book show common practices of teacher learning and demonstrate trends that other teachers should consider in their journey to get better and to meet the complex needs of their students, many of whom are very different from them. Thus, the book provides opportunities for readers to examine the teachers in these cases as well as their practices as they critique and adopt curricula, pedagogical, relational, and assessment moves.

In chapter 5, I discuss the learning of six teachers learning to teach in elementary through high schools. As I reflect on my many years of working with teachers in different preservice teacher education programs, I believe their experiences represent the kinds of challenges and successes that those learning to teach tend to face.

After showcasing these teachers and how they come to more deeply understand and work through opportunity gaps, in chapter 6, I shift the discussion to what I call Opportunity-Centered Teaching (OCT). OCT has four interrelated features: (1) OCT is about relationships, (2) OCT is about building community knowledge to inform practice, (3) OCT bridges students' outside-of-school practices with in-school practices, and (4) it addresses psychological, mental health, and social needs. OCT practices work to disrupt gaps in opportunity.

I conclude the book with some reflections and summations of the main themes and recommendations. In the epilogue I explain my research process so readers can learn in more depth about the journey that led me to share these narratives about the people and social contexts of the schools presented.

Finally, although broad and structural changes can make a powerful impact on students' opportunities, individual teachers can also play a significant role in their classrooms every day! Indeed, teachers *can* make a difference even when they are operating in institutions and systems that do not support their passion and commitment to meeting the complex needs of all students. It is in this vein that I hope educators read this book. Systemic and broad-level change is ideal, but individual-level changes in mind-sets and practices among teachers is a place to begin the journey to construct those moments that become experiences students never forget. Thus, I invite you, the reader, to Start Where You Are—but Don't Stay There!

1

An Opportunity Gap Explanatory Framework

OPPORTUNITY GAPS, especially those linked to diversity, exist at all levels in education and in the lives of both educators and students. The Opportunity Gap Framework that I introduce in this chapter and expand upon throughout the book serves as an alternative paradigm—a different way for educators to make sense of and approach their work with young people. Rather than focusing on gaps in achievement, test scores, or other outputs, the Opportunity Gap Framework shepherds educators into reflective spaces where they consider inputs—the mechanisms, practices, policies, and experiences that influence students' opportunities to learn. The simplest explanation of this framework is that it focuses on how educators think about and conceptualize their work to center opportunity over outcomes. The Opportunity Gap Framework is anchored in the principle that young people succeed when opportunity structures are in place to support their learning and development. Moreover, outcomes improve when opportunity gaps are addressed.

The case studies in the following chapters have important implications for how educators can address opportunity gaps in a range of school contexts across US society—urban, suburban, and rural; public and private; independent and parochial. But while these cases demonstrate how educators address opportunity gaps and exhibit opportunity-centered teaching, it is important that educators approach this work as a way of thinking and carrying out practices over a prescribed way of teaching. In other words, addressing opportunity gaps requires that educators develop the mind-sets, dispositions, and belief systems to do so. There is no magic potion to disrupting centuries of oppression, White supremacy, and inequity.

In this chapter, I introduce a conceptual framework that creates a context for and serves as an analytic tool to explain these case studies in subsequent chapters. Moreover, the framework can be used to help schools and districts organize and operationalize practices that better align with the needs of their students. I describe, analyze, and discuss these cases to illuminate complexities of teaching and learning through a lens of diversity and equity. In addition, the cases demonstrate how teachers listen to the lessons from their students, colleagues, and broader community and change their practices to better meet the needs of their students. Perhaps most important, the educators in these cases recognize the power, potential, and need to get better—to start where they are but not stay there.

The issues raised throughout this book are grounded in, related to, and shaped by many of the concepts presented in this chapter. These concepts emerge from theory, research, and practice established in the literature as well as my own empirical work. While this explanatory framework will be used to analyze and describe the reported thinking of these teachers and students as well as my observations of their practices, it is also meant to challenge educators to broaden their belief systems, shift their mind-sets, and transform their practices in order to better address opportunity gaps that persist in preK–12 and teacher education contexts.

Addressing opportunity gaps requires that educators think about mechanisms and tools to build opportunity-centered practices with young people that may improve outcomes. However, the goal of addressing opportunity gaps is not primarily focused on outcomes but on educational and related experiences and structures. That is, addressing gaps in opportunity can help young people (and educators) build a stronger sense of identity and purpose based on their current experiences rather than waiting on a particular outcome that can be determined by an outside entity. It is essential that those in schools—students and educators alike—find joy, peace, love, and optimism in their educational journey. Addressing opportunity gaps requires that educators construct learning environments where students experience what they deserve and need to thrive. Indeed, educators' mind-sets, beliefs, and overall paradigms about students and their capacity influence the ways in which they address gaps in opportunity.

In the first edition of this book, I outlined five essential tenets of the Opportunity Gap Framework. Since the publication of the first edition in 2010, I have studied additional classrooms, interviewed more educators and students, and read more about opportunity gaps. Thus, the Opportunity Gap Framework covers five interconnected areas that I believe are essential to helping educators shed light on and address opportunity gaps, and I enhance and advance my previous discussions and descriptions of the principles based on my expanded knowledge and understanding: (1) rejection of color blindness; (2) ability, willingness, and skill to understand, build on, and work through cultural conflicts; (3) ability and willingness to understand how the meritocracy myth operates; (4) ability and willingness to recognize, disrupt, and shift low expectations and deficit mind-sets; and (5) willingness to counter and rethink context-neutral mind-sets and practices.

1. *Reject color blindness:* Educators are challenged to rethink persistent notions that they should avoid recognizing and interrogating race and racism.[1] They deeply consider how race and racism operate on individual, structural, institutional, and systemic levels in education. Educators are determined to understand and acknowledge how our race-central experiences can influence our ideologies, attitudes, and belief systems, and consequently our practices in classrooms with young people. Rejecting color blindness allows educators to build insights about how fundamentally *race matters* for all involved in education, even White people. Rejection of color blindness also means

that educators comprehend the ways in which race and racism intersect with educational practices—particularly teaching. Educators are particularly encouraged to move beyond individualized ideas about race and racism to examining and analyzing how systemic barriers and inequity continue to marginalize certain groups of students. For instance, if educators believe that they are not personally, individually, racist, they may also believe that racism does not exist inside and outside of education. However, rather than perceiving racism as a consequence of abstraction, I am also stressing the necessity for individual educators to consider how their own practices contribute to racist actions, systems, institutions, and policies that maintain the status quo. In addressing opportunity gaps, educators consider individual realities as well as systemic and structural causes related to race and racism, and they are challenged to think through how race shapes what happens in society, schools, and classrooms.

2. *Understand cultural conflicts:* To address gaps in opportunity, educators build knowledge about how conflicts emerge in classrooms as a result of educators' and students' different cultural experiences and ways of seeing and being in the world. Because our cultural experiences influence our worldview, how we think, how we approach the world, what we decide is essential for teaching and learning, and how we organize curriculum practices and why, it is essential for educators to consistently reflect on, make sense of, and rationalize why they are making particular decisions at particular times, with particular people. Moreover, our cultural experiences inform policies that are constructed, how those policies are interpreted and enacted, and on behalf of whom they are conceived and operationalized. Thus, it is essential for educators to understand the role of culture and cultural practices as they work to address opportunity gaps in education. Cultural conflicts can cause inconsistencies and incongruence between teachers and students, for instance, which can make teaching and learning difficult. These conflicts include but go beyond race. Cultural conflicts should be viewed as a consequence of individual and collective characteristics and

practices that manifest due to religion, race, gender, sexual orientation and sexual identity, and/or language, for instance. Cultural conflicts result because of practices among people.[2] However, it is important that we do not define culture solely as a trait of individuals. Cultural practices can be adopted across different communities.

Opportunity gaps can persist because educators' cultural ways of knowing, which are often grounded in Eurocentric paradigms and ideologies, take precedence over those of their students. It is important to note that educators across different racial and ethnic groups may have adopted Eurocentric world views that manifest through their practices. Thus, understanding cultural conflicts requires educators to understand the ways in which privilege and power emerge in classroom settings to maintain the status quo. The point is not that educators who do not have the same or similar practices or who are outside the cultural group of their students cannot be successful. To the contrary, this book demonstrates that teachers across cultural groups can be and are successful teachers of students who are different from them. However, they must work diligently, deliberately, and persistently to understand cultural conflicts in order to address them. To address opportunity structures in a constructive way, educators must be willing to build knowledge, attitudes, dispositions, and skill sets to understand the important role culture plays in curriculum development, instruction, relationships, assessments, and broader decision making.

3. *Recognize the myth of meritocracy:* When educators approach their work through meritocratic mind-sets, they believe that student performance is primarily and summarily a function of hard work, ability, skill, intelligence, and persistence. Educators believe that student success is a consequence that they have earned and deserve. That is, the idea is that students and educators deserve their success or failure in school and/or society because they have earned it. Educators are sometimes unaware of how situations far beyond people's control influence success. To address opportunity, educators become mindful of, or are at least willing to acknowledge, the many factors beyond merit that

shape students' academic and social success, or lack thereof. Such a way of thinking about success requires that educators shape opportunity structures that better align with student needs. For instance, when educators build knowledge about and deepen their understanding of the myth of meritocracy, they reject standardized assessment tools and construct measures that more appropriately align with students. Because students do not have the same historical experiences due to economic, social, and racial privileges, educators adapt, adjust, and respond to where students are—even when they have experienced the same curriculum and instructional experiences. That is, educators understand that past inequitable experiences give particular groups of students unfair advantages that will surely impact their outcomes.

4. *Disrupt low expectations and deficit mind-sets:* Educators may have low expectations of particular students and see them through deficient lenses, which can become a self-fulfilling prophecy. Put simply, low expectations and deficit mind-sets lead educators to doubt the capacity of their students and to construct learning opportunities that are far from engaging and challenging. Educators who do not believe in high expectations for their students or who do not see students and their expertise, experience, and contributions as assets tend to focus on what students do *not* bring to the classroom rather than the multilayered, nuanced, deep, and complex strengths that students have and offer when the classroom ethos is conducive. That is, educators may focus on student deficits rather than their many assets. When addressing opportunity, educators embrace the insight that students will generally meet the expectations that are co-constructed with them—including high ones. In short, students bring assets into the learning environment that should be valued and capitalized on in the design of learning opportunities.
5. *Counter context-neutral mind-sets:* Educators sometimes approach their work with students without understanding, attending to, or caring about the complexities and idiosyncrasies inherent to their particular teaching environment. This approach fails to consider the

social contexts of teaching and learning, such as the state, the city, the local community surrounding the school, or the sociology of the school itself. For instance, a teacher may learn to teach a subject such as math, history, or science but fail to understand how to teach that subject well, responsively, relevantly, and effectively in a particular location, the social context. Educators newer to the profession may especially desire to return to the school district where they attended school themselves. They may have rich experiential knowledge about that context as they experienced it as students. However, building professional knowledge and capacity requires that they understand the broader range of districts in which they might teach: urban, suburban, and rural. To address opportunity, educators are deliberate and consistent in becoming more aware of contextual realities that influence their current and future students and their environments. By recognizing the ways in which the social context can influence students, educators are better able to draw from the many outside-of-school assets that can be used inside to shape student learning. Building tools to consistently learn about their social context is an important endeavor, as communities are dynamic and always evolving. Moreover, as educators build capacity to reimagine deficits among students and families, they also shift their perceptions of the communities where their students live.

Rather than seeing students' environments as lacking and inferior, educators see and identify the richness and resourcefulness of their communities. These assets may include *places* (health and wellness institutions, worship centers, park and recreation spaces, recycle institutions, job and career services, and so forth). Identifying strengths and the overall ethos of a place also means that educators deeply study the *people* in the community (community leaders and activists, families, siblings of their students, medical providers, clergy, and so forth). In short, educators who reject context-neutral mind-sets are those who continuously examine the places, people, and resources of a community—both inside and outside of a school. And rejecting context-neutral mind-sets requires that educators understand how the people in the community are the experts of their experiences. In essence, educators learn from and with the community and avoid their subconscious propensity to espouse their value judgments of community realities. When they recognize the challenges and problems in a community, they should understand how structures and systems have caused and perpetuated them and educators should become advocates to support the community in addressing the problems and challenges as they show up.

The following sections expand on these five concepts. I begin with color blindness—a way of describing how educators dangerously respond to issues of race and racism—because I have come to understand that many educators seem to struggle most to understand the role and relevance of race and racism in their work. Rather than including race in the subsequent discussion of cultural conflicts, I have parsed it out as its own tenet because I suspect that it would be glossed over, treated on the surface, or completely ignored if it were not included as a stand-alone feature of the Opportunity Gap Framework.

COLOR BLINDNESS

Educators' beliefs and ideologies impact what they do. When teachers operate from racist, xenophobic, or otherwise discriminatory belief systems, these ideologies show up in their interactions and actions with students. Thus, it is essential for educators to reflect on, bring to the fore, wrestle with, and control their practices that may have harmful ramifications for young people. It is important to note that troubling beliefs and ideologies among educators may be implicit, covert, and tacit. The research literature suggests that student learning opportunities can be hindered when teachers fail to consider their own and their students' racial backgrounds and to think carefully and critically about how race and racism emerge in classroom learning opportunities. The research also suggests that teachers who adopt and embrace color-blind beliefs, worldviews, ideologies, mind-sets, and consequently practices can neglect important dimensions of curriculum practices that influence student learning and identity.[3] When teachers ignore students' racial identity, for instance, they are in effect interacting with their students as incomplete beings. If teachers are not conscious of students' racial background, students of color may not see themselves in or be reflected in curriculum practices because the curriculum may be constructed mainly to reflect and meet the needs of White students almost by default.

In short, rejection of color blindness and race consciousness allows educators to co-construct curriculum and instructional practices that connect to, align with, engage, speak from the point of view of, embrace and celebrate students of color, their communities. But color blindness tends to result in curriculum practices that are static and that reinforce Whiteness—preferences, points of view, and historical insights, for instance, that place White people, their practices, and contributions at the center of teaching and learning. Moreover, when a color-blind worldview is adopted, instructional practices, similar to curricular ones, may be Eurocentric in nature and focus and not take into consideration non-White students' lived experiences.

There is also a sociological dimension to color blindness, beyond curriculum and instruction, that can prevent teachers from empathizing with racially and ethnically diverse students. Consider, for instance, a Brown (Latinx) student who has been racially profiled and followed around a corner convenience store in which he stops before going to school. Also consider a Black student who is called a nigger by a group of older students from a car window as she walks to school. These two experiences may have powerful emotional and psychological impacts on these students and can influence how they interact with their classmates, their teacher, and the curriculum. And these students' experiences likely determine how they feel about themselves and the world around them. Still, many teachers refuse to acknowledge the prevalence and salience of race and racism in their work as teachers because, in their minds, race and racism are inconsequential, and they often believe that we live in a post-racial society. Thus, race-conscious practices are essential for all teachers—not just those in the social studies classroom and not just White teachers. All teachers need to be aware of the racism experienced by the Brown and Black students as described above.

Feminist theorist Audre Lorde maintains that individuals who adopt color-blind ideologies and approaches to their work believe they can "conquer it [racism and discrimination] by ignoring it."[4] I have heard educators, including teachers of color, proclaim in many different contexts that they "do not see color," they "just see students." Multicultural education researcher James Banks explains that "a statement such as 'I don't see color' reveals a privileged position that refuses to legitimize racial identifications that are very important to people of color and that are often used to justify inaction and perpetuation of the status quo."[5]

Furthermore, teachers who adopt color-blind mind-sets and practices can lack the racial knowledge, sensitivity, and empathy necessary to successfully teach racially diverse students, especially those who are often relegated to the margins of teaching and learning. Because teachers may fail to attend to the multilayered identities of students and may even intentionally avoid race as a central identity marker in their decisions regarding curriculum and instructional designs, students may be expected to just assimilate and adjust to expectations that do not consider the role and relevance of their own and others' race. And acknowledging and having conversations about racism can be considered blasphemy because so many educators worry that they may be seen as or be called racist. Thus, many educators avoid thinking or talking explicitly about race and racism in their work.

Teachers with a color-blind mind-set may not recognize how their own race and racial experiences shape what they teach, how they teach it, and how they assess what has been taught. For example, when teachers do not include curriculum content related to indigenous communities such as Native Americans (as an ethnic group), that omission itself teaches students something about the importance (or lack thereof) of Native Americans.[6] Omitting Native American content from the curriculum not only denies Native American students the right to recognize their contributions to the fabric of the curriculum, such as those related to property and land rights, but it also denies students from other racial and ethnic backgrounds the opportunity to deepen their knowledge of that group. The result is that students very often learn from a curriculum dominated by White contributions and White norms to the exclusion of contributions from other racial and ethnic groups. Moreover, students are learning something based on the null curriculum—what is *not* included in the curriculum. What is absent in the curriculum is actually present in student learning opportunities. At the heart of what is and is not emphasized in the curriculum is teachers' racial identity—who teachers are, how they represent themselves to others, and how they come to see themselves as people who benefit from or are discriminated against due to matters associated with race in society. Consider the teacher and student racial demographic data in figure 1.1.

FIGURE 1.1
Racial diversity of students and teachers

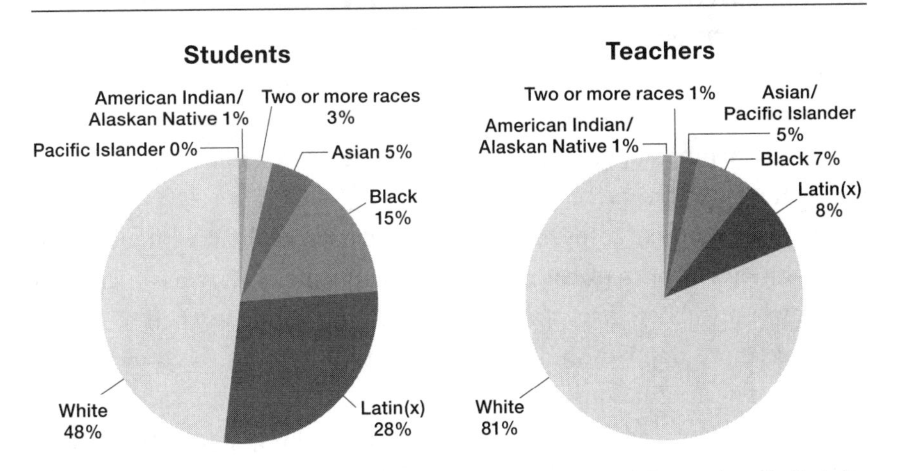

Source: National Center for Educational Statistics, 2018, (students) https://nces.ed.gov/fastfacts/display.asp?id=372; (teachers) https://www2.ed.gov/rschstat/eval/highered/racial-diversity/state-racial-diversity-workforce.pdf.

Indeed, teachers remain mostly White while student racial demography continues to diversify. Racial demography incongruences can impact teaching and learning. The research literature is clear that a racial demographic divide between teachers and students in preK–12 classrooms, as illustrated in the figures, can result in disadvantages for teachers and students alike.[7] In other words, opportunity gaps can emerge when White teachers do not understand or are unwilling to understand how students of color live and what they experience in the world. The point here is that when educators do not build the knowledge, expertise, and understanding to address their own racial biases and racism it can be difficult for them to address opportunity gaps. Addressing opportunity gaps related to race and racism means that educators build knowledge of (1) their own and their students' racial identity, (2) their own and their students' ways of experiencing racism and other forms of discrimination inside and outside of school (and how White people do not experience such racism), and (3) how discriminatory experiences may result in trauma, which can inadvertently influence student learning and development. Educational researcher Adam Alvarez has described traumatic experiences students of color face and how educators can and should work to respond to those experiences inside the classroom.[8] In response to this racialized trauma, White teachers may not possess the tools or the ability to build classroom contexts that can aid in healing these students. This racialized gap may create roadblocks to learning opportunities and consequently roadblocks to students' academic and social success.[9]

White educators, accordingly, must understand their whiteness and how whiteness works to ensure hegemony in different forms.[10] The idea is that when teachers have the same racial background as their students, there are more opportunities for teachers and students to connect, and there are fewer situations for misunderstandings to occur in the learning environment.[11] With important goals of building students' identity and cultivating an ethos of learning and development, educators should reject color blindness in order to build instructional practices and learning opportunities that center students' race and racial identity rather than attempt to ignore, neutralize, or diminish them. As they are developing examples, illustrating points, building rigor, and cultivating inquisitive stances among their students, educators should view race and opportunities to learn about racism, xenophobia, and other forms of racism as important spaces for all to learn and develop. Rejecting color blindness is essential for all teachers across the curriculum, including math, science, technology, physics, and chemistry teachers. In fact, it can be argued that these are disciplines that need to center race and racism the most, given the disturbingly low number of Black and Brown students fully participating in career opportunities in these disciplines.[12]

However, as Gay stresses, even if students and teachers are of the same race, it "may be potentially beneficial, but it is not a guarantee of pedagogical effectiveness."[13] An essential goal of this book is to demonstrate, through empirical case studies, that educators across racial backgrounds and demography can be, and indeed are, successful with groups of students outside of their own racial background when the educators have (or are willing to garner) the knowledge, attitudes, dispositions, and skills necessary to understand and be responsive to their students' social, instructional, and curriculum needs.[14] In other words, it is what teachers know, are willing to learn, and actually do that matter most in practice as educators work to cross racial inconsistencies between them and students.

However, it is clear that teachers of color, because of their racialized experiences in the world, often have a deeper understanding of students of color, and are accordingly able to co-create learning opportunities that students can relate to and connect with.[15] Consequently, given the racial demography of students, increasing the percentage of teachers of color who also build the knowledge, attitudes, mind-sets, and skills essential for student success is an important aim for public and independent schools across the United States. Moreover, we need additional studies that examine practices among successful teachers of color and White teachers working with students of color to bolster the knowledge base about teaching and learning with students of color. For instance, teachers of color often possess life experiences that allow them an insider's perspective to understand and interpret what students of color are grappling with, working through, connecting on, and committed to.[16] The reasons for paying attention to racial demography are copious. The research literature tells us, for example, that teachers of color

- can relate to their students of color and empathize with them during race-related experiences, such as feeling discriminated against or experiencing acts of racism by others (such as classmates or teachers) in the school;
- consciously decide to transform and incorporate a curriculum that showcases and speaks from the point of view of their students of color;
- develop examples that align with the experiences of students of color to illustrate unclear or difficult aspects of the curriculum;
- are more likely to address conflicts in the classroom to avoid sending students to the office;
- build sustainable, authentic relationships with their students, families, and communities in order to connect and learn with students of color;
- see learning as an evolving, developmental, iterative process and do not claim they are the arbiters of knowledge;
- recognize the expertise among students of color and their communities and bridge that expertise in teaching and learning;
- serve as role models for all students, including students of color; and
- recognize "diamonds in the rough" and embrace a wider spectrum of brilliance, talents, and excellence that students possess and may demonstrate.[17]

Where color blindness is concerned, I have discovered at least three common dangerous conceptions among teachers who do not understand the ways in which color-blind mind-sets, belief systems, and overall practices can perpetuate opportunity gaps:

Mind-set 1: If I acknowledge the racial or ethnic background of my students or myself, I may be considered racist.

Mind-set 2: If I admit that people of color may experience the world differently, I may be seen as "politically incorrect." I may offend others in a teacher education classroom or my preK–12 faculty meeting if I express my beliefs, concerns, and reservations about race.

Mind-set 3: I should treat all my students the same regardless of their race. Race does not matter and racism has ended; thus, racial considerations have no place or relevance in the design and enactment of classroom learning opportunities.

These misguided assertions and mind-sets can manifest in seriously destructive ways in the preK–12 classroom. Sociologist Amanda Lewis found in her study of a mostly White school, for instance, that many educators and adults refused to discuss or even acknowledge the ever-present social and institutional race-related matters in their social context.[18] When Sylvie, a student of color, brought up her experiences of racism in the school, educators in the community ignored her concerns and rationalized that the student was "playing the race card" (whatever this means!). Lewis explained that the White adults essentially adopted a color-blind approach and mind-set to their work and lives. The adults in Lewis's study believed that issues of race and racism were not important in their learning environment because most of the students, educators, and parents were White. Consequently, as her study found, some educators believe that when there is not a critical mass of people of color in an environment, then race is insignificant. Such educators may fail to understand that race affects all people in society and in education, even White people. White is in fact a race, and it is the White privilege that educators experience that allows systems, institutions, and structures to virtually never change. Moreover, their White privilege and power allow them to rationalize that a young child would "play a race card" in describing her experiences and thus not take the student's comments seriously.

The two-term election of Barack Obama to the presidency led too many people in the United States and abroad to believe that his election transcended centuries of racism, oppression, marginalization, and discrimination. White Americans as well as those from other racial and ethnic groups, including some Black Americans, proclaimed what seemed to be a modern cliché: that it was "a new day" in US society. Some believed that we as a country had arrived at a post-racial, post-oppressive, post-discrimination era because White voters had helped elect an African American president. However, it is very clear that racism is alive, well, and permanent in the very fabric of US society.[19] The post-racial position does not recognize the pervasiveness of race, racism, and other forms of discrimination and prejudice. While individual educators may not believe they are racist, broader policies and practices (constructed by a collective of individuals) are often rife with racism. To be clear: on an individual level, when educators do not work deliberately to combat racism and injustice, they are complicit in maintaining racist policies and practices. *There is no room for neutrality in this work—either educators are fighting against racism or they are contributing to it.* Accordingly, educators who do not view themselves as racist individuals can have trouble recognizing how racism works and how it can manifest in broader systems and institutionalized structures to prevent certain groups of students from succeeding in the classroom and beyond. In particular, educators who voted for President Obama may find it difficult to believe that we are still living in a racist US society. The recent election of Donald Trump and especially the stark divisions that have emerged since his election send a particular kind of message about where we are in this country regarding race, racism, and inclusion.

In short, it is critical that educators recognize their own and their students' racial backgrounds in order to treat their students as complete human beings rather than fragments of their full identity. Viewing students as "just students" and not as raced students contributes to opportunity gaps.

How do teachers contribute to individual and structural forms of racism that can influence student opportunities? Clearly, color-blind ideologies, orientations, and practices make it difficult for educators to recognize disparities and dilemmas in education, such as

- an overrepresentation of students of color in special education, particularly for behavioral challenges;
- an underrepresentation of students of color in gifted education;
- an underrepresentation of students of color in schoolwide clubs, organizations, and other prestigious arenas, such as the school's homecoming court, Beta Club, honor society, and student government;
- an underrepresentation of faculty and staff of color in school positions, including professional staff, teaching, and leadership positions;
- an overreferral of Black students to the office for punishment; and
- an overwhelming number of Black students who are expelled or suspended.

These disparities and dilemmas are complexly important and seem to persist despite decades of clear evidence of their existence. Yet, one might be surprised at the number of schools I currently walk into across the United States where teachers and other educators boast about the fact that they do not, have not, and will not address race in their talk, curriculum practices, or work more broadly. In my discourse analysis of their feedback to me, they share that they believe that (1) race is inconsequential to their curriculum and instructional practices;[20] (2) they must focus on teaching math or English language arts for the upcoming state test;[21] (3) we are living in a post-racial society;[22] or (4) the issues they face are mostly about poverty, not race.[23] And of course, we should interrogate and think deeply about the intersections of race and other factors.[24] But power and privilege can allow some to avoid that which makes them uncomfortable while others suffer the consequence of their silence, shallow engagement, and/or downright arrogance.

The lack of microlevel race-conscious policies and procedures can be dangerous for students if schools do not centralize matters of race as a proxy for who is representing the school in organizations and in what ways. For instance, if students of color continually do not hold offices such as president of the student body or are not represented in the student government association, school officials and educators should be concerned and take steps to address these and similar patterns. Similarly, they should take corrective action when students of color participate primarily in athletics and rarely in accelerated academic programs. Some believe that the students themselves cause their underrepresentation, not the school's race-neutral, color-blind policies, procedures, and practices. But the schools that make the most progress toward racial justice tend to be those that care about and work toward eradicating racial injustice. Thus, it is critical that educators remember race and racism in their work with students on both individual and systemic levels. By adopting color-blind ideologies, practices, and mind-sets that ignore the importance of race, educators can contribute to and actually exacerbate the persistence of opportunity gaps.

CULTURAL CONFLICTS

Like color blindness, cultural conflicts in classroom practice are widespread.[25] Researchers have found that the conflicts, incongruence, and inconsistencies that educators and students encounter in the classroom can limit students' learning opportunities.[26] When teachers operate primarily from their own cultural ways of knowing, the learning milieu can be foreign to students whose cultural experiences are different from educators' experiences. Such cultural conflicts can have negative consequences because there are few points of reference and convergence between teachers and students. A student may be immersed in hip-hop culture, for instance, and her teacher may have no interest in or awareness of it. This can result in a cultural conflict and, consequently, a missed opportunity for teacher and student to develop a meaningful relationship. Moreover, teachers may miss the opportunity to incorporate aspects of hip-hop into their curriculum and instructional practices in order to explain an idea or to help students solve a complex math problem. Hip-hop or another cultural form might also be the curriculum site. The idea is that "some groups of students—because their cultural characteristics are more consistent with the culture, norms, and expectations of the school than are those of other groups of students—have greater opportunities for academic success than do students whose cultures are less consistent with the school culture."[27]

Educational researcher and educator Lisa Delpit advanced the idea of a "culture of power" that exists in classrooms and that can have lasting influence on the types of learning that can take place in a classroom.[28] Cultural conflicts sometimes result in a resistant, oppositional, or confrontational environment in which educators are fighting to control students and to exert their power, and students do not want to feel controlled.[29] Students can similarly work to be heard and to have some power in the classroom. Consequently, educators and students can *work against* each other, which can leave students feeling that their preferences, interests, insights, expertise, and experiences are insignificant, disrespected, irrelevant, or subordinate to educators', and to classroom and school life. As a result, students may refuse to engage in the classroom culture and refuse to learn.

It is important to note that I am not suggesting that culture should be seen as a characteristic or trait of an individual, but rather as the ways in which collectives of people come to practice, live, and represent their interests and preferences in the world.[30] In this way, culture should be viewed in relation to practices and not generalized based on stereotypes or preconceived notions of an individual or group of people.

Cultural conflicts and power struggles carry important associations. Delpit outlines five aspects of power, culture, and conflicts:

> (a) issues of power are enacted in classrooms; (b) there are codes or rules for participating in power; that is, there is a "culture of power"; (c) the rules of the culture of power are a reflection of the rules of the culture of those who have power; (d) if you are not already a participant in the culture of power, being told explicitly the rules of that culture makes acquiring power easier; and (e) those with power are frequently least aware of—or least willing to acknowledge—its existence. Those with less power are often most aware of its existence.[31]

In this way, educators create a culture of power in the classroom because they do in fact have some power over what happens there. Several common mind-sets and assertions can reinforce conflicts of power and culture between teachers and students:

Mind-set 1: I must teach students based on how I teach my own biological children, not based on their culture, cultural practices, and experiences in the world (which may or may not be consistent with my own).

Mind-set 2: All students should behave the same. I'm not going to tolerate students joking around during class. If they misbehave, I'm sending them to the office—period!

Mind-set 3: "Those" students need to adapt and assimilate into the culture of "my" classroom and accept the consequences if they do not.

What constitutes acceptable and appropriate behavior for students at home can be significantly different from the rules and expectations in a classroom.[32] At the core of these cultural conflicts is what it means to be "normal." Normal classroom behavior can be informed by different cultural frames and cultural practices outside of school. For example, students may be accustomed to joking around with family members when a conflict arises in order to de-escalate or to avoid tension. They may have found that using humor helps family members ease away from or work through confrontation and conflict. Teachers, on the other hand, may consider it inappropriate when students invoke humor to perhaps implicitly defuse a conflict, which can then escalate cultural conflict between a teacher and a student.

Delpit reports that students deserve to be overtly exposed to the "rules" and codes of power as well as the consequences of breaking them.[33] For students to have a chance at success in the classroom, and thus in society, they must understand that they live in a system that can be oppressive and repressive. My point is not that they should simply accept these systems that may subordinate and confine them. Students should work to disrupt and eradicate systems that do not value their difference or those that maintain the status quo.

Those in power such as educators tend to decide what is normal behavior and conduct. If joking around to resolve a disagreement in the classroom is not acceptable, then students need to be taught this and not be punished for using a coping or resolution ideology and practice that they have found effective at home or in their community. Students too often are punished for not behaving or interacting with others like their teachers' own children or even like their teachers would. The onus, therefore, is on educators, those in power, to explain to students expectations that the dominant culture finds acceptable. Hopefully, students will still make decisions that do not compromise their humanity in deciding how to respond to what is outlined as "acceptable." Teachers committed to helping students should expose them to strategies that help them push back against expectations that feel oppressive. Otherwise, conflicts can emerge, and students almost always lose unnecessary *cultural battles* in the classroom. In short, it is irresponsible and simply unfair to expect students to behave in a way that has not been well explained to them.

If the goal is for students to be able to code and culture-switch based on the environmental ethos, then students need opportunities to build that skill set and decide how they will proceed. To be clear, although the culture of power carries limitless oppressive features such as educators attempting to control students, if educators in schools are not willing to change and create the types of learning environments where students want to be, then they should at least help students navigate and survive the spaces for which they (as the adults) have the power and control. Teachers should not assume that students understand the culture of power; teachers must teach it! And a central dimension of teaching the culture of power is helping students disrupt and change it.

In sum, even while students are told explicitly about the culture of power and are learning to survive and thrive within it, they should be encouraged to challenge and question oppressive structures, rather than conform to systems that make them feel, according to urban educational researcher Pedro Noguera, like "prisoners."[34] In essence, Noguera's research suggests that some students in some schools, particularly those living below the poverty line, are treated more like they are inmates than students learning to negotiate educational structures. Educators in these schools are obsessed with straight lines, hand raising, and control of students.[35] Such educational institutions, where young people are treated like inmates, are inundated with instructional practices that teacher educator Martin Haberman calls the "pedagogy of poverty"—teaching practices that reinforce and prepare students to take orders and to eventually assume roles in the larger society either as prisoners or as those trained to take orders.[36] A pedagogy of poverty results in young people moving into the world of work in low-paying jobs that contribute to a cycle of poverty. Educators' practices of control can result in young people eventually working against expectations. These students are eventually referred to the office for misbehavior or noncompliance. Results from office referrals range from detention, time out, in-school suspension, and outside-of-school suspension or expulsion. There is an obvious school-to-prison pipeline where bodies that do not conform end up in correctional facilities that do very little to rehabilitate people. These prisons are designed to kill the bodies, minds, and spirits of people—not to help them necessarily improve.

Educators in Noguera's study identified students they believed would eventually end up in jail. Such a mind-set, where educators predict who will eventually experience firsthand the juvenile justice or prison system, is grounded in a culture of hate that surely has bearing on opportunity structures. If teachers believe their students will fail and become incarcerated, they likely will treat them in ways that essentially guarantee such an outcome. Again, students usually meet the expectations educators establish—whether high or low. In fact, structural practices can covertly be designed to prepare students for "jail-bound" paths. In this sense, schools can structurally produce and perpetuate inequity and poverty while pretending to be designed to do the opposite.[37]

Although students should be encouraged and supported to counter oppressive practices that place them in situations of prison-like insubordination, they must also be able to operate within these cultural systems in order to change them. Knowing what the culture of power actually is, how it works, and how power can be achieved is an important tool for students to develop. Not only should students be taught explicitly about the culture of power, but their parents, family members, and community should also have opportunities to build knowledge about what expectations educators have for their children. Again, educators cannot maintain tacit beliefs about expectations, assuming that families know what is expected of them or of their children. Thus, simply assuming that students will be taught a culture of power about schools and classroom norms and expectations can be considered irresponsible because students' families may operate from a different worldview regarding expectations in their homes and what should happen in schools. Moreover, students' families may not fully understand (or embrace) how to negotiate and live in a dominant culture or may not possess those dominant cultural views and values about how to function in society themselves.

Cultural conflicts are apparent when examining patterns of school punishment and office referrals, especially those that occur in the classroom. The findings in the research literature are straightforward in that most disciplinary student referrals (1) originate in the classroom and (2) are disproportionately for students of color and those from lower socioeconomic backgrounds. Researchers Russell Skiba et al. analyzed disciplinary documents for 11,001 students in nineteen middle schools in a large midwestern urban public school district during the 1994–1995 academic year. They reported a "differential pattern of treatment, originating at the classroom level, wherein African American students are referred to the office for infractions that are more subjective in interpretation."[38]

For instance, if a Latino/a student talks back or mouths off to an educator, the behavior may be interpreted as disrespectful, based on the educator's cultural worldview. However, the student may be behaving in this way (mouthing off) because of peer pressure—not wanting friends to see him/her/them as weak—rather than out of disrespect; malice may not be at the core of the student's actions. Skiba et al. point out that students of color received harsher punishments for the exact same infraction than their White peers.[39] Thus, understanding the role and salience of cultural conflicts is essential to addressing opportunity gaps.

MYTH OF MERITOCRACY

The third feature of the Opportunity Gap Framework, the myth of meritocracy, is another critical area of consideration when addressing opportunity gaps. While many educators, White educators in particular, have a difficult time confronting matters of race, they tend to more readily identify disparities in students' socioeconomic status as a cause of opportunity gaps. Educators appear to be more confident and comfortable with the idea that socioeconomic factors, particularly resources that determine wealth and poverty, influence educational inequities, outcomes, and opportunities. However, they sometimes misunderstand the historic and structural forms of resources that grant people their positions in society. Further, educators sometimes struggle to understand how race intersects with poverty and socioeconomic status.[40]

Educators may embrace the notion that their own, their parents', and their children's success, achievements, and status have been earned. Conversely, they may believe that failure and lack of resources result from individual effort, ability, or will. Educators may equate lack of success to wrong or bad choices over which individuals have control. Unearned opportunities and consequently success, however, are often passed down from one generation to the next; yet many educators believe that their own success is merited because they have worked hard, followed the law, had the ability and skill, and made the right decisions. They have little or no conception of how privilege and opportunity manifest (see McIntosh's article "White Privilege" for an excellent discussion of the nature of privilege).[41] For instance, White educators may fail to see that they are privileged based on their race and the opportunities whiteness has afforded them. Such affordances result from home and business loans made available to White people and denied to people of color. These affordances can result from redlining, in which lending agencies and insurance companies refuse to service particular communities due to the perceived financial condition of the community. Moreover, wealthy educators of any racial background can fail to recognize their economic privilege and to understand how they have acquired that privilege. People rarely become wealthy overnight or based on their own merit. Wealth and related resources are built and established over time and tend to be passed through generations of families. Teachers in general can fail to understand that they have gained their status through a wide range of unearned advantages. In contrast, students who grow up in poverty or from a lower socioeconomic status generally do not start their educational or life experiences in a fair or equitable position. In this way, meritocracy is a myth.

In wealthier families, inherited wealth may afford opportunities that are not directly "earned." Consider the following examples of what generational and family wealth and resources afford people:

- Trust funds established and passed down through generations
- Property (as in homes and land) that is passed down from one generation to the next
- A financed college education (undergraduate and graduate) without student loans
- Private and independent school tuition and education
- Private tutoring in academic subjects
- Exposure to different cultures and languages through travel
- Counseling and therapy clinicians to help support psychological, mental health, and emotional stress and strain
- Kaplan and tutorial programs to prepare students for the SAT, ACT, and GRE
- Vacations and getaways, both domestic and international, to recharge and reboot
- Zoned school systems with superior educational resources and curriculum materials

At the center of the meritocracy argument for student success is opportunity. That is, US society is predicated on the philosophical ideals expressed in the Declaration of Independence, that all people are created equal and have the same opportunities for success. In reality, however, educational practices and opportunities are anything but equal or equitable. The enormous variation in students' social, economic, political, and educational opportunities is in stark contrast to the "American dream," which has meritocracy as its core. Still, many educators believe that if people just work hard enough they will be rewarded and achieve their full potential, regardless of historic or contemporary economic structures. To be sure, educators should encourage students to do their very best—to work hard to succeed, for instance. However, they should also be honest with students—we live in a world where meritocracy is in fact a myth and that there are many forces at play that maintain a caste system. A caste system suggests that structures are in place for people's socioeconomic status to remain constant from birth. That is, those born wealthy remain rich throughout their lives, as do their children. Educators can fail to recognize systemic barriers and institutional structures that prevent opportunity and thereby hinder success. Several mind-sets and assertions regarding meritocracy are common and can impede our efforts to reduce and ultimately eliminate opportunity gaps:

Mind-set 1: All people are born with the same opportunities. If students work hard, put forth effort, and follow the law, then they will be successful.

Mind-set 2: If students do not succeed, it is because they are not working hard enough, not because of other factors that may be outside their control.

Mind-set 3: Some students just do not have the aptitude, ability, or skills for success; the "system" has nothing to do with academic achievement.

However, if the meritocracy argument were accurate, as sociologist James Henslin writes,

> [A]ll positions would be awarded on the basis of merit. If so, ability should predict who goes to college. Instead, *family income* [my emphasis added] is

> the best predictor—the more a family earns, the more likely their children are to go to college . . . while some people do get ahead through ability and hard work, others simply inherit wealth and the opportunities that go with it . . . in short, factors far beyond merit give people their positions in society.[42]

The meritocracy argument is a myth because it maintains that people—any person regardless of race, socioeconomic status, religion, sexual orientation, and so forth—living in US society can achieve the "American dream," as long as they have the ability, work hard, follow the law, and make good decisions. However, one could argue that many talented people remain imprisoned, both figuratively and literally, for offenses that have little to do with their aptitude, ability, or hard work. The system works to reproduce itself. Thus, opportunity gaps can "undermine one of our most powerful and core beliefs that we as Americans cling to: that no matter what circumstances children are born into, all have the opportunity to become educated and, if they work hard, to pursue their dreams."[43] To rationalize a meritocratic philosophy and position, successful, isolated cases are offered of individuals such as successful athletes and celebrities who have supposedly pulled themselves up by their bootstraps.

This philosophy can reject institutionalized and systemic issues and barriers that permeate policies and practices, such as racism, sexism, classism, and discrimination, both in the classroom and in society. Teacher education researcher Marilyn Cochran-Smith explains that "U.S. society writ large is not a meritocracy but is embedded in social, political, economic, and educational systems that are deeply and fundamentally racist."[44] Indeed, the meritocracy argument does not appropriately take into consideration resources, advantages, and privileges that wealthier students often inherit.[45]

A pervasive theme of a meritocratic mind-set centers on a we/they binary that some adopt as they position themselves and their "earned" success in opposition or in relation to others. Critical theorist Michael Apple maintains that

> the binary opposition of we–they becomes important . . . For dominant groups, "we" are law-abiding, hardworking, decent, and virtuous. "They"—usually poor people and immigrants—are very different. They are lazy, immoral, and permissive. These binary oppositions act to exclude indigenous people, women, the poor, and others from the community of worthy individuals.[46]

Thus, dichotomous mind-sets can allow people to rationalize and view their successes as having been "earned" by being law-abiding, hardworking, and virtuous. However, Ladson-Billings has stressed that it is unfair and inconceivable to expect all students to finish their education in the same place when they do not begin their education in the same place.[47] In other words, how can we expect equal outcomes on achievement measures when structural inequities place some groups of students in poorly run schools with fewer resources and underqualified teachers? Bafflingly, we wonder why populations of students who have been poorly served in education cannot necessarily overcome an educational system that is not designed for them to succeed. Ladson-Billings maintains that rather than focusing on achievement gaps in education, we should instead work to address the education debt as the system continues to fail particular groups of students. This failure is not a function of merit but a function of injustice and inequity in education.

Figures 1.2 and 1.3, based on the 2000 and 2010 US Census data, capture the correlation between people's earnings and their level of education. These graphs summarize unemployment and annual salaries as well as lifetime earnings. It is clear that people's ability to pursue higher education and earn a degree has serious implications for the amount of money they will earn in their lifetime. A central challenge is removing gaps in opportunity so that more people can have access to high-quality education. These graphs provide an important picture of the educational and economic landscape that has direct implications, I believe, on the kinds of experiences and opportunities people have in society. Logically, education level as well as family/generational legacy are strong predictors of economic success. Understanding the roots and genesis of economic resources is crucial for

FIGURE 1.2

Unemployment rates and earnings by educational attainment, 2018

	Unemployment rate (%)	Median usual weekly earnings ($)
Doctoral degree	1.6	1,825
Professional degree	1.5	1,884
Master's degree	2.1	1,434
Bachelor's degree	2.2	1,198
Associate's degree	2.8	862
Some college, no degree	3.7	802
High school diploma	4.1	730
Less than a high school diploma	5.6	553
	Total: 3.2%	All workers: $932

Note: Data are for persons age twenty-five and over. Earnings are for full-time wage and salary workers.

Adapted from U.S. Department of Labor, Bureau of Labor Statistics, *Employment Projections*, 2018, https://www.bls.gov/emp/chart-unemployment-earnings-education.htm.

educators as they work to level the playing field and remove obstacles and barriers that contribute to gaps in opportunity inside schools.

However, as ethnographer Jay MacLeod explains, sometimes "schools actually reinforce social inequality while pretending to do the opposite" because educators refuse to see meritocracy for what it really is, and they blame students for issues far beyond their control.[48] Moreover, when educators do not understand (or when they understand but do not acknowledge) how educational opportunity and economic patterns are linked, they are unlikely to make decisions that help students build knowledge about inequity and learn how they can transform their lives to break cycles of poverty as a result of low-paying jobs and careers. Elementary-age students cannot control how much money their parents and family earn, the school zone in which they live, their zip code, property taxes, or the availability of private tutoring. Although educators may understand and empathize with such young people, curriculum theorist Beverly Gordon explains it

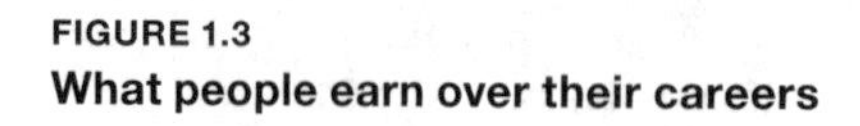

FIGURE 1.3
What people earn over their careers

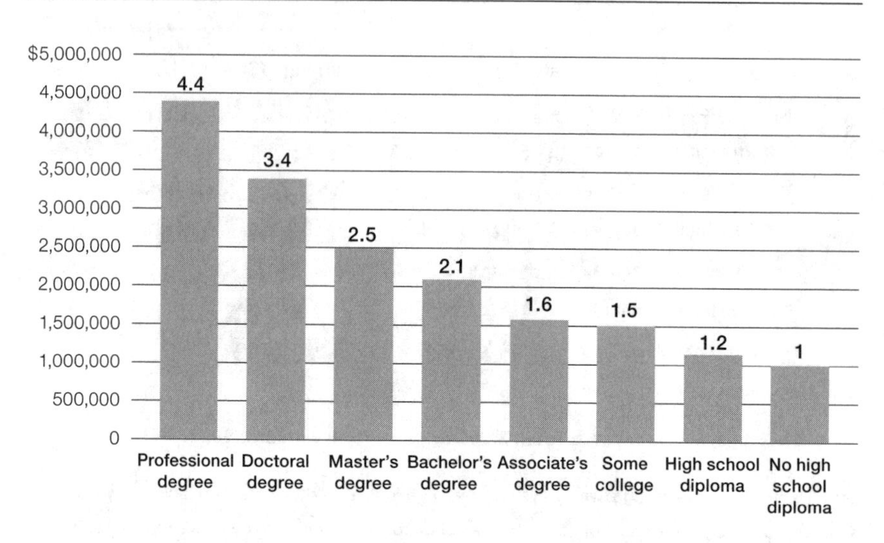

Adapted from U.S. Census Bureau, Current Population Reports, Special Studies, *The Big Payoff: Educational Attainment and Synthetic Estimates of Work-Life Earnings*, July 2002, http://www.census.gov/prod/2002pubs/p23-210.pdf.

is difficult for educators to critique the world and work to change it when the world works for them.[49] Thus, although educators may understand and empathize, when the world works for them, they may not consciously do anything to change their practices or better advocate for and with their students. Indeed, to address gaps in opportunity, educators must understand how meritocracy is a myth by interrogating their own lived experiences and building practices designed to create equitable opportunities for students to learn and thrive.

LOW EXPECTATIONS AND DEFICIT MIND-SETS

Thus far, I have explained three tenets of the Opportunity Gap Framework, designed to assist educators in addressing opportunity gaps, that I believe are essential to helping educators build the knowledge, attitudes, mind-sets, and ultimately practices to support all students for academic and social success: reject color blindness, understand cultural conflicts, and recognize the myth of meritocracy. In this section, I expand upon the fourth explanatory lens for analyzing and addressing opportunity gaps that educators should consider: disrupt low expectations and deficit mind-sets. Where cultural deficit theories are concerned, Ford writes, "These theories carry a 'blame the victim' orientation, and supporters look upon Blacks and other minority groups as not only culturally but also intellectually inferior. According to deficit theories or perspectives, 'different' is equated with deficient, inferior, and substandard."[50]

Low expectations and deficit mind-sets make it difficult for educators to develop learning opportunities that challenge students. For instance, teachers may believe that some students cannot master a rigorous curriculum, and consequently may avoid designing important learning opportunities for those students. They may see the knowledge and skills that students possess as irrelevant or inconsequential rather than important and central to build on in a classroom environment. For instance, in education, we tend to determine what students do not know or cannot demonstrate and work to remediate or fill in the areas of need. I am suggesting, however, that educators determine what students actually know and are able to do and build on those experiences as a foundation for supporting their learning and development over time. In this way, because all students are knowledgeable and capable, educators approach the teaching and learning exchange from a position of strength because they recognize that, in fact, all their students have assets from which they can build and learn. Throughout this book, educators demonstrate how they learn about the assets of the young people with whom they work.

However, even when educators do recognize student assets, they sometimes struggle to understand how they can build upon those assets or strengths to co-create learning opportunities. At times, student assets are not appropriately used as anchors to make instructional connections in the classroom. Consequently, educators continue teaching in ways that avoid or overlook the brilliance and talents that students possess because they may not align with educators' own worldview of what excellence looks like. They may not see how hip-hop, graffiti art, music composing, and other assets that students possess are talents and strengths from which they can build instructional practices. Moreover, rather than viewing argumentative students as troublemakers, an asset-based approach would require educators to encourage strong, verbal students to build their debate skills through research and evidence substantiation.

Educators' beliefs that can lead to low expectations may materialize out of (1) conversations about students they have had among themselves in the teachers' lounge or hallway, reflecting on previous experiences they have had with students or even their siblings or relatives; (2) their interpretations of student results on standardized tests; or (3) their disdain for or lack of relationships with family members of their students. Regardless of the source, deficit mind-sets and low expectations can result in practices that do more harm than good for young people. Indeed, students need and deserve educators who believe in them and refuse to allow them to give up. These educators see education as a developmental process that helps to cultivate growth and learning over time. Several common beliefs are related to low expectations and deficit mind-sets:

Mind-set 1: I need to distance students from the "horrors" of their home conditions. Students lack so much, and their home environments make it difficult for me to teach them.

Mind-set 2: I feel sorry for my students because they need so much. If I expect too much, then I am setting them up for failure.

Mind-set 3: I cannot co-construct rigorous and engaging learning opportunities with my students because they are so far "behind" and they "bring so little."

Mind-set 4: "Those" poor students cannot meet high expectations because they do not have the resources to do so.

Because of a deficit mind-set, educators sometimes believe they are actually doing students a favor by not challenging them to think deeply, engage fully, and do their very best. These lowered expectations emerge in how and what is taught, when, for how long, and for what purposes. Educators who operate from deficit mind-sets and low expectations

- assign mountains of work sheets, developing unchallenging, mundane tasks for students to complete;
- have rigid expectations for what success and improvement look like; and
- use outdated unidimensional assessment tools to gauge student learning and development.

Many students in classrooms with such educators function like they are completing an independent study. Students need teachers to teach and engage with them, not occupy their time with busywork. But when teachers do not really want to engage with students and push themselves, they tend to rely on instructional methods that distance, rather than unite, them with younger people.

However, when educators disrupt deficit mind-sets and low expectations, they realize and acknowledge that students are developing beings, and they have a chance to help students learn and grow when they see them as human beings with limitless potential. For example, educators can give students multiple opportunities to succeed, not give up on them, and work with students to create the type of learning environment where all students succeed. They can provide students space to be creative, exert their voice, or offer views that differ from those presented by a teacher, a textbook, or other classmates.[51]

Deficit mind-set contributes to an unending, troubling cycle that has been described by Haberman: educators do not teach with rigor and high expectations; students do not learn; students' test scores suffer; and then all involved wonder why.[52] I have learned that the blame for failure is too often placed on students, their families, and communities without any serious interrogation of the role that educators and school structures play. In short, deficit mind-sets and low expectations can have negative outcomes for both educators and students. Indeed, justice where teaching and learning are concerned has to be realized on both sides, as Winn has explained.[53] In other words, sometimes teachers get it wrong and should work to address areas of development on their (educator's) part as well as students'.

Additionally, stereotypes can play a huge role in educators' expectations and students' mind-sets. Social psychologist Claude Steele's research points to the psychological burdens that marginalized people have endured as a result of stereotypes about them "in the air."[54] His research shows that people's performance and achievement, such as women in mathematics, can be hindered due to what he calls "stereotype threat," where members of the stereotyped group worry that they will reinforce or confirm a negative stereotype through their performance in a particular domain. The stereotype becomes an additional burden that people believe they must counter. Educators' expectations coupled with students' understanding of their "deficiencies" have direct consequences for students' psychological, social, and emotional well-being. Stereotyped students know what is being said about them through the media, for instance, and their performance can be influenced by these views because they may be working overtime to counter or disrupt the stereotypes. Students understand when teachers buy in to pervasive, negative stereotypes about them, and they realize when low expectations and deficit mind-sets shape what happens in the classroom. Consequently, as a feature of the Opportunity Gap Framework, educators are urged to think carefully about the ways in which deficit mind-sets and low expectations position the most vulnerable students as inadequate. Addressing gaps in opportunity means that educators move away from deficit mind-sets and low expectations and consequently avoid placing young people neatly into a predetermined box for what it means to be a successful student and human being. People are diverse and our practices should honor the positive aspects of human identity as students develop and learn.

CONTEXT-NEUTRAL MIND-SETS

A fifth dimension of this Opportunity Gap Framework, a counter to and disruption of context-neutral mind-sets, is also essential to transform educational facilities into ones that honor and support student wholeness, emancipation, and success. Social contexts have a huge bearing on human development and opportunity structures, for both educators and students. Communities can be classified as suburban, rural, or urban. Urban and rural communities have many similarities.[55] Suburban communities often offer educational material resources that many urban and rural contexts do not. The social context of schools and communities therefore reinforces opportunity and the status quo. Although suburban schools tend to have more material resources, technology, and working spaces than rural and urban schools, suburban schools are not excluded from problems. Students in these schools still struggle with all the challenges that adolescents encounter and sometimes more. These include dating; conflicts with parents, step-parents, and family members; drug and alcohol abuse; bullying, including cyberbullying and body shaming; self-esteem issues; and psychological and social difficulties. Thus, educators in suburban schools, like those in other settings, must consistently consider the ways in which where they are teaching/working can influence student experiences. It is educators' responsibility to understand the role, importance, and salience of place as they work to address gaps in opportunity. However, context-neutral mind-sets do not allow educators to recognize the nuances embedded in a particular place, such as a school in a particular community—what multicultural education researcher Francisco Rios calls the cultural context.[56]

The social context should be taken into account when attempting to understand opportunity and diversity and the impact they have on educators' and students' performance and outcomes. The broader context of student learning—the geography of opportunity—is essential for educators to study and understand as they help to build a village of resources inside of school to support students.[57] Such a village from which educators might learn includes school counselors or social workers or even coaches from a community who have worked with a young person. Centralizing the role of place provides educators with opportunities to build on what they are learning from and with students in the classroom.[58]

As they consider their own identity and those of students and families, policy makers and school board officials must also carefully study the place of their work. Consider the following contextually grounded realities that inevitably influence the nature of opportunity for both educators and students. I have adapted many of these examples from Paul Barton's policy analysis, *Parsing the Achievement Gap: Baseline for Tracking Progress*:[59]

- Urban and high-poverty schools have a disproportionate number of new teachers; students whose teachers have five years of experience or more make three to four months more progress in reading during a school year.
- Teachers in urban and high-poverty schools are absent more often than teachers in other locations; as a result, students in urban schools are taught by substitute teachers, many of whom are not trained in the subject matter domains of their teaching.
- There is often a lack of commitment and persistence among educators in urban and high-poverty schools. Graduates of college/teacher education programs work in urban and high-poverty schools until another position becomes available in a "more desirable" location.
- A disproportionate number of educators teach outside their field of expertise in urban and high-poverty schools.

In addition, money and resources are unequal in different social contexts: high-need districts where resources are low too often receive the same assistance as districts with much higher resources.[60] Some districts distribute "equally funded programs into schools regardless of how many students need them. For example, a district might allocate $100,000 to each school with English language learners, even though one school might have 200 students with limited English proficiency and another—often a more affluent school—might have only 20 [students]."[61]

Clearly, it is no secret that urban and high-poverty schools face persistent challenges that can put student learning opportunities in jeopardy. Educators' understanding of how the factors presented above influence students' opportunities is important, as this awareness allows us to examine how a social context shapes opportunity rather than focus primarily on the students themselves, on achievement gaps, or on an outcome, such as a test score. Indeed, we must consider factors beyond test scores if we are serious about seeing a more nuanced picture of what it takes to support student learning and development.[62]

Studying rates and patterns of absenteeism among educators in urban and high-poverty schools can help us make sense of student achievement when we consider that students have received instruction from a substitute teacher who may or may not have the educational credentials (especially the knowledge of the subject being taught) to teach. In a similar vein, it is not enough for educators to have deep subject-matter knowledge if they lack strong context-centered knowledge. Sadly, many education researchers treat these two important dimensions of knowledge (subject matter and social context) separately, in terms of both research and practice. But I believe these two areas should be treated, understood, and addressed together.

An added problem arises when educators believe that issues of race and diversity are insignificant in mostly White learning contexts. Researchers and theoreticians agree that teaching about race, diversity, and multicultural education more broadly is a necessity for the intellectual, academic, and social success of students across different spaces.[63] Understandably, because the number of culturally, racially, and linguistically diverse students in the United States is increasing at a high rate, emphasizing race and diversity has consistently focused on White educators teaching in predominantly African American or other settings with large populations of students of color—namely, urban settings. However, Banks explains that diversity studies and multicultural education are "to help *all* students, *including White mainstream students* [emphasis added], to develop the knowledge, skills, and attitudes they will need to survive and function effectively in a future U.S. society in which one out of every three people will be a person of color."[64]

Issues of race, diversity, and multicultural education, then, are important not only for students of color, linguistically diverse learners, and students who have a special learning need, but also for students in the mainstream of learning; White students and students who grow up with some degree of wealth and privilege in a range of social contexts should also focus on these matters. However, in suburban and mostly wealthy schools "in which the population is basically white and middle-class, multicultural education is often viewed as unnecessary."[65] The idea that racial discrimination and cultural misunderstandings do not exist in predominantly White settings is a fallacy. Moreover, students who attend mostly White settings do not live in a vacuum; they will experience matters of race and diversity in the broader world, and they must be prepared to function effectively in that world in order to understand their own position and opportunities, as well as those of others. Moreover, White people are not a monolithic group, and students need opportunities to think about the diversity among them.[66]

I have learned that too many current and future teachers operate from a context-neutral mind-set:

> *Mind-set 1:* It does not matter where my students live; I will teach them all just the same. Kids are just kids. If I teach my subject matter well, I can get all my students interested in the subject; the type or location of the school and who is enrolled do not matter.
>
> *Mind-set 2:* It is not necessary for me to rally the local community to help me learn, to energize and motivate students inside the school and classroom.
>
> *Mind-set 3:* There are few differences between the various school types in the United States. It is not necessary for me to develop skills to study and deepen my knowledge and understanding of the historic and contemporary realities of the school communities where I teach.

To address opportunity gaps, it is necessary and important for educators to deeply understand both the broader and the more localized social contexts that shape their teaching. Relevant, effective, and responsive teaching requires that educators know more than their subject matter; they must understand the differences, complexities, and nuances inherent in what it means to teach in urban, suburban, and rural environments. Such an understanding of the context in which they teach can assist in moving educators beyond stereotypes to mind-sets that allow them to learn continuously about their communities and the people in them. While I support educators' learning about the social context in which they teach, I am also stressing that teachers refuse to accept commonly held ideas that place particular communities in a negative light. Educators need to learn about the social context so that they are able to grasp how communities are classified and what they might encounter; concurrently, educators need to be deliberate in their efforts to locate the "good" in social contexts that others have written off as hopeless. One way to think about the assets of a place is to study its history. For instance, engaging with elders of a community allows educators opportunities to understand when shifts occurred in a community, for what purposes, and for whose benefit. Moreover, understanding the social context also means that educators are aware and critical of the ways that gentrification has redefined neighborhood structures and displaced those indigenous to communities. As families are pushed out of their homes and communities (similar to how Black and Brown students, those with disabilities, and those in poverty are pushed out of classrooms) for little profit while those who occupy the spaces receive considerable profit, educators understand how forces are at play for economic interests of the elite and powerful. When educators deepen their knowledge and insights about a sociopolitical context, they also recognize and honor histories and perspectives of those placed on the margins in the community because they may not have the resources to maintain their communities.

In essence, educators need to understand that they are working in service *with* the community. As Brazilian critical theorist Paulo Freire explains, those of us in education are working with communities to improve individual circumstances and ultimately the human condition.[67] Educators are not the only or the most important knowers in a community or a school. As curriculum theorist Gail McCutcheon reminds us, we must take control of our beliefs and positions before they control us.[68] Indeed, community context knowledge is an essential aspect of understanding opportunity, and educators must be vigilant and steadfast in their efforts to learn about the social context of their work.

Table 1.1 summarizes the five core interrelated tenets of the Opportunity Gap Framework discussed throughout this book. The table includes a summative explanation of each concept, several mind-sets or assertions educators may hold that substantiate and define each tenet, and possible instructional and related consequences connected to opportunity drawn from the feature.

The following chapters showcase teachers in particular social contexts and how they address issues of opportunity and diversity in their practices.

TABLE 1.1
An explanatory framework on opportunity

Tenet	Explanations	Educators' mind-sets	Instructional consequences
Color blindness (conceptions of race matter)	Educators avoid and reject their own and their students' racialized experiences in their decision-making. Educators see race as a taboo topic that is irrelevant and inconsequential to the success of students. White educators do not recognize the multiple layers of privilege associated with their race and how race can manifest in teaching, learning, and curricular experiences.	M1: If I acknowledge the racial or ethnic background of my students or myself, then I may be considered racist. M2: If I admit that people of color may experience the world differently, I may be seen as "politically incorrect." I may offend others in a teacher education classroom or my preK–12 faculty meeting if I express my beliefs, concerns, and reservation about race. M3: I should treat all my students the same regardless of their race. Race does not matter and racism has ended; thus, racial considerations have no place or relevance in the design and enactment of classroom learning opportunities.	Educators teach their students in a myopic manner; they do not consider how racially diverse students experience the world inside the classroom, inside the school, and in society. Curriculum and instructional decisions are grounded in a "White norm" that students of color have to just "deal with" and adapt to. Race is seen as a marginal, not central, aspect of developing lessons and enacting those lessons (teaching).
Cultural conflicts (conceptions of culture matter)	Inconsistency emerges in the teaching and learning context based on (among other factors) race, gender, age, geography, and socioeconomic disconnections between educators and students. Conflicts may be historically or currently shaped. Educators see their culture as superior to that of their students.	M1: I must teach students based on how I teach my own biological children, not based on their culture, cultural practices, and experiences in the world (which may or may not be consistent with my own). M2: All students should behave the same. I'm not going to tolerate students joking around during class. If they misbehave, I'm sending them to the office—period! M3: "Those" students need to adapt and assimilate into the culture of my classroom and accept the consequences if they do not.	Educators refer students of color to the office when they "misbehave." Educators refer culturally diverse students to special education when they are not grasping instructional material rather than attempting to adjust their instructional practices to better meet the learning styles of those students. A disproportionate number of African American students are suspended and expelled.

(*continued*)

TABLE 1.1 *(continued)*

An explanatory framework on opportunity

Construct	Explanations	Educators' mind-sets	Instructional consequences
Myth of meritocracy (conceptions of socio-economic status matter)	Educators accept the idea that people are rewarded based (solely or mostly) on their ability, performance, effort, and talents. Systemic and institutional structures and barriers are not considered. Individual achievement is seen as an independent variable.	M1: All people are born with the same opportunities. If students work hard, put forth effort, and follow the law, then they will be successful. M2: If students do not succeed, it is because they are not working hard enough, not because of other factors that may be outside their control. M3: Some students just do not have the aptitude, ability, or skills for success; the "system" has nothing to do with academic achievement.	Educators do not give students multiple chances for success because they believe the students are not working hard enough. Educators do not delve deeply into the reasons behind students' lack of engagement or the reasons why students do not complete their homework. The reality that performance may be a consequence of students' financial problems is not considered as a source of "problems" in the classroom.
Deficit mind-sets and low expectations (belief systems matter)	Educators approach their work focusing on what students do not have rather than on the assets students bring into the learning environments. Educators have a narrow view of what it means to be "normal" or "successful"; these views are based on their own cultural references, which may be inconsistent with others.	M1: I need to distance students from the "horrors" of their home conditions. Students lack so much, and their home environments make it difficult for me to teach them. M2: I feel sorry for my students because they need so much. If I expect too much, then I am setting them up for failure. M3: I cannot co-construct rigorous and engaging learning opportunities with my students because they are so far "behind" and they "bring so little."	Educators spend their time remediating students instead of building on the knowledge students actually bring into the classroom. Educators refuse to allow students to develop their own thinking skills. Students are expected to regurgitate a right answer that the educator or a textbook has provided.

(continued)

TABLE 1.1 *(continued)*

An explanatory framework on opportunity

Construct	Explanations	Educators' mind-sets	Instructional consequences
Deficit mind-sets and low expectations (belief systems matter) *(continued)*	Educators do not believe that culturally diverse students are capable of a rigorous academic curriculum, so they provide unchallenging learning opportunities in the classroom.	M4: "Those" poor students cannot meet high expectations because they do not have the resources to do so.	Very little discussion and creative learning opportunities are available. Students are given busywork in hopes that they will not talk; the classroom is viewed as the educators' space, and students are expected to conform and to be quiet. Educators water down the curriculum and have only minimal curricular expectations. Educators focus on basic skills only and push students to get a "right" answer in all academic subject matters. Students are not allowed to think outside the box, to develop critical and analytic thinking skills, or to question power structures in order to improve unfair, inequitable realities.
Context-neutral mind-sets (social contexts matter)	Educators approach their work without a keen sense of how contextual, ecological, and environmental realities shape opportunities to learn. Educators concentrate on learning subject matter (such as math, science, social studies, and language arts) and consider it unimportant to understand the complexities inherent in teaching that subject matter in different contexts, such as urban, suburban, or rural spaces.	M1: It does not matter where my students live, I will teach them all just the same. Kids are just kids. If I teach my subject matter well, I can get all my students interested in the subject; the type or location of the school and who is enrolled in the school do not matter M2: It is not necessary for me to rally the local community to help me learn, to energize and motivate students inside the school and classroom. M3: There are few differences between the various school types in the United States. It is not necessary for me to develop skills to study and deepen my knowledge and understanding of the historic and contemporary realities of the school communities where I teach.	Educators do not build on or draw from the knowledge or established resources of the local community. Rather than constructing knowledge with the community, educators act as if they are omniscient and miss or possibly consciously avoid opportunities to build substantive partnerships in the social context that can assist them in supporting the learning and development needs of students.

2

White Teacher, Diverse Urban School

Relationships, Expectations, and Race Matter—Even in the Science Classroom

The students were resistant [to me] because they did not know me when I first started teaching here. There was all this pushback because the kids were like: "I don't care who you are, I don't know you."

—MR. HALL, MIDDLE SCHOOL SCIENCE TEACHER IN AN URBAN SCHOOL

MR. HALL, a White science educator, had been teaching for three years at Bridge Middle School when he made the above comment. He explained that when he first entered the teaching profession, his students were sometimes unwilling to engage in class and were resistant because, as his students stated, they did not "know" him. In this chapter, I demonstrate the important transformative nature of Mr. Hall's work in the science classroom by focusing on the role and relevance of race and relationship building in addressing opportunity gaps. As discussed in the previous chapter, relationship building is essential to working through cultural conflicts, racism, and deficit mind-sets. Some students in Mr. Hall's classes struggled to make a connection with him, which had an influence on the kinds of learning opportunities that Mr. Hall was able to co-construct with them. However, rather than accepting that tensions would emerge and that opportunity gaps were inevitable, Mr. Hall learned from his students and adjusted his practices accordingly. He demonstrated a level of vulnerability as he worked with his students and allowed them to teach him what they needed in order to learn and succeed in the classroom. In reality, what I learned from his practices was that Mr. Hall started where he was but refused to stay there. He was willing to look at himself, his own life experiences, and examine his classroom practices in order to address broader issues related to opportunity structures. Had Mr. Hall not been tenaciously vigilant in addressing problems and tensions as he experienced them, opportunity gaps could have taken several serious forms. But he refused to allow tensions to win. He learned and got better.

To maximize opportunity and avoid serious opportunity gaps in the classroom, Mr. Hall realized early in his career that he would need to (1) learn from his students and adjust his practices, through instructional agility, based on what they taught him; (2) develop a deeper understanding of the impact of race in the science classroom; (3) create as many opportunities as possible to develop relationships with his students to work through cultural differences; and (4) understand how uncomfortable situations could become opportunities to learn for his students and about himself.

The growth in this educator's conceptions, mind-sets, and practices was driven by the students themselves—the very students who insisted that Mr. Hall did not "know" them when he arrived at Bridge Middle School. Like many educators early in their careers, Mr. Hall had not thought about how or why race, culture, or diversity was important in his teaching practices, especially in a science classroom. He explained that he went to work to "teach science," and had to work to understand that teaching science would require much more than knowledge of his subject, particularly at Bridge Middle School. He realized as he listened to his students that he had to understand the environment in which he was working and could not adopt a context-neutral mind-set. Moreover, Mr. Hall learned that he would have to address race, even though it was not something he necessarily wanted, expected, or felt comfortable doing as a science teacher. But, as a White teacher who grew up outside the Bridge community with very different cultural experiences and practices, he *had* to think about race because the students needed, expected, and ultimately demanded that he do so.

In my work preparing teachers, I have learned that preservice educators are sometimes skeptical or uncertain about the relevance of race and other dimensions of diversity in the preK–12 classrooms. For years, I have been met with persistent and assertive resistance from preservice educators who struggled to understand how race or, more broadly, diversity would matter to their teaching practices. In their defense, I should note that many of the educators with whom I worked had not experienced firsthand what it meant to teach in a diverse classroom. By diverse, I mean a context that included a range of different racial and ethnic backgrounds, students who lived below the poverty line, those whose first language was not English, and those who had learning differences such as "disabilities." Although contexts with large numbers of Black and Brown students are often viewed and talked about as "diverse," I want to stress that understanding diversity requires that teachers build capacity beyond a black-white dichotomy. Still, other preservice and in-service teachers with whom I have worked seemed to recognize that they would experience diversity among their students but were unclear about how diversity, and race in particular, might influence their actual teaching practices.

In the case study in this chapter, I describe how a White, middle school science educator, Mr. Hall, developed into what one of his Black colleagues called a "shining star" and what a group of students called a "with-it" teacher. His story shows how a White educator was able to learn from his students, build relationships with them, and transform his teaching in the process. Mr. Hall demonstrates how he was able to learn, change, and grow to reject color blindness, work through cultural conflicts, and disrupt his context-neutral mind-set. In essence, the case demonstrates how the students themselves helped their teacher become responsive to what they believed they needed to learn from and with him. Mr. Hall was able to transform his practice by learning from and with his students about how to deal with the challenges and roadblocks that they faced together in their journey to teach and learn. The case addresses some critical questions: What experiences shaped Mr. Hall's shifting mind-set, beliefs, and consequently his practice in an urban classroom? Why and how did his thoughts, beliefs, and practices change over time? What might other educators learn from this case about teaching in similar contexts?

INTRODUCING MR. HALL

When I met Mr. Hall, he was in his early twenties. He usually dressed in blue jeans or khakis and a polo shirt. Describing his own identity and background, he proclaimed that he was a part of a "rural Southern" culture. Approachable yet firm, Mr. Hall projected a "tough love" demeanor that was also what some students called "cool" and "with-it." I observed that, over the years, his disposition seemed to intensify as he developed into a more attentive, conscientious, confident, and conscious educator; as he built knowledge about the idiosyncratic needs of his students, he transformed his practices with zeal and attentiveness. Whenever I interacted with him as a "university professor," in his words, he would always ask me how he could improve. In some cases, he would ask me about a particular episode I had observed or an interaction he had the previous day or week that he was still trying to make sense of. He was "cool and with-it" enough that students enjoyed hanging around him between classes or before and after school.

While Mr. Hall rarely raised his voice, when he did, from my view, it was not in a condescending, demeaning, disrespectful, or arrogant manner. His interactions with students reminded me of a parent or older sibling who clearly was not willing to accept nonsense but who also realized that every situation was not going to be perfect, and that occasionally he would have to let some things go and negotiate with his students in order to succeed. In this sense, Mr. Hall reminded me of a father or older-brother figure to his students (a point I will expand upon later). Mr. Hall seemed to realize that he needed to choose his battles wisely and that his real challenge would be to co-create learning opportunities, not to dominate his students or make them feel as if their preferences and needs were inconsequential. As he learned and improved as a teacher, he did not try to control his students based on some predetermined rules or expectations that were often out of date and irrelevant to his particular students and context.

Throughout the two years I observed at Bridge Middle School, I never saw Mr. Hall take much of a break. During his planning time, he was in his classroom talking with students or preparing for the next class: cleaning lab materials, grading papers, or writing on the board. During an assembly I attended, Mr. Hall sat with his students and was constantly making sure they were being respectful to their classmates, whereas some other teachers used the occasion to take a break. In 2008, Mr. Hall was chosen by his colleagues as Teacher of the Year—a major feat for someone in the profession for only a few years. However, I was not surprised by this honor because Mr. Hall not only knew his subject matter well but also was astute enough—and perhaps more important, open enough—to realize that knowing his students well was equally important. His instruction, curriculum development and enactment, assessment, classroom management, and vision for his students and related learning opportunities were dynamic, responsive, iterative, relevant, and always evolving.

KNOWING SCIENCE, KNOWING STUDENTS

Teachers cannot teach science until they understand and acknowledge who they are teaching science to. Subject-matter knowledge is essential but not sufficient for success in the classroom.

I recently had a conversation with a preservice math teacher who declared, "I respect people who want to deal with all that diversity stuff, but that's not for me. I just want to teach math and help my students develop a love for math." This future teacher explained that what mattered most in urban and highly diverse schools was that students develop mathematical thinking and be able to understand math beyond getting a right answer. He went on to tell me that he was "beyond" and "so past" the diversity aspect of his work. In his view, it was a waste of time for him to engage in diversity-related matters because he believed that his knowledge of math and his ability to teach it would supersede such issues. I reminded him that he would indeed be developing *people* into those who love math and that he would be working with *people*—real human beings—as they developed mathematical thinking beyond getting a right or wrong answer. I explained to him that without *understanding* and *acknowledging* whom he would be teaching, he would probably find it difficult to succeed in transforming students into the avid mathematicians he aspired to create. I reminded him that students are grappling with the demands of living, learning, and thriving in the classroom and also in their broader social worlds and realities. Furthermore, students are individuals with diverse preferences, interests, belief systems, worldviews, experiences, successes, failures, needs, and desires, all of which are shaped by a range of influences, including their race, socioeconomic status, culture, language, religion, sexual identity, gender, geography, and ability.

Like this math teacher who declared that he was "so over" the diversity aspect of his work, science teachers may wonder *how and why race should be considered in the teaching of science.* It is well known that the biological roots of race can be traced through scientific methods. Moreover, as suggested in the previous chapter, there are many problematic spaces to explore in science when we consider the dismal number of Black scientists in comparison to White people. However, science educators may not see the relevance of understanding and thinking beyond the surface. In other words, attempting to wrestle with matters of race as a social phenomenon, construction, and reality in a science classroom can take on much more complex nuances that need to be considered. For instance, we should all be mindful that something is likely going on in science classrooms over time as Black students' interests in the subject decreases year after year. For a science educator, thinking seriously about diversity may seem irrelevant or even inappropriate for the science curriculum. As a teacher educator, I have learned that science teachers often cannot or will not understand how or why learning about race or diversity in a teacher education program or professional development workshop has any real bearing on their work in the classroom. When he first started teaching, Mr. Hall was among this group. He noted, "I came here to do one thing, and that was to teach science."

However, Mr. Hall soon began to understand that he could not teach science until he understood and acknowledged *to whom* he was teaching science as well as the social context in which he was teaching it. Stated differently, teaching science in one context can be qualitatively different from teaching it in another, which means that educators should develop knowledge and skills to address matters beyond the science curriculum. Educators need to be aware that some of their students may have been exposed to scientific ideas for years, others not at all. It became evident to Mr. Hall that he had to be able to respond to a wide spectrum of diversity among his students in order to co-construct optimal learning opportunities.

Although Mr. Hall initially embraced a color-blind and diversity-blind philosophy, his experiences teaching and interacting with his students propelled him to a space where he understood how much race and diversity mattered in his work as a science educator. Outside the school, race seemed insignificant to him. As a White man, he did not *have* to consider race or racism because his life experiences did not necessarily require or warrant it. Indeed, a person who has never experienced racism and does not find race germane to how people function in society may find it difficult to understand why students would invoke racism in situations where it seems arbitrary. For me, as an African American man, I constantly experience racism in my everyday experiences; thus I am empathetic when race and racism emerge in how he engaged in and through situations for others. Although race was not a critical element in his life outside of Bridge Middle School, Mr. Hall's thoughts and beliefs evolved as his students insisted that he expand his notions of race, racism, and diversity.

When he began teaching, several students called him a racist. He explained: "Just coming from a rural country [town] and coming into the urban areas, the first couple years here, if I got onto some of the 'harder' African American kids, you know, who are really into rap . . . because I don't listen to rap . . . they'd say, 'You are racist.' They'd walk out the door saying, 'You're racist, you're racist.'"

Mr. Hall believed that these students saw his attempts to "correct" their misbehavior—that is, his "getting onto them"—as racist. Some Black students viewed him in terms of race, perceived him as racist because he got onto them, and he struggled with this because he did not consider himself a racist. He believed he was just someone who had not thought much about race and racism until he was compelled to do so by his students. Mr. Hall wanted the students to realize that he did not have anything against them. Perhaps the fact that he vehemently did not want his students to call him a racist or anyone to believe he was racist was the catalyst for him to really stop, reflect, and listen. In his explanation, he merely expected the Black students, like all his students, to engage and take advantage of the many opportunities afforded them in class. Mr. Hall rationalized the students' concerns: "I think some [students] have it in their minds that because I am up here, I get on to you, that I am attacking you personally. That is one of the hardest things to get across to children—that I am not attacking you; I am attacking your behavior."

So, even though Mr. Hall explained that he held no malice or racist motives and that he was only correcting students' behavior, not "attacking" them personally, some students still perceived him as a racist. It may be easy for some readers to dismiss the students' claims, insisting that the students were just playing a race card (again, whatever this means!), were being immature, or simply had it all wrong. Others may believe that the students were in fact upset with Mr. Hall and were using race to exacerbate the tension between themselves and their teacher. However, it is critical to remember that the students were expressing their view of reality, which Mr. Hall rightly refused to dismiss. Indeed, the students' perceptions were their realities, which should not be ignored, dismissed, or minimized.

I found that one of Mr. Hall's most compelling attributes was his ability to determine what his students needed by listening to and observing them and to respond to those expressed or demonstrated needs. He wondered why the students would default to race and racism when they had conflicts about his "getting onto them," and how he could reinvent himself and develop a reputation as a caring, committed, and competent educator for all his students through his practices with them. Interestingly, Mr. Hall did not express that he wanted to become an anti-racist. But his language around his experience suggested that he did, a point that I expand upon later in this chapter. I always wonder how education would be if other teachers—more teachers—would take the approach that Mr. Hall took in this situation. Rather than expecting his students to change or accept him without any critical reflection or shifts in his practice, Mr. Hall realized there were some power dynamics occurring in the classroom from which he needed to reflect and learn. What if all teachers/educators were willing to start where they are and deliberately work to get better—to not stay there?

As inaccurate and unfair as he may have considered the comments, accepting his students' perceptions allowed him to develop into an educator I would describe as deeply caring for his students. It was important for him to be willing and able to improve his practices based on what he learned from his students; listening to them gave him that opportunity. Had he failed to consider their reality, he could have missed important opportunities to forge deeper connections with his students. An important question is, how was Mr. Hall able to work through this difficult experience? To be clear, this was a distressing situation because Mr. Hall was devastated when he was referred to as "racist" after he "got onto" his Black students. How was Mr. Hall able to use this experience of being called racist as a critical site for him to learn and transform his thinking and actions?

In essence, although Mr. Hall struggled at first to understand the "racist" allegations, he more readily realized that his students were right in expressing their observation and belief that they needed to get to know one another. He realized that he needed to build and cultivate relationships with his students in order for them to grant him entry into their worlds, and to see that he challenged them not because he was racist but because he wanted them to reach their potential; he cared whether they decided to do what was necessary for them to succeed. However, saying that he cared without demonstrating that care would prove to be insufficient in the relationship-building exchange (a point I will expand on later in this chapter).

Mr. Hall realized that while there were differences between him and his students, there were also commonalities that could become anchors for bridging connections in the classroom. In searching for those common threads with his students, Mr. Hall remembered his poverty.

POVERTY

Educators must recognize cultural and other points of connection that allow them to bridge differences; shared experiences between teachers and students enable students to see their teachers as real people who have known and worked through difficult circumstances, such as poverty.

After being called "racist" by some of his students, Mr. Hall learned that it was essential for his students to learn more about him and to think about some of what they had in common. Based on his reflections of his experiences, Mr. Hall stressed that talking about, sharing, and demonstrating past and present "commonality" would allow his students to see that when he was "getting onto them" it was because he expected excellence from them—not because he was a racist or did not care about them. He needed to get his students to understand that they were on the same team. To build such trusting relationships, he and his students had to learn to share aspects of their lives, points of convergence that they may not have considered. In other words, Mr. Hall needed some *points of reference* and *points of convergence* that would enable them to open up to each other.

When he began his career at Bridge, some students had questioned Mr. Hall's loyalty to them, in part because he was not into rap music/hip-hop, but primarily because they felt they did not know him. Moreover, because he did not live in their community, the students suggested that he did not "know" what it was like to "be" them. As a White teacher, he later realized that while race was an important identity marker, his students needed to see him as a real person who could connect with and relate to their experiences on other levels. Indeed, Mr. Hall could not change the fact that he was White, and initially he saw this as a potential roadblock to the connections he hoped to build with his students.

Mr. Hall explained: "I grew up in rural west Tennessee, and I've told a couple of kids—I said, I grew up poor and we didn't have anything, you know? I told them I didn't know what real money looked like until I was about fifteen and had my own job because . . . my family bought food with food stamps . . . I thought all money was purple, green, and brown. I didn't know what real money looked like."

Mr. Hall started to see that the difficult economic conditions he faced growing up were a bridge to some of his students. Indeed, many of his students lived below the poverty line, and Mr. Hall believed they originally thought he might have grown up with socioeconomic privilege. Having a sense of his history living in poverty, he believed, ended some of their assumptions that all educators have "had it easy" and have not had to struggle to reach their current positions. However, although Mr. Hall wanted to reveal the fact that he had indeed grown up in poverty, he also projected a discourse of meritocracy among his students. For instance, he often talked with them about "working hard" and how it was not until he got his "own job" that he was able to transition out of poverty. Still, he pointed to his sharing of his tough financial upbringing as essential to building relationships with his students.

Once his students realized that he had had difficult times similar to their own, they became more receptive to what he was attempting to build in the classroom. Mr. Hall had learned that students had to *allow* teachers to teach them. It now seemed impossible for the teaching of science to occur until students were ready and willing to learn it from or with their teacher. In short, Mr. Hall could teach once the students were in a posture to learn.[1] Sharing his own story about poverty allowed his students to see the links between his growing up, in his words, "in the woods" and their growing up in a "tough neighborhood." Mr. Hall came to understand that some of his personal experiences could be incorporated more seamlessly into his teaching practices as a way to facilitate interactions with his students. It is important to note that Mr. Hall stressed that he needed to be deliberate in what he shared with his students. Had he not thought carefully about how his lived experiences connected with theirs, he likely would not have shared points of connection that began to make an observable difference.

Mr. Hall recognized that sharing his childhood poverty experience with some students could provide an important learning perspective for them: "I haven't brought that [childhood socioeconomic status] out to everybody, but every once in a while you'll get a couple of attitudes, and you know, you just kind of sense that [the students think], 'You don't know where I'm coming from . . . You don't know what it's like to live here' . . . You know? I told them it's like living in the woods is similar to living in a tough neighborhood. The house I grew up in for about three years didn't have indoor plumbing. It was an outhouse. We went outside to go to the bathroom. And a lot of them find that kind of amazing . . . because even they have never not had a toilet." Revealing his early poverty seemed to precipitate students' "opening up"; by sharing some of his life experiences that linked to theirs, they, in turn, began to grant him entry into their lived experiences and ultimately engaged the science learning opportunities.

Mr. Hall believed it was those situations of struggle that often helped him connect with the students in his classes. He stated: "The struggle of being a human being is that every day is not going to be sunshine and roses—that's what I told them . . . I said every day is not sunshine and roses; some days it clouds up; some days it rains; but hey, there's always tomorrow. So don't worry about it." Because some of his students struggled with finances and grappled with other tough situations outside the classroom, Mr. Hall believed they would "give him attitude." They saw him in his present successful position as a teacher and didn't realize that he too had struggled with basic resources and poverty in the past. Despite their outward bravado, some of the students were hurting on the inside. Their pain appeared to increase their need to feel confident that their teachers understood what it was like to "be here" and to "be" them. In some situations, science learning seemed to be irrelevant to their humanity, and

Mr. Hall needed to see his students as human beings and adjust through instructional agility accordingly. Eventually, Mr. Hall's connections with his students deepened and improved, and the claims that he was a racist subsided, but the accusations remained sharply entrenched in his mind. Perhaps it was because he wanted so desperately not to be seen as a racist that he kept developing deliberate practices to better connect with his students. Had he not been called racist, I wonder if he would have worked so hard to learn from and connect with them. In this sense, this challenging situation for Mr. Hall became fuel for him to reflect and get better.

In sum, Mr. Hall attempted to inspire his students with features of his own story: he grew up living in deep-rooted poverty and yet was able to persevere. His students had an opportunity to glance into a window on his past and to think about his developmental journey to his present professional situation. At the core of Mr. Hall's vision and decision-making for his students were *possibility, optimism, hope,* and a *commitment*—not just to help students work through difficult science-related content, but also to help them deal with situations outside of school. According to Mr. Hall, sharing that he had to use an outhouse for nearly three years was a real eye-opener for his students. And thus, he refused to allow students to feel sorry for themselves but insisted they own the fact that they indeed were capable of making a better life for themselves.

Mr. Hall developed high expectations for his students—even though he realized his middle school had fewer resources than many neighboring schools. One of his goals was to prepare his students with a toolset to work through difficult situations outside of school as well as give their best effort in the classroom. He wanted his students to anticipate life beyond their present situations and to realize that if he could transcend poverty, they could, too. He came to know that he could not teach the students if they felt too distant from him, so he used his experiences as *opportunity anchors*—sites to build and scaffold relationships with his students that would be critical for teaching and learning to occur.

Mr. Hall refused to be defeated by the challenges of his work and instead used the difficult situations (such as being called a racist) as an opportunity to learn, to sharpen his pedagogical skills, and to grow. Admirably, Mr. Hall never complained about the limited resources at Bridge Middle School. While he worked to increase the resources available for his students, he realized from the beginning that he would need to do more with fewer material resources and that he should not expend his energy on matters (such as scarce resources) beyond his control.

DOING MORE WITH FEWER RESOURCES

Student and teacher potential cannot be limited by a lack of material resources. Material resources matter, but teachers cannot allow inadequate resources to deter them from challenging students to reach their potential or from exposing them to the types of experiences necessary for success.

Mr. Hall did, in fact, do more with fewer resources, such as laboratory equipment—but he also did something about the problem. When Mr. Hall was uncharacteristically absent from school, I learned that he was participating in professional development workshops offered by local universities in order to earn laboratory equipment for his school. His participation forced him to miss school, which placed him in a quandary—he wanted to be with his students, but he also realized what having more sophisticated laboratory equipment could mean for them and for the school. So, distressed by the lack of resources in his lab, he did something about it. His actions are consistent with Freire's view that those who are marginalized and treated unjustly cannot wait for others to rescue them or act on their behalf.[2] Rather, those on the fringes of dominant economic structures must do what is necessary to improve their own situations. Mr. Hall worked to bridge the resource opportunity gap by earning lab equipment for his students.

It is important to note that I am not excusing the inequitable funding of urban and highly diverse school contexts. At a minimum, all students in public schools deserve equitable funding—not even the same—resources and materials, which can make a huge difference in terms of their learning opportunities. In other words, I am suggesting that students in urban contexts such as Bridge Middle School deserve more material resources than students in other contexts that are rife with privilege and advantage. But Mr. Hall understood that some inequities were structurally unavoidable, and he was unwavering in his commitment to address the resource gap in the school.

Although he was disappointed by the lack of resources, Mr. Hall was not willing to merely complain about them and play the role of victim. In practice, Mr. Hall believed that if he and his colleagues were to succeed, they would have to "never give up . . . You got a lot of people here who are bound and determined to succeed no matter what obstacles are put in front of them . . . even though we are at one of the oldest buildings in the [school] system. We've got [fewer] materials than anybody else, and it's just like—so what—who cares? You know the kids can do it; so *we're going to find a way to do it. I think that's it, you know? They never give up, never surrender—we're going to make it work no matter what*" [emphasis added].

Clearly, Mr. Hall did not feel defeated by the lack of resources or by the outdated building. Perhaps most important, he did not want his students to feel defeated or to adopt a victim mentality. However, he realized they were not blind to the inequities, and that they needed to understand and critique what they may have perceived as inequitable facilities and resources. A critique of the resources appeared to be a first step to addressing a much more complex array of issues. He did not make excuses for the fact that he was teaching in one of the "oldest buildings in the system." He just taught in spite of this reality. He was able to build confidence in himself and confidence in his students because he placed opportunity at the core of his mind-set and practices. For instance, when they engaged in laboratory experiments, students participated without any real consideration of the quality or age of the equipment they were using. In my observations, Mr. Hall's confidence was portrayed by his tireless energy, displayed from the beginning of a class period to the end. He taught with the equipment that he had, was enthusiastic about the content he covered, and never complained publicly about the quality of the equipment or materials the students had to use. He was teaching and the students were involved in learning activities from bell to bell. The students had few chances to think about the lack of resources or the building's shortcomings because there was work to be done.

Another issue related to resources was the size of Mr. Hall's classes—he was teaching more students than most science teachers in the district and with fewer resources. His classes were even disproportionately larger than others at Bridge Middle School. He told me, "These are actually the smallest classes that I've had in my three years that I've taught. My largest class was last year, and it was at one time thirty-nine, but then it went up and down as the year went . . . People transferred out and transferred in . . . usually I average about thirty-one or thirty-two [students] per class. I do have one class this year, sixth period, and it is sixteen students. I am used to big classes; it's all I've ever known." Mr. Hall estimated that he had taught as many as one hundred fifty students throughout the day in previous years. My inquiries revealed that an average science classroom at neighboring suburban schools enrolled twenty to twenty-five students.

When I asked Mr. Hall what he considered his greatest success, he stated, "My greatest success would be with my high school class [eighth graders preparing for high school] . . . The first year that I got here [I learned that] the high school science class . . . had three people who passed the high school exam the year before . . . My first year only five people passed. Last year, I had thirty-one students who passed the exam." He knew that many science teachers in other schools had a higher percentage of students who passed the exam, mainly because they had more resources to work with. However, even with fewer resources, Mr. Hall was able to significantly increase the passing rate among his students. Think about it: six times as many students passed the high school science examination after just one year of teaching. The students' engagement and performance increased as Mr. Hall continued to bring innovative materials into the school. But it was the connections he made with his students that allowed him the space to be able to teach in ways that students would learn. Clearly, learning was taking place in Mr. Hall's classroom, despite the inequities.

EQUITY IN PRACTICE

Educators need to understand that equity does not necessarily mean sameness. Equality tends to connote sameness, while equity implies parity. To achieve equity, educators provide resources, take actions, and make decisions based on particular needs in a particular context. This means that it may be necessary to distribute more resources in a school based on the needs of those in that space.

Mr. Hall appeared to understand equity, and he worked to achieve it in his practices. He seemed aware that he would need to develop different learning opportunities and curricula for his students and establish individual connections with them, based on their specific needs. Mr. Hall worked to build solid and sustainable relationships with all of his students, both individually and collectively, paying close attention to where they were cognitively, socially, emotionally, psychologically, intellectually, academically, and behaviorally. His interpretation would require him to respond to students in different ways. He explained: "I think that you have to develop a relationship with *each student* [emphasis added]. Every kid that you have has a different story, and if you show interest in what they've gone through, they're going to show interest in what you're trying to convey to [teach] them. Then they will show interest in what you're doing."

Mr. Hall was known for giving students multiple opportunities for success. He did not want to place a student's destiny in the hands of another, such as an administrator who had the power to suspend or even expel a student from school for "misbehavior."[3] Clearly, the kind of learning necessary for success is not taking place when students are outside the classroom, so Mr. Hall was serious, deliberate, and attentive to doing everything possible to keep students in the classroom and not refer them to the office. He believed it was his responsibility to work with his students and to make the classroom environment "right" for them to succeed. From my observations, it appeared that some students' "misbehavior" showed up through jokes with their classmates. But these jokes seemed to be made to offset pain they were experiencing; in a sense, it appeared that these students were laughing to hide their hurt. In at least three observations, it seemed that a person was joking to keep from crying. It was obvious that what his students needed was counseling support, not exclusionary practices such as suspension. The students I observed wanted to appear strong and jovial when they were in fact experiencing turmoil.

In general, it seemed that students cared more about how they would be perceived by their friends than by their teacher. Being disrespectful to teachers when they joked or played around seemed not to matter as long as they felt they were receiving praise for being the class jokester. During one class session, one student continued to be disruptive, joking around as Mr. Hall was lecturing. I asked the student after class why he had chosen to be disruptive, and the student made it plain for me: "It was all good for me. Mr. Hall is cool; I have no problem with him. He's all right. He can't take what we say personally. We are just trying to get through the day and have some fun, that's all. Sometimes we have a lot on our minds and we are just letting off steam, that's all." Understanding that students were dealing with a range of difficult realities (some he was aware of; others he was not), Mr. Hall gave disruptive students multiple opportunities to "straighten up"; he also gave them multiple opportunities to succeed on their assignments and was not quick to allow a student to fail. During my entire study at Bridge, I never witnessed Mr. Hall refer a student from the classroom to the office (although this does not mean he never did—I just never observed it). From my observations, though, he likely would have been justified in doing so, as at times the students pushed him and each other to a point where he could have decided to refer them. However, his point was that these are "my kids" and we have to figure "this" out together. Based on my conversations with him, he refused to give up on students and continued to work with them, even when they made it difficult.

This approach—giving multiple opportunities to some students and responding to each student's particular needs—could lead some to question how Mr. Hall was able to avoid problems associated with equity. In other words, how could he treat all students fairly if he treated them differently? I asked him how he responded to adults or other students who questioned the equity of his practices. He explained:

> Well, I'd ask: who hasn't gotten a second chance in life? I mean, everybody messes up, and not everybody messes up at the same time [and in the same way] . . . It's a different situation for everybody. I mean, I know there are times in my job that I said the wrong thing, did the wrong thing, and . . . alarms didn't go off and the swat team didn't come in . . . People, my peers—people above me—pulled me aside and said: "Hey, you know, we don't do it this way." You know, I wasn't terminated on the spot . . . You know I'm not going to [give them failing] grades or hurt their self-esteem right there on the spot just because they did it wrong that time . . . Everybody's different, you know . . . We are not robots . . . we can't all just crank out the same stuff every time. It's going to take one kid five times to get it . . . and it's going to take one kid one time.

Importantly, Mr. Hall connected how he dealt with and interpreted the needs of his students to his own experiences. For example, he himself had received multiple opportunities to succeed, even at Bridge Middle School, and he transferred these professional and life lessons into his teaching practices. The idea that teachers can empathize more fully with students when they have had parallel experiences is a constant theme of the teachers portrayed in this book. However, what should teachers do if they do not have similar experiences from which to draw? Thinking about Mr. Hall's narrative and how he made decisions for students based on his own experiences reinforces the idea that teaching is identity work. That is (as will be demonstrated throughout this book), it can be difficult for teachers to separate themselves and their own life experiences when making decisions that affect students. Thus, teachers must consistently reflect on their decision-making when teaching students.

Mr. Hall's approach of providing multiple opportunities for success seemed to support and propel his students to participate in classroom activities and discourse without worrying so much about the consequences of their off-target responses. Based on what I observed in his classes, it appeared that he had designed the learning environment around an opportunity structure that valued different cognitive and social spaces that students were in at a particular time. The students seemed unafraid to participate in the classroom learning opportunities because they understood that while Mr. Hall expected them to do their best work and to excel academically, he recognized that excellence would show up in different forms, among different students at different times, and at different developmental stages among his students.

He seemed determined not to "tear the students down" when they were (mis)interpreting scientific content and context. For instance, based on my observations, students regularly participated in class discussions, and Mr. Hall consistently pushed them to think deeper about the content by not accepting answers that were off-target; but at the same time, he never belittled or dismissed student comments. One student, for instance, was consistently off base for several weeks, but as Mr. Hall put it, he "never gave up," and this is what was most important for him—the persistence, the never-quitting attitude. Some teachers might have grown weary and frustrated by the student's consistently off-track responses, but Mr. Hall appeared excited that the student continued to put forth effort and develop scientific thinking. Whenever the student's hand was raised, Mr. Hall called on the student: "Tell me more about your thinking here. Why might we want to measure the mass here? What other information do we need to know?" Indeed, Mr. Hall continued to invite the student into discourse even though his participation seemed to complicate the discussions for everyone else. He refused to allow others to attempt to silence the student, and the student continued to give his all. Later, I learned that the student was being mainstreamed into the classroom, and Mr. Hall shared that it was essential for the student to feel accepted and cared about. Because of Mr. Hall's approach with the student, other members of the class seemed to give this student a bit of a "pass" when he contributed to the conversation.

When other students had the "wrong" answer, Mr. Hall and other students would pose additional questions to guide them to think more deeply.

It was obvious, based on my observation, that Mr. Hall had co-constructed this type of ethos in the classroom. It was also obvious that Mr. Hall and his students had developed a disposition of support and inquiry rather than one of silence, worksheet completion, and targeted "right" answers. Overall, students did not appear intimidated by the scientific teaching and learning or threatened by the expectations and discourse because the classroom context supported participation and engagement. Mr. Hall had created a classroom context where many of the students (including some society might not expect) appeared confident, capable, and enthused about what was happening. Mr. Hall also shared that for some of his students, this was the first science classroom where they could get "excited" about the subject. No question, the students wanted to learn, and they seemed to realize that even if it took them multiple times to "get it," Mr. Hall was not going to give up on them. In Mr. Hall's words: "I think as long as they get it—that's the ultimate goal. It doesn't matter how fast you get it; it's that you do get it."

In sum, Mr. Hall cared deeply about ensuring that each of his students was able to master the information and skills being taught. This meant that he regularly allowed his students multiple opportunities to turn in work and that he would explain a concept or lab procedure repeatedly until they understood: "Maybe that's bad—[that] I give so many second chances, that I care about them too much—but I think it works for me. And I wouldn't know how else to do it. I couldn't be one of those who say, 'Uh oh, Timmy, you didn't get your homework done; well, that's your fifth zero.' You know I couldn't be like that."

However, he would not accept "nonsense" or allow his students to "run over" him, in his words. He had high expectations of his students but also would do everything in his power to help them succeed as long as each student was putting forth the effort necessary for both academic and social success—a clear demonstration of his care for them. He gave multiple opportunities for success, but he would not accept mediocrity; he pushed his students to produce and he expected their best work. An important feature of Mr. Hall's work was his ability to understand equity and to design learning opportunities that were responsive to students' individual, academic, and social needs.

To be responsive to his students, however, Mr. Hall had to work through cultural conflicts.

WORKING THROUGH CULTURAL CONFLICT

Unavoidably, there will be times when conflicts between teachers and students will emerge in a range of social and cultural contexts. The real questions are, how do teachers work through those conflicts, whom do they blame for them, how and what do they learn from them, and how do teachers use conflicts as opportunities to grow and support student learning?

Inevitably, there were times when Mr. Hall had conflicts with students who did not want to engage in class, refused to complete their assignments, and were disruptive. He told me about one such conflict:

> [There was one student]—he was a foot and a half taller than me, a big old guy. He wanted to chitchat and talk about sports and basketball and stuff, and he didn't like me coming up to him telling him "get on task, get on task" every five minutes. And one day he stood up to me and just went off. And I went off [too]—you know, it's like two brothers fighting. He let me know what he was thinking. And I let him know what I was thinking, and we went our separate ways . . . It took us about a week, but one morning he just walked up to me, and said, "We're cool now." It was almost like, "I didn't know what happened." I was cool from the minute he walked out the door. That's just me: I am going to tell you how I feel, what I didn't like, and I am done [with it]."

Mr. Hall expressed his feelings, allowed the student to do the same, and the two moved forward.

Mr. Hall realized that his students, regardless of their grade level or physical height, were still adolescents dealing with all kinds of developmental matters of which he might or might not be aware. As a teacher and as an adult, he understood also that he could not allow misunderstandings to hinder his relationships with his students. He explained how important it was for him to not hold grudges, that when students walked back into the classroom after a previous misunderstanding with him or a cultural conflict, he did everything in his power to move forward and not hold the conflict against the student: "If I get upset at you or if you screw up . . . tomorrow is going to be new. I'm not even going to mention it. Unless you do the same thing . . . Every day is a new slate." Moreover, he also was not one to gather with colleagues to discuss his students' faults. Such gathering and "gossiping" about students simply was "not [his] style." He wiped the "slate" clean each day.

Mr. Hall explained that he had to constantly reset the parameters in the classroom so that students realized he expected them to do their best work at all times; he was willing to accept *only their very best.* Mr. Hall had to establish his motives and his vision with the students by making explicit why he was "getting onto them." Making rules and expectations explicit is consistent with Delpit's suggestions about how power works and should work in the classroom.[4] Although one could argue that students should have a voice in making decisions and setting expectations in the classroom, it is also essential for teachers to make their goals clear so that students do not have to guess what is expected of them. Ideally, students and teachers together will co-construct the goals and expectations of the classroom, but at a minimum teachers need to overtly share their views on what is expected with students. Mr. Hall had developed some meaningful relationships with his students partly because they understood what was expected of them and what would be acceptable in the learning environment.

Another important reason for Mr. Hall's success was the way he "sowed seeds" with his students to build lasting relationships with them that seemed to be impactful for student learning and development.

SOWING SEEDS

Building, cultivating, and sustaining relationships means that teachers develop knowledge and understandings of students, to enhance both present learning and future opportunities. Teachers need to establish powerful relationships with students as a way to "plant seeds" that will enable a teaching and learning relationship to grow over time.

I have learned, based on my research over the last twenty-one years, that at the heart of good and effective teaching is teachers' ability to develop solid and sustaining relationships with students. The relationship factor, as I will describe in subsequent sections of this book, can be the difference maker for students who do not organically feel connected to their teachers, the learning environment, or school in general. As the adults, it is educators' responsibility to develop the necessary skills and tools to build relationships with students. When opportunities to develop meaningful relationships emerge, educators must be prepared to identify and seize them. Mr. Hall recognized the importance of relationships as a foundation for the kinds of learning opportunities that he hoped to design. I suspect his focus on relationship building developed in some ways from being called racist early in his teaching. This teacher did not want to be thought of as a racist—period. After students called him a racist and insisted that he needed to "get to know" them, he realized that he needed to develop the skills to center relationships with his students so that they could recognize him as someone who was fighting for and with them, who wanted to provide opportunities to enhance their lives both in and out of school. Developing this ability required him to deeply reflect about who he was (indeed, he was White) and who his students were (the majority of the students he taught were students of color). He needed to think about how his and his students' multiple and varied identities emerged and converged, and how he wanted to grow as a teacher. He discovered that personal and professional reflection was critical as he concurrently planned and taught science. Thus, this case would suggest that, as a foundation, educators preparing to teach science have to consider the sociological, geographical (spatial) facets as well as the relational aspects of their practices.

Mr. Hall described the evolution of his relationship with one student: "I had a kid named Mike, and last year, he was one of the biggest trouble-makers that I had. I couldn't get him to do homework. I couldn't get him to study for a test or anything. And this year he made the basketball team and made the football team. And every week I was asking him, 'Hey, how you doing [with basketball]? Did you score a basket? What did you do in the game?'"

The now solid relationship between Mr. Hall and Mike took some serious work—lots of seed sowing—before Mike's engagement, participation, and ultimately learning in the science classroom increased. Mr. Hall would query Mike about his games in the classroom and also in the corridors when he saw him. He took an interest in Mike outside of school (in athletics) in order to build a stronger relationship with him inside the classroom. He was constantly asking Mike about what was happening in his games, which gave Mike a sense that Mr. Hall was interested in his life experiences beyond academic success and beyond what was expected of him in the science classroom.

Out-of-school experiences and extracurricular activities mean much more to some students than their classroom experiences. With Mike, Mr. Hall needed to engage in the "extra" curriculum to get Mike to engage more fully in the science curriculum. *The idea that Mike was experiencing any curriculum—albeit extra—is important.* He was learning something from the athletic curriculum. Beyond simply asking questions about Mike's performance in games, Mr. Hall realized that he also needed to more assertively sow seeds to ultimately get Mike to "grab onto" learning opportunities in the classroom: "I've gone down to a couple basketball practices and played one-on-one against him, and he missed two assignments the whole year in homework. And his grade, average-wise, from last year is up about fifteen points. He's gone from being a C student in my class to being an A student. He's just one example of how you show interest in a kid and how [his, her, their] output goes up in your class." In short, Mike refused to learn from Mr. Hall until he believed that Mr. Hall was concerned about him as a person, not just a student in the science classroom. Mr. Hall clearly credits Mike's increased participation, engagement, and improved science grade to the relationship factor.

Ultimately, Mr. Hall came to understand that some of his students, like Mike, would refuse to perform, engage, and provide "outputs" for educators they did not believe had an interest in them. Basically, some of his students refused to learn from him and to engage in the classroom until they felt that he cared about them. Moreover, they did not seem to realize or care about the consequences of their (in)actions when they refused to complete learning tasks and assignments or were disruptive. (This was perhaps a function of where the adolescents were developmentally.) Interestingly, it seemed that the students believed they were "hurting" the educator they did not like when they were disengaged, underprepared, or disruptive or when they missed assignments or did not study.

One day when I visited the school to do observations and was waiting to sign in at the front desk, I had a conversation with a student, Jazmine, who had been sent to the office by another teacher. I asked what happened and why she had been sent to the office to be reprimanded. Her response was quick and direct: "[The teacher] doesn't like me, and I don't like her." For this student, what precipitated her dismissal from class was a consequence of the "like" factor. I learned that some other students were battling teachers because they did not believe their teachers had their best interests at heart or felt teachers simply did not like them. In this way, teachers similar to Mr. Hall had to make conscious efforts to demonstrate that they indeed "like" their students. For some students, the lack of likeability of and from their teachers could be a detriment to student learning and success.

I have spoken to countless educators, both preservice and in-service, who give up on students like Mike and Jazmine. These educators place most or even all of the blame on their students, and rarely examine their own beliefs, mind-sets, attitudes, dispositions, and practices as sites that could and perhaps need to be transformed to strengthen their relationships with students. Some teachers may rationalize that it is not their responsibility to build a "likeable" interaction between themselves or their students, for instance. Might teachers' practices or lack thereof stifle the participation, and, ultimately, the achievement and success of students like Mike and Jazmine? Or should all the blame lie with the students? An educator working with a student like Mike could easily put all the blame on Mike, his parents, or other external factors. They could see Mike as one who is unmotivated, lazy, and/or incapable of success. However, Mr. Hall took some responsibility and initiative, decided to learn about the areas of Mike's life that piqued his interest, and then used that deepened understanding to build a relationship with him. Although certainly not as simple as asking about basketball or football, Mr. Hall was intentional about helping Mike see him as someone who cared about him and who wanted him to succeed.

In other words, Mr. Hall realized that in some cases he would have to go *beyond* the walls of the classroom before he could connect with a student *in* the classroom. Based on my observations and my conversations with students, it is clear that Mr. Hall was an educator students came to know and respect. Of course, this took time and required Mr. Hall's willingness and developing skill to recognize opportunities to build meaningful relationships when they presented themselves. In my conversations with students, they would tell me what they thought about the teachers at Bridge Middle School, both positive and negative. As for Mr. Hall, the students saw him as "cool," "with-it," and a "good teacher." At the same time, they perceived his class as "hard" but "fun." The students commented on how Mr. Hall watched the Discovery Channel, and many of them had developed an appreciation for the channel as well. In class, students would often reference a recent program, and Mr. Hall was right there with them. A television channel had become a *bridge* to learning in the classroom. Such bridging seemed essential to the development of meaningful relationships between Mr. Hall and his students.

In short, Mr. Hall wanted what was best for his students, and he would not allow them to get away with actions that could be destructive or disadvantageous to them in the present or the future. As he put it, "One thing

I try to let kids know this year is that I really do care about them, you know, whenever [and wherever] I see them. You know, I love you. I want to see you play basketball. I want graduation invitations. You know, that's not going to happen though, if you don't straighten up in class. And I've tried to be more expressive, but at the same time, stay on them." As Mr. Hall developed his teaching repertoire at Bridge Middle School, he found that sowing the seeds of strong relationships was vital to his success in the science classroom.

Mr. Hall also learned that constructing narratives was an important way to forge deeper connections both with students socially and within and through the curriculum.

POWER OF STORY

The sharing of personal narratives allows students a window into an educator's life. Personal and professional stories can be powerful tools for building connections with students and bringing the curriculum to life. Story sharing can be a compelling connection tool in the classroom.

It appeared that Mr. Hall's students developed a heightened interest in his class when he shared narratives that connected his own life with the course content. For instance, students seemed to become more attentive when Mr. Hall shared aspects of his home life. When he described a recent episode with one of his own children or a debate with his wife about an issue, student interest seemed to escalate. Mr. Hall explained: "If you can relate what [the students] want to know and put some science in there with it [then you have a better chance of success] . . . I mean everybody remembers what happened Tuesday whenever Ricky and Jane broke up. There was a big screaming match outside; they will remember that for six months and make connections to science."

Mr. Hall stressed that he had begun to share personal stories that enhanced the learning opportunities for his students. The lesson here is that it is important for educators to bring not only students' cultural experiences into the classroom, but some of their own as well. As Mr. Hall related,

> I've gone real personal. I mean, my second year that I was teaching here, me and my wife [sic] were expecting our second child. We were talking about reproduction. I brought the little video from where they show the little baby before birth; we talked about how whenever an embryo is developing . . . the cells are multiplying, and we showed how it [the baby] looked like a real person, but it was only two inches long. And just that connection—the kids really have never seen a picture [video] like that . . . It was just amazing to them that it could be two inches long and yet still have all the features and characteristics of a person. You can see the outline of the head. [The narrative] gives them *something to hold on to* [emphasis added], and it puts a picture in their mind that they're not going to forget.

According to Mr. Hall, the students needed something to hold on to during lessons, and sharing personal (appropriate) stories helped make the content real and relevant to their lives. According to Mr. Hall, students seemed mature enough not to intrude and pose inappropriate personal questions. While it can be advantageous for teachers to share aspects of their own story with students, it is also important that teachers maintain professional distance between themselves and students. My point is not that educators should share personal stories that are irrelevant or inconsequential to students' experiences. Rather, I am stressing that based on what I learned from Mr. Hall, educators have an opportunity to share aspects of their personal lives with students that can help them think differently or more deeply about, or with stronger connections to, the content being covered. Mr. Hall said that eventually students would ask, "How is the baby doing? How is your wife doing?" By granting students entry into his personal life through the power of narrative, he said that he was able to both sharpen his relationships with his students as well as use the stories as pedagogical connections in science. Mr. Hall shared how some of his students saw him as someone extraordinary—they did not realize how "human" and "real" he and his family actually were. He used narratives as opportunities to demystify who his students had perhaps come to believe he was. He was a "regular" person who cared about them.

Put simply, Mr. Hall discovered ways to support students; he just refused to allow his students to fail.

JUST CAN'T LET THEM FAIL

When educators truly understand the stakes for students if they fail, they simultaneously should understand that their mind-set, attitudes, dispositions, belief systems, and practices must be to do what it takes not to let them fail. When students fail, teachers, in a sense, fail too.

Mr. Hall seemed to embrace the idea that he could not let his students fail because they were "like family." Moreover, he believed it was important that he demonstrate "good" behavior so his students would understand that he was not only telling them what kinds of practices he expected for success, such as treating oneself and others with respect, but practicing them himself. He stressed that educators often have to play various roles with their students: "For some kids you are going to be mama, daddy, brother, auntie, uncle, grandmother, and granddaddy. I mean, you're going to be the one person who they're going to tell everything to. Some of them, it's going to be almost like a big brother. They're going to do what you do. Now if you're modeling good behavior, they're going to act like you, almost like a younger sibling would."

Mr. Hall stressed that family members are not willing to let other members fail. They do "whatever it takes" for their family to succeed: "I like the family aspect because, I mean, if family's not important to you, then what [or who] is? I mean, family should be the thing that's most important to everybody. And I mean that for some people it's not, so hopefully in here [in Mr. Hall's classroom] they kind of get that aspect . . . I care about everybody; I love them all . . . just like I would my own . . . If I holler at you it's because I know you can do better. And if I get on to you, I know that you're slacking; you're not pulling your weight."

Mr. Hall added that family and community are established not only with students in the classroom; he also developed and modeled relationship building with colleagues at the school:

> Another thing [I] started doing last year is, we had a couple of new teachers who were on the first floor. And during my planning time I'd just walk in and check on them. So kids who I didn't even have, they were seeing me. And if they were acting crazy, I was taking them, and we were coming up here, and we were doing sixth-grade science in my room. And I think just to gain that reputation now, you know, you might not teach them that year but you're always watching them. And if you're around they'd better be acting right. So the school is the community.

Thus, Mr. Hall believed that he needed to develop relationships (1) with the students in his classroom, (2) with other students in the school, even those he did not teach, and (3) with his colleagues, particularly new teachers, in order to build a school community. Communities are established and nurtured by the people in them, and Mr. Hall seemed committed to building the kind of school community in which students and teachers alike understand that they are on the same side.

Mr. Hall clearly believed that "if you quit caring about what you're doing, that's when you stop improving. You [can't] quit caring about the kids." Therefore, he was constantly thinking of ways to connect with his students and others in the learning environment. When he was teaching he felt he was fighting for his students: "You've got to fight against everything else in their life for their attention for that one hour. And if you can win the battle, you've won the child for that one hour, and 99 percent of the time they are going to remember the important things you talked about."

In Mr. Hall's interview, his point is consistent with Ladson-Billings's idea that educators in schools across the country are actually fighting for the lives of students when they are teaching.[5] It is not enough to simply teach their subject; educators must think about the enormous responsibility that working with students entails. Mr. Hall realized the possible consequences his students might face if he did not teach them and if they did not learn. An undereducated and underprepared student from an urban school (and possibly any school) could too easily fall into destructive and dangerous activities, possibly leading to drug abuse, prison, gang activity, or, unthinkably, death.

In the next section, I conclude this discussion with suggestions for explicit reflection regarding diversity, opportunity gaps, and teacher identity. I also provide heuristics to guide educators as they build the knowledge and expertise to transform their practices in ways that can make a difference for their students.

RECOGNIZING RACE, RECOGNIZING CULTURE

In teacher education courses I have taught and in professional development sessions I have led for more experienced educators, I have observed great resistance to acknowledging the importance of diversity (especially race) and its relationship to teaching. Thinking about race, culture, or diversity requires educators not only to consider others, such as their students or their students' parents, but also to reflect on themselves. Reflection on race, in particular, I believe should center the self. Educators must deeply reflect on their own experiences, worldviews, and mind-sets as they are working to understand and support others; such self-reflection on race can help them build a positive personal racial and ethnic identity and also think about how their racial identity can influence their work with students.

To build a positive racial identity as a teacher, I have discovered that educators, all educators, must engage in deep, explicit reflection about matters of race. When examining their own privilege and their experiences as educators, it can be easy for teachers to engage in general self-reflection and to avoid reflecting on race altogether. However, thinking about the role race plays can be a critical dimension of teachers' work, as Mr. Hall learned from his students. Mr. Hall's experience as a White teacher working with many Black students who called him racist suggests that White teachers need to be especially well prepared to confront matters of race in their classrooms.[6] But it is also important for teachers of color to engage in race reflection. In fact, race reflection is essential for teachers of color as well because they can be "kidnapped" into believing negative untruths—or flat-out lies—about themselves and other people of color.

All teachers need to reflect about themselves as people who operate in and through systems that are shaped significantly by race, racism, and racialized mind-sets. It may be difficult for some educators, especially science educators, to find the relevance of race in their work or to understand how to make pedagogical, curricular, and relational connections centering race. Table 2.1 provides a list of questions and a brief explanation of each to help educators engage in race reflection as they contemplate issues of racism and avoid color-blind mind-sets and practices.

The purpose of this table is to support educators in the necessary work of reflecting about race. Reflecting about race and racism can serve as a forerunner to more deeply meeting the needs of racially diverse learners (and explain why, for example, a student could perceive a teacher as being racist). It is important that educators from all racial backgrounds think beyond simplistic and/or static answers to the questions. Revisiting the table over time can support teacher thinking as their contexts, experiences, and situations shift. The potency of this exercise lies in provoking analysis of such critical questions, not in the answers per se, which will vary from person to person and from situation to situation. This important reflection relates back to the idea that teaching is a journey; therefore, educators should work to answer the questions more thoroughly and provocatively throughout their careers. The questions are critical because they ask educators to contemplate higher-level, deeply contextualized issues that go beyond closed-ended, simplistic queries. In short, the power of the table is in actively engaging in the questions, not necessarily in articulating finite answers. Again, I focus on race and racism here because they tend to be the areas that are most challenging for educators. Other constructs such as gender and sexual identity can be substituted for race.

TABLE 2.1
Questions to guide teachers' self-reflection about race

Critical questions	Reflective purpose and significance
How might my race influence my work (relationships, curriculum development, instruction, assessment practices) with my students?	This question prompts educators to think about how their race might inform how, whether, or with which students they build relationships. It also encourages educators to consider how their race might impact their curriculum, instructional, and assessment practices with students.
What are some of the privileges I have experienced as a result of my race? What are some of the challenges I have faced because of my race?	These questions shepherd educators into reflective spaces where they think about privilege and challenge areas that they are able to identify as a result or consequence of race. Understanding how their race impacts them outside of school can serve as a reflective space for them to think about how their students might experience privilege and challenges. For instance, if White educators understand how their own privilege manifests, they should be able to consider how their White students and families experience the world through a privileged frame and system—providing advantages that might lead them to falsely believe that they have meritocratically earned their academic and social success.
How do I help students more deeply understand their racial identity, and why is students' racial identity important to teaching and learning?	This question attempts to push educators to think about making explicit connections between race and racial identity in the classroom. Because students' sense of racial identity is essential to their achievement and outcomes, it is important for educators to consider practices that enhance students' sense of racial and ethnic identity.
How do I continue building knowledge and understanding of my students' and their families' racial background and experiences outside of school that can inform what happens inside of school?	This question challenges educators to think about specific strategies they should employ to continue learning from and with their students and families about their experiences and practices related to race outside of school.

As educators reflect on themselves and build knowledge about themselves, their own experiences, and worlds related to race and racism, they should eventually engage in reflection about their students' race and racial experiences and also about the context in which they are teaching. Table 2.2 provides questions that support teachers' reflections about race relative to their students and also the teaching environment.

I hope educators find the questions in tables 2.1 and 2.2 useful as they work to transform their mind-sets and practices from color/diversity/culture/context blindness to those that are race/diversity/culture/context

TABLE 2.2
Questions to guide teachers' reflection about students, race, and social context

Critical questions	Reflective purpose and significance
How might my students' race influence their experiences and outcomes with me as the teacher? What conflicts might emerge due to racial differences and disconnections between my students and me?	This question challenges educators to reflect on the way students' race might influence their perceptions of the teacher and also their experiences in a classroom. The question also encourages educators to think about how racial dissonance might emerge and why.
Have my students experienced racism? How do I know? How can I support my students who have experienced racism and help them build tools to advocate for themselves and work to end racism and discrimination?	This question pushes educators to think about how racism may have been prevalent in students' experiences and how educators can support those who have experienced racism. The question also encourages teachers to equip students with tools to combat racism and advocate for themselves.
How does our classroom environment promote a context that is racially just and inclusive?	This question encourages educators to build a racially inclusive classroom environment—beyond the individual—where there is a classroom ethos of justice and equity.
How might school or district policies enable or stifle the academic and social success of students of color?	This question requires that educators think about race beyond their local classroom to consider how policies such as zero tolerance influence students of color disproportionately in comparison to White students.

conscious. Again, the term *race* in the tables can be replaced with a range of different identity markers such as culture, gender, socioeconomic status, sexuality, or religion. Still, I have included the term *race* because so many teachers find it difficult to confront it in their personal and professional lives and because I believe that until we begin to really penetrate race and its role in teaching and learning, we will continue to see significant disparities in education.

SUMMARY

An overarching theme of this chapter is that opportunity gaps related to race, culture, meritocracy, expectations, and social context can emerge if a teacher is not conscious of ways to address the gaps, even in the science classroom. There were many encouraging facets of Mr. Hall's thinking, mind-set, disposition, attitudes, and practices related to his work. He learned from his students and consistently readjusted his practices based on what they taught him. He developed a deeper understanding of how race mattered, even in a science classroom, after being called racist by some Black students. He created opportunities to develop relationships with his students that allowed him to work through cultural conflicts and differences. Importantly, he did not necessarily view cultural conflicts with his students as impediments to teaching and learning. Rather, he perceived these as opportunities that he could learn from and work through.

Mr. Hall understood that knowing science—that is, having deep subject-matter knowledge—was absolutely necessary but also insufficient for success in the classroom. He needed to come to "know" his students in order to teach science. He needed to develop knowledge about whom he was teaching science to, and this effort had to be ongoing and not seen as a destination. Many of the students with whom he worked claimed that they would not learn from a teacher they did not like or who did not know them. So, much of the work for Mr. Hall involved getting to know his students and for his students to feel confident that Mr. Hall cared about them. Demonstrating this care was essential to the relational, social, and academic success of his students.

To connect with his students and build sustainable relationships with them, Mr. Hall decided to share areas of his life that would help them recognize some of the commonalities that existed between them. For instance, he revealed to some of his students how he grew up in poverty, worked his way out of it, gained an education, and became a teacher. But he also demonstrated a meritocratic way of thinking about his capacity to get out of poverty. Although his hard work likely played a role, suggesting to students that they too can or will transcend poverty through hard work may be misleading. In other words, hard work is necessary for most people to build financial resources, but there are many other forces beyond merit that people must understand as well.

Mr. Hall connected his experiences growing up "in the woods" with growing up in a tough neighborhood. He not only shared stories about his youth that he believed connected with his students but also told them about his own family. He found that sharing personal narratives about his wife's pregnancy, for instance, provided connections on at least two levels: (1) in developing relationships with his students and (2) in helping students make subject-matter (here, science) links in the classroom.

In essence, Mr. Hall worked through racial and cultural conflicts, using them as opportunities to learn, and he developed relationships with his students by sowing seeds that he would nurture and develop over time. He understood that at times he needed to take an interest in students outside the classroom in order for them to perform and engage inside the classroom. Finally, Mr. Hall understood what it meant to maintain high expectations despite limited resources. In his view, the students were capable of academic success and of meeting rigorously constructed learning opportunities. So, Mr. Hall did more with fewer resources, and he participated in professional development to earn additional materials and supplies for the school. While I am not condoning, by any means, inequitable funding in urban or any schools, Mr. Hall did not allow the scarce resources to deter him from what he was confident that his students needed. He attempted to avoid opportunity gaps by developing very high expectations for his students. He taught in spite of the resource shortage.

Finally, Mr. Hall treated his students equitably and realized that he needed to be responsive to his students as individuals. He provided them with multiple opportunities for academic and social success. Even when students were "off-target" with their comments or thinking, he invited them to continue contributing to the discussion rather than attempting to silence them. Mr. Hall was tough but did everything possible to keep his students in the classroom, even when they were being disruptive. Mr. Hall simply refused to let his students fail. More than anything, Mr. Hall started where he was, but he did not stay there!

3

Black Teacher, Suburban White School

Addressing Cultural Conflicts

You teach what you know; you teach what you've experienced; you teach who you are . . . My students know me. They know how I live, and there's no misunderstanding, no misinterpretations about that. I am a Black woman, and they need to understand that there are some differences between myself and them.

—DR. JOHNSON, HIGH SCHOOL LANGUAGE ARTS TEACHER IN A SUBURBAN SCHOOL

IN THE QUOTE ABOVE, Dr. Johnson, an African American language arts teacher with twenty-six years' experience, eleven of them at Stevenson High School, explained how important it is for her students to understand her racial and gender identity in her predominantly White teaching space. In our conversations, she also explained how teachers' various identities, experiences, and values shape what they teach, how they teach, why they teach what they teach, the amount of time they spend on issues, and why they emphasize what they do through curriculum practices. Dr. Johnson was very deliberate in deciding to teach with race, gender, culture, and diversity at the center of her curriculum.

In contrast, consider Mr. Hall's initial approach to teaching. In chapter 2, I shared the story of Mr. Hall's transformation, especially regarding the centrality of race and relationship building in his science classroom and his ability to bridge opportunity gaps. But when Mr. Hall first began his work in his school, he purposely avoided race and adopted a color-blind orientation to his work. He also did not fully understand the relevance and importance of developing relationships with his students. Initially, he declared that he came to Bridge Middle School to do one thing: "to teach science." He transformed his practices by listening to the voices and requests of his students. The Black students, in particular, expected Mr. Hall to think about race and "get to know" them, although such a focus was not his goal in the beginning. In essence, Mr. Hall learned that he had to know more than science in order to teach it in his context. He needed to know whom he was teaching science to in order to be successful in his work.

Dr. Johnson, on the other hand, did not begin her work at Stevenson High School consciously avoiding issues of race and diversity. Because of what she had observed and experienced both within and outside the school context, she had come to understand how important race and diversity were to her teaching practices. She found that although she was teaching in a predominantly White setting, issues related to race, culture, and gender were still salient to her work. In some ways, she believed that conversations about race in particular were essential in her environment.

In this chapter, I focus on an African American teacher working in a context that might easily be overlooked in a discussion of race and diversity, in that her school has a small population of students of color, children living in poverty, or English language learners. There is scant evidence about the nature of multicultural education, particularly matters of race and diversity, in suburban, primarily White school environments. Opportunity gaps related to diversity exist in many such schools, but few people working in them seem aware of the interplay among race, diversity, and opportunity, leading to a lack of understanding of how diversity curriculum and instructional opportunities can and should manifest in mostly White spaces.

In this case study, I demonstrate how issues of race and diversity are incorporated into a school's curriculum even though most of the students, faculty, and staff are White. Students live in a multicultural society, which requires them to be able to understand their own and others' privileges and power, or lack thereof, and the many varied ways in which people experience the world. Some believe that race and diversity are inconsequential and insignificant in mostly White spaces, until they actually confront uneasy and unsettling situations, such as these:

- Someone in the community makes a racist, sexist, xenophobic, or homophobic comment.
- Parents become uncomfortable with interracial dating among students.
- Adults in a school start to question why all the members of one racial group sit together during free time, such as at lunch, at an assembly, or during sporting events.
- Parents insist that their students not be taught by a teacher of color.
- Children of color are not invited to outside-of-school gatherings, such as parties and sleepovers, held by their White friends.
- It becomes evident that students of color are showcased in sports, while White students are showcased in honors courses, in honor clubs and societies, and/or with academic awards.
- The number of teachers of color is disproportionately low in comparison to White teachers.
- Students and parents become concerned that the school curriculum is Eurocentric and male dominated and excludes contributions from other ethnic groups and women.

According to Dr. Johnson, avoiding discussions of race and diversity can make it difficult for teachers to provide optimal learning opportunities for all their students. For instance, educators and administrators are sometimes not prepared to respond to parents or family members when students select to date outside their race. They may not be able to rationalize why students of color—such as Black and Brown students—excel in football or basketball while their White students are showcased in academic subjects. Inside the classroom, educators may struggle to understand how to build a curriculum that offers opportunities for students to learn about others as they are learning about themselves.

Students from all racial and ethnic backgrounds will interact with multicultural, multiracial, multilingual, and multiethnic people in the United States and in a global society for the remainder of their lives. It is essential that all students have the opportunity to develop knowledge, skills, awareness, attitudes, belief systems, and understandings of what it means to function effectively in society in order to understand diversity and live healthy lives. Research has found that "both children of color and White children develop a 'White bias' by the time they enter kindergarten."[1] This means that if educators are not working against these biases, students' beliefs about Whiteness may intensify. They may believe that White people are superior to others in terms of intellect (smartness), social status (who plays with whom), and personality traits (likeability). These biases, assumptions, and worldviews need to be recognized as problems and disrupted in order to help students broaden and complement their mind-sets related to themselves, others, and how the world works. Students' unexamined biases, assumptions, and worldviews can make it difficult for them to understand oppression and how various oppressive forces leave some people discriminated against, undervalued, and ostracized while other groups are privileged and positioned for success both in schools and in society.

As Dr. Johnson suggests in the quote that begins this chapter, teachers' identities and experiences shape their curricula and instructional decision-making. Who they are and how they see themselves in terms of their racial, ethnic, cultural, socioeconomic, gender, and linguistic background are perhaps the most important dimensions for teachers to consider when developing learning opportunities for students. This point may be contested by those who suggest that high-stakes testing and "scripted" curriculum guides prevent teachers from making decisions about what they emphasize in their teaching. However, by deciding what is germane and central to student learning opportunities, teachers still play an enormous role in what goes on in the classroom. Despite structural and instructional limits caused by high-stakes testing, teachers bring their own perspectives and experiences into the classroom based on their own backgrounds, paradigms, and worldviews. Indeed, teacher identity is a critical facet of teacher and student work, and this case study demonstrates how Dr. Johnson addresses gaps in opportunity by centering issues of identity.

INTRODUCING DR. JOHNSON

Dr. Johnson, an African American English teacher who lived in the Stevenson County School District, understood quite well how central her own and her colleagues' identities were to the learning opportunities available to their students. Having earned her doctorate from a large midwestern institution, she had a rich array of language arts subject-matter knowledge and was well equipped to connect with her mostly White students, although cultural and racial conflicts did emerge from time to time, as will be discussed in this chapter.

Dr. Johnson was the only African American teacher at Stevenson High to teach in the academic core; two others taught in the vocational/elective departments. Energetic and passionate, Dr. Johnson kept her students entertained and engaged in learning from the beginning of the class period to the end. She enjoyed reading, traveling, and, most of all, caring for her two biological children. Typically wearing slacks and a blouse, Dr. Johnson was well dressed and maintained a professional appearance.

REFLECTION ON SELF, OTHERS, AND SOCIETY

There is value in facilitating student reflection of social realities, particularly those regarding opportunity and privilege. Students need to understand how they are positioned in relation to others and how their worldview is shaped by forces both in and beyond their control.

Much has been written in the educational literature about the importance of teachers' taking time to reflect on a range of matters, from subject matter and curriculum development to issues of race. Dr. Johnson used reflection, however, as an instructional tool in her classroom to facilitate discussion with students about broader issues they face in society. For instance, as most of her students were "wealthy," she created opportunities for them to reflect on how free they were to enjoy their social and economic status and helped them understand themselves in relation to others who did not have the same economic status. These reflective discussions enabled her students to start thinking about their connections to those who are not in positions of economic privilege. In Banks's words, "Students need to understand the extent to which their own lives and fates are tightly tied to those of powerless and victimized groups."[2] And I would add that students need to understand that their own positions are a consequence of broader social and economic systems of privilege, which dictate social mobility in society. It is essential for them to think deeply about the fact that, as high schoolers, they have not "earned" their financial status. Students need to understand, as explained in chapter 1, that success and failure (and socioeconomic status) are determined by realities far beyond merit.

Banks also suggests that when poverty exists, all in society are affected; students need to understand this, especially those who believe in a meritocracy. That is, students and adults who believe that people earn their positions in society and that hegemonic systems have little to do with socioeconomic status need to deepen their ideology and look at the evidence to help them broaden their positions and belief systems. Dr. Johnson thought deeply about the privileges she and her students enjoyed, a reality she considered important when making decisions for their learning. This point is particularly interesting if we consider the fact that the majority of her students were White and wealthy. She interpreted as central to their needs an understanding of how wealth, poverty, race, and culture work, especially in the broader society. She believed that her students needed to gain a level of self-knowledge and awareness as they attempted to understand others. It is important to note that Dr. Johnson skillfully orchestrated such reflection to help her students understand power relations and matters of equity without making the students feel they were to blame for society's inequities. Because her students were in high school, Dr. Johnson was clear that she needed to provide a caring and nurturing environment and not make students feel or believe that they had necessarily done something wrong. However, she also wanted her students to understand that they could use their influence to make the world better for others.

She clearly created a safe and welcoming classroom environment in which students were given opportunities to think through the curriculum and draw connections to their own experiences and worldviews. I believe the creation of such inviting and caring contexts is critical for both high school and grade school students. Dr. Johnson would likely not have had the same level of success with her students in a less welcoming environment. She co-designed a space where her students felt comfortable expressing their views and beliefs, even when they disagreed with Dr. Johnson. The students were savvy and deliberate in exerting their voices and perspectives even as they disagreed with the multiple "texts" available in the classroom. These varied texts included the teacher, their classmates, their books, society, and other curriculum materials, including computers.

I asked Dr. Johnson what she thought about when she was designing lessons for her students. She replied, "I try and go beyond the Eurocentric literature. Most of the contributions to literature [they have read] were made by White men. The main thing I consider, then, besides my kids, is the importance of exposing the kids to writers who make up the world: the Hispanics and the Hispanic Americans, the Asians and the Asian Americans, the Africans and the African Americans." Dr. Johnson clearly had an idea of what she believed her students "needed," and she was always thinking about whom she was teaching. As evident in her statement, she believed that helping students understand the role of ethnicity learning is critical. Ethnicity is aligned with the home cultures and communities of indigenous people. Dr. Johnson wanted her students to understand the ethnic origins among groups of people as well as those who now live in "America." Her commitment to exposing students to ethnic origins was likely a function of having being married to an African and having children who well identified with their African roots (as did she).

Reflection on gender was an important element of her teaching practice as well: "Women are also important because most of the writers were White men. I want my girls to read about women, too. I try to broaden their horizons. They are on their way out into the real world, and everybody they meet in the world might not look like the people here. To me, this is what's important in the decision-making."

At the heart of Dr. Johnson's decision-making for her students was opportunity. She facilitated their reflections to provide opportunities to think about important matters, which she worried they otherwise would not have—new experiences that could enlighten them about issues of race, ethnicity, culture, and gender. She especially wanted the girls to be exposed to women writers, a point that the research literature describes as a necessity for maintaining student interest and engagement. As feminist theorist bell hooks explains, girls and women too often are left out of classroom conversations and content even when the discussions are about them.[3] Dr. Johnson still included the "White men"—the male authors who make up much of the traditional literary canon—but she also wanted her students to be exposed to women writers and writers from other ethnic groups. In sum, issues of culture were central in Dr. Johnson's thinking about students' opportunities for learning and reflection.

Dr. Johnson understood the importance of making lessons relevant to students. She asserted: "If I were an Asian student, I would want my teacher to know something about Asian writers. It is important to make lessons relevant to students . . . these kids know so much nowadays, so you have to make the work fit into their scheme of thinking." While Dr. Johnson did not claim to know everything she needed to know about Asian writers, for instance, she was unwavering in her position that she was willing to learn about them and also to learn about "Asian culture" with and from her students. In fact, she believed that it is a teacher's responsibility to engage in this kind of learning about other cultures. As she stressed, "So, that means that I got to learn about Asians by asking the right kinds of questions, because you don't want to get too personal, but you want them to know that you [as the teacher] care about them enough to learn about their culture." Exposing students to "the self" and "the other" was important to her given the fact that "many of these kids don't have any idea about how other people around the world live. They are sheltered. They are good kids, but they just don't *see it* [emphasis added]; so because for years I've been the only Black teacher they encountered, I try and plan and develop a set of experiences for my students that will make them better human beings when they leave."

Dr. Johnson's push for self-reflection and self-understanding as a way to enhance how one relates to others connected to how she thought about herself in relation to her students: "I work hard to make all my students feel like they are a part of the learning environment. *This might be because I haven't been made to feel like I am accepted in this school* [emphasis added] . . . I have been hurt here, and I don't want my students to feel hurt for being different—you know, we need to celebrate our differences." Thus, Dr. Johnson understood that her own identity, experiences, and mindset—the ways she interpreted her own (mis)treatment by others, mainly adults, in her school—played an enormous role in what she taught, how she taught it, and how she treated, connected with, and engaged her students. She was especially sensitive to the students who seemed to be on the margins of the school context. Her decision to have her students reflect about justice and treating all people well regardless of their racial, ethnic, or gender identity or background was clearly shaped by her own experiences and reflections about what she believed to be important. In this sense, as she taught the expected curriculum, Dr. Johnson was teaching herself her own identity in the school.

Dr. Johnson felt she had not been "accepted" at her school because of a range of experiences, which are discussed below. In her words, "When they ask me to teach the seniors who[m] no one else wants to teach, I accept. That's right . . . I gladly accept because I bring out the best in them. And they [the students] see that I am different, and I have come to love myself for being different because wherever we go in life, there will be people who have problems with us." Thus, even at the mostly White and affluent Stevenson High School, there were students who were considered to be in the socially constructed bottom tier, referred to as the "low group." There also were students considered gifted, or the "top group," as well as those in the middle. Such social stratification was not invisible to students and faculty. There was also a social hierarchy among the students. Dr. Johnson enjoyed teaching the students considered to be in the "low group." She believed in creating opportunities for them to reflect about themselves, others, and society in order to be better equipped to thrive in the real world and also to navigate what could be seen as challenging times among their classmates.

Astutely, Dr. Johnson was able to help students think about localized situations of marginalization and connect them to broader ones. According to Dr. Johnson, the students felt that being ostracized by their classmates made them better able to understand and empathize with others who might be seen as lower on the social strata. As she facilitated learning opportunities through reflection for her students, she also worked to address cultural conflicts that emerged in the classroom and school.

CULTURAL CONFLICT

While cultural conflicts are inevitable in a range of social contexts in education, the ability of teachers to recognize those conflicts as learning opportunities is a promising component of developing the kinds of knowledge and practices essential to teach all students well. It is largely teachers' responsibility to bridge, work through, and address cultural conflicts in order to get to the heart of the content/subject matter they are teaching.

The research literature often presents cultural conflict as tensions and inconsistencies that surface when White teachers teach culturally diverse students. Dr. Johnson's case demonstrates how cultural conflict can emerge between a Black teacher and mostly White students. Although there were many cultural differences, tangible and intangible, between Dr. Johnson and her students, they worked through them as Dr. Johnson, similar to Mr. Hall, used these conflicts as opportunities to get better.

In many ways, Dr. Johnson addressed cultural divides and created opportunities to connect with her students as she examined conflicts when they emerged. Her success in dealing with the conflicts was evident in her students' participation and engagement in the classroom as well as their interactions with her in the hallways. But the power of her relationships with her students was made crystal clear when the graduating seniors asked her to present them with their diplomas at commencement each year. Dr. Johnson prided herself on the fact that she awarded, proportionally, more diplomas to graduating seniors than did any of her colleagues. Because the students selected their "most influential" teacher to award their diplomas during commencement, she interpreted her students' invitation as a sign that she was making a positive impact on them and their experiences.

Dr. Johnson clearly stood out as "different" in this mostly White context. She had felt ostracized and undermined at times because she was quite vocal about issues of racial and cultural diversity, which she believed had made some of her colleagues and supervisors "uncomfortable." Dr. Johnson drew from her own experiences to connect to how her socially constructed "low group" of students must feel as "seniors who[m] no one else wants to teach."

Dr. Johnson discussed her thinking about decision-making and cultural conflicts in terms of balancing the "self" with that of the "other." In a sense, she was stressing philosopher Cornel West's position that we cannot work for freedom (or social justice) on behalf of others until we are free and unbound ourselves.[4] The balance of self and other manifested itself in how Dr. Johnson developed lessons, the types of activities she developed to carry out those lessons, and how she tried to help her students understand their multiple (yet intersectional) identities. She also attempted to provide space where students understood the many contributions of the people and places she presented in the curriculum. Connecting to these multiple identities was central in understanding her students' sense of belonging and acceptance in the larger school community. Her attempt to understand herself in relation to others and what her students were experiencing was important to the kinds of relationships she developed.

When addressing cultural conflicts, Dr. Johnson pushed her students to think about their own role in the school in relation to others. Her aim was to help them gain knowledge about how people may feel silenced or placed on the fringes of what society (or the school) expects and accepts. As Dr. Johnson explained, "These students will be stronger if they find a sense of belonging. They know that Dr. Johnson cares about them, and I'm not willing to let them get away with mediocrity." Thus, Dr. Johnson demonstrated that she cared about her students and had high expectations for them, despite the fact that many of her seniors were considered undesirable to teach. She shared, "Just because they [the students] are not all on the football team or the most popular kids or the kids on the honor roll does not mean that they are not good students."

Moreover, she built connections with her students and addressed cultural divides because she empathized with, not pitied, them: "I know how they must feel." She too has felt ostracized, undermined, and marginalized, not only as a Black woman in society but also in her school. She used her past experiences and the students' experiences as a foundation as she planned assignments, tasks, and related learning opportunities: "I plan assignments like the self-portrait that allows them to think about themselves in positive ways. I also do self-portraits with them so they can see that I too am different and yet I'm OK. Kids like this, and they do it because they can relate. This helps me every time I [write a self-portrait], so it probably helps them as well." Dr. Johnson attempted to propel an ethos of self-care and healing among her students. She wanted her students to engage in the deep self-reflective work necessary for them to disrupt negative stereotypes they may have bought into about themselves. She also wanted to help them build stronger self-confidence and self-awareness.

The content of her class could easily have been more general or focused on different topics, but she was deliberate and mindful in helping students make connections to and draw from their own experiences of marginalization. In essence, consistent with the research literature about good practice, Dr. Johnson's efforts helped her students link the head (cognitive) with the heart (affective).

Thus, Dr. Johnson addressed cultural conflicts by doing the following:

- Making explicit connections with her own and her students' experiences of feeling marginalized in the school. Although Dr. Johnson and most of her students were not the same race and had many cultural inconsistencies, they bonded from and through their experiences of difference in their local context.
- Allowing students to see her as a real person. Dr. Johson shared aspects of her personal life with her students to help them see her humanity.
- Perceiving conflicts as opportunities to learn and develop. Drawing from her many years of teaching, Dr. Johnson knew she would have conflicts with her students. She used those conflicts as anchors to learn.
- Building relationships with students and developing lessons and experiences that helped them recognize their worth, intelligence, and connections to her life as teacher. Dr. Johnson also recognized that students would not perform at their academic highest if their personal worth or self-esteem was not strong. She attempted to support her students as people developing their own self-esteem.
- Demonstrating her care for them, having high expectations of them, and not accepting mediocrity. Although Dr. Johnson understood and empathized with her students, she held them to high academic and social expectations.

Dr. Johnson further addressed cultural conflicts with her students by not allowing them to develop "White or cultural guilt" and by helping them see how a range of people have been mistreated and have experienced hate in society. This point is elaborated on in the next section.

CREATING SAFE SPACE FOR OPEN DIALOGUE AND POSITIONING

Many differences between teachers and students exist just as many similarities are present. It is in those spaces of commonality that curriculum and instructional practices can meaningfully connect with all those in a learning environment. Providing high school students the chance to examine their own lives and worldviews safely in a space that is not antagonistic or hostile can be essential to facilitate open and honest dialogue and help students position themselves in classroom and broader discourses regarding difference.

Dr. Johnson also worked through cultural conflicts by helping students understand that they are not directly responsible for situations beyond their control. However, although her mostly White students were not directly responsible for racism or White supremacy, for instance, she stressed that her students had a responsibility to address these issues and make the world a better place for all. Although some would argue the classroom space equity should not be "safe" but "brave" spaces, brave because of the developmental level of her students, Dr. Johnson created a safe space with them. She provided opportunities for students to move beyond White and cultural guilt by exposing them to "hate against White people." She explained: "I want to teach them about hate and how hate is relegated to all groups of people, including the White race. I often discuss with my students how the Irish were mistreated. The Italians, you know, they were lynched and could only work in farming and agriculture." When Dr. Johnson exposed students to how their ancestors had been mistreated, they were more open to understanding how hate works and more willing to discuss its manifestation in current society. Ultimately, though, Dr. Johnson wanted her students "to eradicate hate. I want them to love themselves because when we hate ourselves, we hate others." She wanted her students to learn "more than what's in a book" and take action in a quest for social justice.

It is essential to clarify that in classrooms where the students are adults, or more developmentally aware of injustice, such as in teacher education programs, tensions and uncomfortable conversations may be necessary for transformation. The research literature suggests that classroom contexts with some hostility can serve as an additional tool in helping White people and particularly men build knowledge about their deep-rooted racism prejudice, xenophobia, and sexism. However, Dr. Johnson believed that students in elementary, middle, and high school should experience a curriculum that would shed light on discrimination from a broader, historical landscape. The classroom settings needed to be "supportive" and "safe" for her students, especially if there was not a collective school culture that supported tense classroom interactions as a pedagogical tool for transformation and deep change. From my observations, Dr. Johnson treated her students with care and concern, and they seemed to feel safe and supported in the social context, which allowed them to open up about difficult issues related to equity, wealth, gender disparities, and diversity in general.

Dr. Johnson explained: "Kids are into drugs; kids are, you know, smoking marijuana; they're not always being quiet when you tell them to be quiet. Homes are different. We have what they call a 'blended family.' We have divorced families. So, all of those things are important in kids' lives." These "important things in kids' lives" were where Dr. Johnson was able to draw connections and to build relationships with her students, which ultimately became central to addressing cultural conflicts that otherwise could have overshadowed, disrupted, or derailed learning opportunities.

As a point of connection and relationship building, Dr. Johnson said: "My kids know that I was married and now I'm divorced, and my life goes on, and it's OK, you see? So, I guess part of it is showing the differences, but part of it is showing the similarities. We all hurt. We all cry. We all have bad days . . . when I show them the differences, I show them just how similar we are, too. So, being different is not bad, 'cause we are actually a lot alike. Does that make sense?" In essence, Dr. Johnson was able to demonstrate how she and her students were different and yet very similar at the same time. She found that sharing about her separation from her ex-husband was a particular area of connection for students whose parents were divorced or preparing to divorce.

While Dr. Johnson had the ability and skill to create safe and welcoming spaces for her students to engage in difficult discourses related to race and diversity, she also felt an added layer of pressure to both know and expose her students to multiple literacy worlds. She was a bit concerned that her students would never be exposed to certain writers or genres of literature without her exposure. Thus, Dr. Johnson came to know and represent multiple literacy worlds with her students to build their knowledge and insights.

KNOWING MULTIPLE LITERACY WORLDS

Teachers of color sometimes feel that they have an additional burden to intimately know culturally and ethnically grounded literacy worlds as well as traditional literacy worlds. Women, too, are often expected to be experts on women authors.

As a Black teacher, Dr. Johnson explained that she had to know multiple literacy worlds in order to (1) expose students to literature they would more than likely not read without her and (2) maintain her love and appreciation for both Eurocentric and African and African American–centric literature. She noted that while she was expected to know traditional literature, she also read and deepened her knowledge of African American–centered literature. She added:

> Culture plays a role. Because if you think about it, why haven't we, in our educational process, taught certain things [and people] in the classroom? I mean, if you look at White teachers—how many of them know about Toni Morrison? How many of them know about Terry McMillan? How many of them know about bell hooks? And they are not teaching that kind of stuff. bell hooks is a literary genius; she's more intellectual than many other writ-

> ers, but *my White colleagues teach what they know* [emphasis added]. They teach Hawthorne, you know, and it's a cultural thing. But with me, you know, we [Black teachers] have to know [and teach] Hawthorne too, and that makes me . . . flexible because we know both worlds.

In essence, she maintained that teachers' identities are intricately tied to what they come to know, understand, and decide to teach. Because of Dr. Johnson's identity, she reminded her students that "people have stories that are not a part of the White story."

Dr. Johnson believes that the worlds teachers know, live in, and negotiate influence how they conceive and represent curriculum matters both inside and beyond the classroom. In discussing her knowledge about multiple roles and the range of literature she has come to know, she suggested that she "knows" at least two worlds or realities. It became evident from my observations that Dr. Johnson had built a strong knowledge base of multiple literacy worlds. For instance, she was as comfortable talking about Asian and African writers as about African American and White American writers.

Her notion of knowing multiple worlds points to what educational pioneer W. E. B. DuBois in his seminal text, *The Souls of Black Folk*, referred to as *double consciousness*.[5] Double consciousness suggests that Black Americans have at least two deep levels of awareness and consciousness—they are African and they are also American. These levels of consciousness are sometimes at odds, but they are in communion as well. Tensions around what it means to be Black in America can make life complex and difficult. At the same time, their African consciousness allows Black Americans to operate at a deep level of awareness because it affords them the opportunity to look at situations, texts, and worldviews as insiders as well as outsiders.

Dr. Johnson maintained that she was expected to know more than her colleagues because of her African American identity, and she expressed how difficult it was to deal with these added expectations: "It's like Black teachers have to know more—we have to know about what's accepted and expected from a European perspective, and we are expected to be the expert on everything Black too. It's hard work." Dr. Johnson shared how whenever questions emerged about Black writers or other writers outside North America, she was expected to "know" them or learn about them. Her White teacher colleagues, according to Dr. Johnson, did not have that same pressure or expectation.

Dr. Johnson realized that she needed to be able to teach the multiple forms of texts available in the classroom and the broader community. She recognized that text-based learning opportunities extended far beyond traditional definitions of what a text is. Moreover, she realized that she and her students would need to examine texts from various vantage points.

TEACHING MULTIPLE TEXTS

It is important for teachers to recognize that they should be prepared to teach multiple forms of texts that range well beyond a traditional novel or textbook. Students themselves are texts, teachers are texts—people in society are texts. Moreover, society itself is a text. These various forms of text manifest inside and outside of a school. These texts need to be examined and explicated in order to complement and build on learning opportunities that may or may not emerge through the exploration of traditional literary texts.

In this section, I attempt to capture some of the powerful qualities of Dr. Johnson's teaching. I describe how deeply she understood the texts she taught. The works that Dr. Johnson taught so brilliantly included:

- Traditional printed reading texts expected to be part of the curriculum, such as *To Kill a Mockingbird*
- Nontraditional printed reading texts that related to Dr. Johnson's own experiences, such as when she lived in Africa
- Traditional and nontraditional printed reading texts that represented her students' experiences both inside and outside of school, such as

when students felt ostracized because they were not the most popular students

- Nontraditional human-experience texts through oral sharing, which allowed her to expose students to her own textual experiences and for them to share aspects of their experiences with her and their classmates

A Snapshot of Dr. Johnson's Teaching of Multiple Texts

Dr. Johnson prepares the class for the day's reading—Alice Walker's "Everyday Use," a short story that focuses on the cultural and historical legacy embedded in patchwork quilts and the art of quilting. She provides some brief information about Alice Walker and the story, which she calls "setting the stage." "You see," she explains, "Alice Walker is a brilliant African American woman who wrote the novel *The Color Purple*, which was made into a movie. Has anyone in this class read that novel or seen the movie?" Only two students raise their hands (all of the students are White). "I see," Dr. Johnson responds. "Well, let me tell you a bit about that novel before we move on." She spends approximately ten minutes discussing the time period of the novel and points out some of the major themes, after which she returns to the story at hand—"Everyday Use."

The students read the story aloud, with Dr. Johnson orchestrating the reading. She calls on students, one by one and by name; there is no choice in the matter—you either read or you are not participating, which means points are deducted. After a few paragraphs, Dr. Johnson breaks in with her own memories:

> I remember when I was a girl. My grandmother made me a quilt when I went off to college. I still have it today. That quilt is old and dingy now, but it'll be in my family forever because it means something to me culturally. I see that quilt as more than pieces of cloth sewn together. And I miss my grandmother—the food she cooked, and her smell, you know, all the things that remind us of the good times, when my sisters and I would play

> in her yard, and the clothes on the line outside flew in the wind. Those were some great times. And so, when I run across that quilt in my basement, I think back to those times and I get full [emotional]. Those are times for me to share about my sisters, my parents, and my grandmother with my [own] kids.

Not a person moves during Dr. Johnson's soliloquy—words cannot describe the calm in the room. Dr. Johnson continues:

> And if my grandmother . . . could see me now as *Dr.* Johnson, her heart would be glad. I was a little Black girl who grew up right outside of [Ohio], and so, yes, it is deeper than just the cloth and the quilt and the fabric. It's about artifacts that we treasure and allow to become meaning makers to remind us to tell stories to our children who I hope will tell stories to theirs, starting from a patch quilt. I cannot help but think about this as we read this story.

The bell sounds to dismiss class, but no one moves. It is obvious that this is an important and meaningful moment—not only for Dr. Johnson but for her students as well. It is evident that Dr. Johnson relied on her memories of family customs and traditions as she interpreted the text of "Everyday Use." During the time I observed her classes, she consistently relied on her history, her multiple identities, and her experiences (here, of quilting) to bring the text to life. At the core of her transformative pedagogical decisions was her ability to share aspects of herself as a way to guide students toward deeper thinking, self-reflection, and understanding. Her personal narratives allowed students to see the themes and experiences in a traditional text as relevant and real. Dr. Johnson told me that she "often invited students" to share similar experiences they had had with their grandparents or other family members—a tool she used to make connections to the multiple texts available in the classroom.

I asked Dr. Johnson to express why she chose to open up to her students about her family history, and she said, "I don't mind sharing my experiences with them. Some of them are hurtful, and others are times to celebrate. [My students] see me for a real person because I cannot present myself in any other way. They know this about me, and I am proud of that." It should be clear from the classroom snapshot above that Dr. Johnson taught at least two texts: a traditional printed reading text ("Everyday Use") and a nontraditional text that showcased aspects of herself and her history. Another text that Dr. Johnson taught related to experiences that both she and her students had outside of the classroom and in their local community. One of her students, Dan, provided an opportunity for her to demonstrate her teaching of a nontraditional societal or community text based on his experience with a person whose first language was not English.

A LESSON FROM A COMMUNITY INTERACTION: ENGLISH LANGUAGE LEARNER

When I asked what she believed her students were learning from the curriculum and instructional opportunities available to them, Dr. Johnson explained that she attempted to help her students build skills—just as they would in someone else's classroom. But the texts she used to help them build those skills tended not to be the same ones used by her colleagues. She helped her students transfer the lessons from the classroom into the community as well as identify and learn from community experiences and make connections in the classroom. She shared this story about Dan, one of her students:

> During another class session [not the session on "Everyday Use"] Dan talked about being upset about the people who are coming into our district. I think he was referring to the Spanish or the Mexicans; I'm not sure what nationality. And Dan was saying that he was upset that this guy couldn't understand him in a convenience store. He said, "Why are these people moving here, and they can't even speak English?" And that gave me a chance to teach—to really get down and teach. I love it—because this kid was very passionate when asking, "Why are these people here?" And I told him that these people are doing things that we don't want to do. He was

> saying that he didn't like these people coming here, and I was saying that his family, his grandparents, great-grandparents, came from different countries. And they don't see that; that's all important to me because I think that sensitivity . . . I have a sensitivity to people who are not like my kids at Stevenson High School—that are not, you know, mainstreamed right away.

Dr. Johnson then related her comments to systemic power structures: "Any time you're part of the ruling class with power, it's likely that you don't see it. You're not as sensitive to minority groups, and that's OK. We have to learn these things from people who live them. It's not just Black and White. I've had many of my Asian students talk about things that they've heard or gone through, too. We all learned from the discussion that day [the "Everyday Use" lesson], even Dan."

Although captivated by Dr. Johnson's lesson on "Everyday Use," the students sometimes struggled to see her points. Given their youth and developmental levels, they had difficulty realizing how power works in the real world. Although Dr. Johnson had some power as the teacher, she was quick to demonstrate broader notions of power by pointing out the advantages her students had by virtue of their race, their White privilege, and their whiteness.[6] In fact, the power Dr. Johnson's students had was demonstrated when they complained about her teaching, and her classes were taken away from her (a point discussed below). At a time in the past, Dr. Johnson's open approach and her decision to have a race/diversity/gender-centered curriculum did not come without problems. The problems she had encountered were most prevalent during her early years at the school, but they still seemed to affect her at the time of my study.

CONSEQUENCES OF DIVERSITY-FOCUSED PRACTICES: SAME TEXT, DIFFERENT INTERPRETATIVE EMPHASIS

Although during my study I saw only that Dr. Johnson was a powerfully transformative teacher and the students seemed to respect her immensely, she shared with me that in the past there had been consequences to her decisions. She explained: "I've become aware of how many of my colleagues look at various [curriculum] selections, and I'm not sure if they understand the whole message of what writers are attempting to do. What I want to talk about is basically how we teach a book called *To Kill a Mockingbird*—how we [many White teachers] don't intently focus on the political, social, and racial aspects of that book." Then she gave a specific example: "There are two parts to that book. There is Boo Radley, and then there is that Tom Robinson situation. When I first started teaching here and I taught that book, my students would run down to the principal's office and tell the principal that I was prejudiced—they thought I was a racist."

She explained that students thought she was spending too much time on some of the broader social ills and situations, and her students were uncomfortable with this emphasis—especially when she first started teaching at Stevenson High. Dr. Johnson's experiences of being called a racist provide additional evidence that issues of race should be incorporated into teacher education programs and professional development opportunities to help teachers work through these challenging experiences.

Dr. Johnson and Mr. Hall both experienced explicit situations in two very different learning contexts that required them to work through and address being called a "racist." What if Dr. Johnson had decided to change her teaching practices and area of focus when students would "run to the principal's office" to complain about her? How do teacher education programs help teachers build the capacity to work through challenging situations that seek to maintain the status quo and silence teachers for teaching social realities of books that may be uncomfortable for some?

Searching inwardly, Dr. Johnson attempted to rationalize why her students complained: "Maybe I did spend too much time on the Tom Robinson aspect, but that's how they [the students] handled our discussions. They thought I was racist for exposing areas that made them uncomfortable. I was trying to get them to see how the female character falsely accused Tom Robinson [a Black male character] of raping that woman [a White character]." Dr. Johnson believed that too many students did not have opportunities to learn about the two important aspects of the book, especially that of the dangers of making assumptions and stereotypes: "And on the other side is how we make assumptions about people like Boo Radley. You know, Boo never came out of that house—the house was all spooky and so on and so forth. And we make assumptions about people . . . my students didn't see all that. And as you know, I'm sort of animated in my classes, and they misinterpreted what was going on in there."

Dr. Johnson stressed that because the students had not previously focused on the nature of assumptions or on matters of race (or even, more broadly, diversity), they were not equipped to address those issues in her class. The students who complained about her teaching were White; the students of color in her class often saw the points she was hoping to make. She explained: "I didn't have any Black students in that class my first year, and I've found that when I do have Black students or Asian students or Hispanic students, they see what I'm trying to do and say because we live those experiences. It is my White students who don't understand, and I have to say that there are cultural differences that exist when you [a Black teacher] teach in a predominantly White situation. They [cultural differences] ought to be explored if we are doing what we need to do—preparing our kids for the real world."

Dr. Johnson makes the point that there "are cultural differences" in predominantly White teaching contexts, although she believed that many of her colleagues did not think so. This reality, of course, is tantamount to Lewis's study outlined in chapter 1, which revealed that in White contexts, issues of race especially are dismissed as insignificant because there is not a critical mass of people of color in the social context.[7]

Dr. Johnson sought out the social and political themes in the class readings and used them to provide learning opportunities that would cause her students to think and act differently—perhaps in line with a social justice agenda. To be clear, Dr. Johnson did not attempt to make her students think or believe what she believed. She attempted to provide space for them to think deeply, substantiate their points, and perhaps expand their thinking and beliefs. For many years she had presented lessons that focused on social and political matters in her classes, but she did so at the risk of being accused of being prejudiced and a racist, as she explained:

"Many of the students took my teaching in this way as an attack on them. And, of course, there is a price you pay when you go outside of people's comfort areas. I was called into the office and questioned about it [from the principal]. And you guessed it—eventually my principal took those freshmen away from me. So, there is a price you pay for decision-making and teaching in this way."

As is evident here, attempting to transform the curriculum in such a profound manner had its consequences for Dr. Johnson. Teaching in a predominantly White context with colleagues who Dr. Johnson suspected rarely thought about such issues likely intensified her being ridiculed and eventually having her freshmen classes taken from her. Teachers like Dr. Johnson must be prepared to negotiate, balance, and sometimes combat pervasive counterproductive discourses and practices that are already in place in a social context, so that they can teach the content and provide related learning opportunities they believe to be germane to issues of diversity (namely, gender, race, and cultural inequities).[8] Dr. Johnson elaborated on the resistance she perceived from her students, colleagues, and other adults in the Stevenson community: "I think that it's due to the privileges of the White population here. Whether children or adults . . . there are privileges that they have been receiving that many of these kids don't understand."

ADMINISTRATIVE ACTIONS TO ADDRESS DISCOMFORT

Dr. Johnson explained that her mind-set and her decision to construct learning opportunities with her students to address deep-rooted assumptions were resisted by many of them, and as a result "that class was taken from me. These were ninth graders, and I don't teach ninth graders anymore; haven't for years now because they [the administration] felt like many of the students were right—that I was a racist. And that hurt me . . . I am not racist. I just wanted to *open eyes* [emphasis added]. I was anxious for the students to *see it* [emphasis added]." This experience has not stopped Dr. Johnson from working to eradicate "ignorance where culture and race" are concerned, and she now provided such opportunities for her seniors. As she explained, "The older kids see it much clearer than the younger ones." In these senior courses, she again explicitly stressed issues that were important to her because of her experiences as a person of color and as a woman.

From my view, there were at least two dimensions to the success Dr. Johnson had with her twelfth-grade students. First, when Dr. Johnson began to teach in the mostly White context and was called prejudiced and racist, the students had not yet gotten to know her, and she had not yet developed the kinds of relationships with them necessary for such teaching and learning connectedness. Moreover, she had not developed a reputation in the school that they could deeply draw from. Second, her senior students were older, and from a developmental perspective they were perhaps better prepared and more willing to think outside of their comfort zones. Pushing her students to think outside that zone was important to Dr. Johnson because she wanted her students to be prepared for college: "So they get a taste of it, and I can openly tell them that I want them not to go away to college not having experienced other people's cultures. But I found that [with] a lot of my ninth-grade students, it was like they were in denial, and I think that it had to do with maturation." Thus, because perhaps younger students are less prepared socially and emotionally to think about these topics, we must consider the ways in which entire school systems (schools that serve elementary, middle, and high school students) can support equitable and justice-centered practices.

It was evident, though, that Dr. Johnson was not as frustrated with her ninth graders as she was with how the administration handled the complaints against her: "What surprised me was . . . not so much the kids; it was my administration that didn't understand because I was constantly being called down to the office and told that the students said that I was a racist for teaching certain books in certain ways." She persistently had to justify what she was teaching and why, and she did not feel she was supported by the administration, which she found frustrating and disappointing. Over time, however, she saw the pendulum shift a bit, and teaching the more controversial aspects of books had become more acceptable because White teachers had begun to do so at Stevenson High. Dr. Johnson said, "You see, they [the administration] see the worth so it's accepted and even expected now. But they [White teachers] are not [necessarily] teaching the social, political, and historical aspects of that book . . . Racism is a major theme that has been blatantly overlooked by most teachers here."

A TEACHER'S TRANSFORMATIVE CURRICULUM AND TEACHING

Dr. Johnson addressed and worked through cultural conflicts in her mostly White school context, and she maintained a diversity-oriented curriculum even when she was called prejudiced and racist by students. Moreover, she persisted even when her ninth-grade classes were reassigned. She helped her students think about themselves and how privilege, power, and marginalization were prevalent at many levels—in the school, in the local community, and in the broader society. Her goal, similar to that of other teachers, was for her students to build skills to analyze, critique, question, substantiate, write, and communicate about what they were learning. Moreover, she wanted her students to learn to read multiple texts intently. Dr. Johnson helped her students understand their economic, racial, and ethnic privilege while simultaneously facilitating their reflections on their own experiences of historical marginalization. Transforming the curriculum also meant that students were exposed to knowledge about others—from other cultures, races, and gender groups.

Dr. Johnson felt it was essential to create a classroom ethos where she could talk about issues of power and privilege without making students feel as if she were attacking them, their parents, or their ancestry. From her view, varying ethnic groups have been discriminated against at some point in history, and she connected with her White students by pointing out that many of their ancestors at one time had experienced discrimination. In addition, when a student complained about the increased number of immigrants who were moving into their district, she reminded him that they (their parents, grandparents, and great-grandparents) had immigrated to the United States from other countries as well at some point in history. Developing what she called a "safe," "supportive," and welcoming space to reflect about themselves, others, and macro-level societal matters allowed her seniors to let down their guards and to think about matters of power, equity, privilege, and discrimination beyond a Black-White divide. She was deliberate in her practices to focus on issues of gender, issues of immigration, and broader themes such as the social construction of assumptions and stereotypes that move far beyond those of a Black and White binary.

In this case, it appeared that "the school culture and social structure are powerful determinants of how students [and teachers] learn to perceive themselves [and others]. These factors influence the social interactions that take place between students and teachers and among students, both inside and outside the classroom."[9] Dr. Johnson's perception of the support—or lack thereof—that she received from her colleagues, the school community, and the broader community seemed to have a profound impact on her. Being called to the principal's office to be questioned about what she was teaching her freshman students could easily have made her want to retreat from such scrutiny. However, she persisted and persevered. The question is: Why and how do some teachers persevere in the face of such adversity while others do not?

Although teachers of color may consider racial and cultural conditions and experiences appropriate and relevant to include in the curriculum because of their personal experiences, the pervasive belief systems, goals, and discourses of a school can derail this desire to provide a more nuanced set of opportunities for students. Early in her career at Stevenson, for example, Dr. Johnson paid a price for the opportunities she attempted to construct for her students. Teachers of any ethnic background may struggle to be justice- and equity-centered in unsupportive contexts.

It is essential to stress that whether or not Dr. Johnson's colleagues were supportive of her pedagogical strategies is not as important as Dr.

Johnson's *perception* of their lack of support. Others in her school could disagree with Dr. Johnson's construction of her experiences. However, her voice and perception are valid and essential to understanding how broader school cultures can advance or disrupt students' opportunities to engage in difficult content. Dr. Johnson had earned a doctorate from a major research institution and she had traveled the world, even living in Africa at one point with her then husband. Her exposure and previous experiences to a wide range of knowledge likely contributed to her persistence even during difficult times. Teachers who cannot rely on such a wide body of knowledge and experience likely would find it more difficult to persevere in their quest to disrupt and expand on established mind-sets, discourses, and practices.

As evident in this research, a teacher's racial and cultural background may surface in their practices. How teachers perceive themselves and what they stand for is reflected in what and how teachers teach. Moreover, this case suggests that a teacher's identities, experiences, and stories often shape their decision-making and practices with students. Thus, teaching is almost always a personal and political endeavor.[10]

SUMMATIVE THEMES AND CONCLUSIONS OF THIS CASE

Teachers do not teach on secluded islands; they teach in a school environment that is shaped by people (other teachers, administrators, students, parents) with varying views on what is and is not appropriate and necessary to consider in curriculum and instruction. When a decision to focus on matters of diversity (xenophobia, nationalism, language variation, and racial, ethnic, and socioeconomic differences) in the classroom is met with dissension, there can be serious consequences for a teacher, perhaps especially for a teacher of color.

I have discussed several important aspects of Dr. Johnson's mind-set and practices, and the opportunities she attempted to co-construct with her students. As a Black educator working in a school with mostly wealthy White students, she believed that many opportunity gaps would have remained in their educational experience without the exposure she could provide. In particular, Dr. Johnson placed matters of gender, race, culture, and privilege at the center of many of her curriculum and instructional decisions because she believed they were important for her students. She taught her curriculum in part by facilitating student reflection, and she was able to address inevitable cultural conflicts by making powerful connections with her students and building solid and sustainable relationships with them.

Dr. Johnson's ability to work through cultural conflicts was guided by the marginalization that she and many of her students experienced. She felt marginalized because she was so vocal about matters of culture among her colleagues; some of her students felt marginalized because they were not the "most popular kids" in the school. Moreover, Dr. Johnson developed relationships with her students, connecting with them as those who felt marginalized. Dr. Johnson also did not "blame" students for issues beyond their control (such as historical racism). She was able to create a safe space in which students could grapple with difficult, sometimes controversial, matters of diversity, be open to dialogue and critique, and avoid "White and cultural guilt." However, she did not let her White students off the hook. She expected them to use their hearts and minds to fight against inequity and injustice. When she demonstrated how various racial and ethnic groups had experienced discrimination, including White people, her mostly White students seemed to be more open to listening, learning, and acting to address discrimination.

I have explained that Dr. Johnson believed that she was expected to know both Eurocentric and African and African American–centric literature while her colleagues were expected to know only the former. In essence, Dr. Johnson stressed that her identity played an enormous role in what she taught and was expected to know; she transformed her curriculum practices to be responsive to students' everyday experiences and also to address what students might experience after they graduated. While

Mr. Hall was called racist for not acknowledging race and exerting color blindness, Dr. Johnson was called racist for focusing too much on race and being color-race-conscious.

In sum, there were serious consequences related to Dr. Johnson's practices when she first entered the Stevenson school district. Nevertheless, she exhibited a level of stick-to-itiveness in the face of serious challenges and adversity that many teachers likely would have found unbearable. The consequences of such interaction and perceptions of colleagues and administration could cause a teacher to revert to or fall in line with common discourses and expectations established in a school (see Buendia, Gitlin, and Doumbia for more on this).[11] However, those experiences, although hurtful, did not stop Dr. Johnson from building "eye-opening" experiences for her students through the curriculum. She eventually had to present these opportunities to her seniors rather than the freshmen, but they were an integral part of what she felt she needed to cover with her students, and so she continued to do so.

Indeed, based on my observations and interviews with her, Dr. Johnson felt a professional and moral obligation to prepare her students for a diverse world and to help them not be color-blind or in denial about our diverse society and world. Teaching and learning are preparation for life. As Banks explains, "The world's greatest problems do not result from people being unable to read and write. They result from people in the world—from different cultures, races, religions and nations—being unable to get along and to work together to solve the world's intractable problems such as global warming, the AIDS epidemic, poverty, racism, sexism, and war."[12] Surely all students, not only those outside of the mainstream, need and deserve learning opportunities that expose them to the knowledge, awareness, and skills necessary to combat these and other social problems and perhaps experience the world more fully.

4

Black Teachers, Diverse Urban School

Recognizing Assets in Unexpected People and Places

The reason I know what is happening in their world is that I live in their world. [As a father,] I have a fourteen-year-old; I have an eleven-year-old; I have an eight-year-old. I know the world they came from with my eight-year-old, and I know where they are with my eleven-year-old . . . I know where they are going with my fourteen-year-old. Because I teach in middle school, I am right around eleven- and twelve-year-old range [students] . . . If I didn't have children their age, I would have to learn about what's happening with them. It's my job to do this.

—Mr. Jackson, middle school math and science teacher in an urban school

You are going to be the social worker; you are going to be the parent; you are going to be the friend.

—Ms. Shaw, middle school social studies teacher in an urban school

In the quotes above, Mr. Jackson, a Black math and science teacher, and Ms. Shaw, a Black social studies teacher, stressed two important dimensions of their thinking and their practices at their diverse urban school, Bridge Middle School. As a father, Mr. Jackson shared how he relied on his own children to help him stay connected to and gauge what was going on with his middle school students. While he admitted that he was at an advantage because his own biological children spanned the ages of his students in his middle school classes, he shared that he believed teachers without such an advantage have a responsibility to learn about what is happening with students in order to teach them successfully.

Ms. Shaw reminds readers that teachers need to assume multiple interrelated roles when they are teaching. Although the role they play will vary according to the students and social context of their work, Ms. Shaw was firm in her position that teachers will assume roles far beyond that of classroom teacher as they develop knowledge about what is necessary for their students to build and sustain positive academic and social identities. Mr. Jackson and Ms. Shaw both taught in the same school as Mr. Hall, whose practices were the subject of chapter 2.

In chapter 2, I shared how Mr. Hall, a White science teacher, developed and improved his pedagogical practices over the years by listening to his students and being responsive to their requests, needs, and actions. For example, Mr. Hall developed meaningful relationships with his students and got to "know" them because they insisted that his knowing them was essential to their learning. Moreover, Mr. Hall started to think about matters of race and diversity, although he began his work avoiding such an emphasis. At the beginning of his work at Bridge, he declared that his goal was to do one thing: "teach science." Through his experiences and interactions with his students, he came to understand what was necessary for success in the classroom—he realized that he could not teach science until he came to know and understand *to whom* he was teaching science.

In chapter 3, I provided a picture of Dr. Johnson, an African American woman high school language arts teacher who developed transformative learning opportunities with her mostly White and wealthy students at Stevenson High School. Dr. Johnson was able to work through cultural conflicts, and she developed powerful relationships with students by building on experiences in and out of school that both she and her students encountered. Although at times she was met with resistance and did not feel supported in the school where she taught among her colleagues, Dr. Johnson was resolute in her decision and her desires to develop and implement curriculum and instructional opportunities that exposed students to matters that are often ignored in mostly White contexts, such as those dealing with equity, diversity (race in particular), and discrimination as well as White and socioeconomic privilege. Moreover, she discovered that it was necessary for her to coconstruct with students a safe, welcoming, and comfortable space for her high school students in order for them to remain open to the multiple themes explored in the classroom. She helped her students understand that all groups of people, past and present, experience hate and discrimination, and Dr. Johnson was cognizant of her goal for her high school students not to feel White and cultural guilt. From a developmental perspective, this approach—not to cultivate a classroom ethos of guilt and hostility—seemed important. However, older (perhaps college) students may find that a more assertive approach, where teachers consciously guide students to feel uncomfortable about difficult, taboo, and controversial issues, is necessary.

Although Dr. Johnson was successful in her work at Stevenson High, she had experienced adversity, especially when she first began teaching there. Some of her ninth-grade students interpreted her curriculum and instructional practices as prejudiced and racist. As a result, her freshman classes were taken from her, and she was assigned a new set of courses with high school students, mostly seniors. However, her instructional and curriculum goals remained the same: she continued teaching with a diversity- and equity-centered focus. Consistent with the general goals for her students, she helped build and cultivate skills among her students that would be transferable to other contexts. Such skill development included reading, writing, critical thinking, analytical thinking, reasoning, and so forth. However, rather than relying on traditional canonical texts, she used equity and justice-centered texts to help her students not only build these skills but also develop a social justice stance.

In this chapter, I showcase the mind-sets and practices of two teachers as they designed learning opportunities for students at Bridge Middle School. In short, these teachers had very different orientations, beliefs, and consequently practices in the very same building. But they were both effective because each identified sites from which they could learn in order to get better as teachers. As he deepened his knowledge and understanding of his students, Mr. Jackson embraced opportunities to use music and hip-hop culture to build relationships with students and develop lessons. As she learned about the shifting culture of the community where she and her students lived, Ms. Shaw constructed opportunities for her students to develop a sense of agency and authority to contribute to improving their local community. For Ms. Shaw, understanding community shifts and patterns meant that she was not solely concerned about test score results but also about helping her students build dispositions to improve their community.

INTRODUCING MR. JACKSON

When I met him, Mr. Jackson had been teaching for seven years. At school, he always wore a shirt and tie, usually a suit jacket as well, and could typically be found standing in front of his classroom door between classes. He often reminded students (both those he had taught and students not in his classes) to "be mindful of the time" and not to be late for class. He had a deep love and appreciation for music—jazz, pop, rhythm and blues, classical, and hip-hop—which filtered into his teaching. Music was almost always playing softly during his classes and students seemed to have become accustomed to hearing it.

Married with three children, Mr. Jackson was engaged, even immersed, in popular culture. He watched music videos, listened to "hip" radio stations, and played video games himself. It was rare that students used formal or informal language he did not understand. Well versed in "slang," he could quickly code-switch to more conventional, standardized language practices when necessary. His interactions with students were never forced;

they were easy and smooth, and he seemed to naturally stay current and relevant about social phenomena that seemed to matter to his students.

SIGNIFICANCE AND INSIGNIFICANCE OF RACE

Race is always a salient factor that educators should consider, but having the same racial background as students will not necessarily sustain teachers in the classroom when they do not have the knowledge and skill to teach all students equitably and effectively.

While I have argued throughout this book about the significance and relevance of teachers' racial consciousness and development, and a rejection of color blindness as they construct learning opportunities with their students, Mr. Jackson added a different spin on the issue. When I first began observing his classes, I assumed he was able to connect with his students—most of whom were Black—because he was Black. Indeed, I wondered about the nexus between his success and the ways in which the social construction of his race and gender, a Black man in a diverse urban classroom with large numbers of Black students in his classes, influenced his interactions, practices, and success in the school. I asked Mr. Jackson, based on his experiences at Bridge Middle School, whether he believed being a Black man provided him a bit of an advantage with his students due to their racial and ethnic match. He replied, "Yes and no. I hate to be ambiguous like that, but . . . yes, initially, because they can relate to me because of my ethnicity . . . Initially. *But the effectiveness comes from my style, how I teach, and how I manage* [emphasis added], and any person of any race can do that if trained properly. Any gender can do that."

I observed, for instance, how one African American student, Ryan, would be disruptive and disengaged from the beginning to the end of a different class, then walk into Mr. Jackson's classroom and behave completely the opposite. While Ryan seemed to yearn for attention in the classroom in general, his actions to gain recognition moved from overwhelmingly disrespectful (hitting other students, using profanity, refusing to sit down, perpetually asking to be excused to the restroom) in one classroom setting to respectful and open and positively engaged in Mr. Jackson's. Ryan was unquestionably a different student in the environment co-created with Mr. Jackson in their science and math classroom. Mr. Jackson was stern in his position that he initially garnered respect, and students seemed to be drawn to him based on phenotype: when his students saw a Black teacher—and a Black man—they were perhaps willing to give him a chance to teach and learn with them. However, Mr. Jackson came to believe that it was his teaching style and the ways in which he managed learning opportunities that made the difference. He believed that a teacher from any gender or any racial or ethnic group could be successful in any environment. What mattered for Mr. Jackson was *how* teachers teach.[1] This point is not only substantiated in the literature, it is also confirmed by Mr. Hall's and Dr. Johnson's success, portrayed in chapters 2 and 3, respectively. That is, although Mr. Hall, Dr. Johnson, and their students were not the same race, Mr. Hall and Dr. Johnson both developed relationships with their students and connected with them; consequently, they were successful in contexts with students who did not share their racial and ethnic background.

Mr. Jackson expanded on his thinking regarding the significance of his race and gender: "So I say yes, [race and gender are significant] because initially they [students] get attached to me, but that is only the start of the race. You can have another guy come in with the same ethnicity, and they may become attached to him at first, but if he is not being consistent, if he is not being fair, if he is not doing everything you are supposed to do, he is not going to be effective." He said that teachers must earn students' respect, and noted that students are sometimes not willing to allow a teacher to teach them if they do not have a deep connection, deeper than just shared race and gender. In Mr. Jackson's words, "I have seen several men with the same ethnicity come in and couldn't quite cut it. But initially [students said], 'He was cool; he's a good guy; he's cool." But then—if you are not being fair, if you are not being consistent, and if you are not effectively managing the classroom, you are not going to be very effective to the whole. Maybe a small group—but not the whole." Mr. Jackson was clear that a teacher's knowledge base and skill would ultimately be sustainable factors that make the difference in the classroom and would surpass initial connections. In his view, "If somebody [a teacher] comes in from a different ethnicity—even if they don't feel like they have a sense of belonging with them [the students] if they [teachers] come in and [are] consistent and fair and stress everything, they are going to be successful, I believe."

STRESSING THE VALUE AND RELEVANCE OF LEARNING

There are competing positions about students' value of and interest in learning in urban and highly diverse schools. Some research suggests that students in these schools do not value learning, while other research points to the importance of context in making such claims; indeed, the sociocultural context of some urban and highly diverse schools fosters a valuing of learning, while other social contexts may not. But just because students do not seem interested in learning in a particular place does not mean they do not value it. Students tend to adapt to the expectations of schools; they value learning when learning is to be valued in an environment.

Given the divergent views on student motivation for learning in urban and highly diverse schools, I was curious about the kinds of challenges Mr. Jackson faced as he tried to design and implement learning opportunities at Bridge Middle School. He said he continually struggled to help his students find the value and relevance of learning and the value of school, and to that end he attempted to help them visualize how learning and school could help them do what they *aspired* to do in their lives outside of school, both currently and in the future. He believed that he needed to provide opportunities for his students to see themselves as capable of success in the classroom and beyond. He stressed that many of his students could not see their current learning expectations as a vehicle to take them where they wanted to go. Too many of his students did not recognize their own genius, and he needed to help them see themselves as both capable and worthy of academic, social, emotional, and educational success. In short, many of his students did not see "successful student" as part of their identity.

Perhaps part of the challenge was what it actually means to be successful. Informally, I questioned one of his students, a Latina seventh grader, Marianna, about what she wanted to do (mostly professionally) in her life post-graduation. At first, I wondered if the student had spent much time thinking about her life after graduation yet, in light of the fact that she was in seventh grade. The student shared rather emphatically with me: "I plan to go to culinary school. I'm in this math class because I have to be. It really won't matter much to me later when I start stacking my papers [earning money] cooking for celebrities." The student clearly had not come to see how learning mathematics in seventh grade would be important or have any real bearing on her future work as a chef "cooking for celebrities." In particular, based on my conversation with Marianna, she wanted to own a restaurant and work with country music stars and other "famous people." But, for Marianna, math had very little (if anything) to do with her future plans to "stack" her money.

Because students tended to care most about impressing their friends and were more interested in what was happening in other areas of their lives, especially the social areas, Mr. Jackson realized that it was important for him to help students see school as a "hip" and "cool" place to be even as he worked to convince them that learning was salient to their current and future experiences and opportunities. He wanted students not only to learn math to align with their interests and future work but also to see the value in learning for the sake of learning.

Mr. Jackson believed that "the biggest struggle in most urban schools is getting over the 'it's not cool to learn' factor. Once you break those barriers and you get your classroom management in check, everything rolls pretty smooth[ly]. But [the idea that school is not cool] is a microcosm of our society." Mr. Jackson observed that there was a hierarchy of priorities in society and at Bridge Middle School, and "academics" were not at the top of the structure. He felt that entertainment was number one in the broader society, and noted, "It's like that in the school system. The biggest struggle would be getting . . . the children to understand how important education is and that it is OK to act cool and be smart and intelligent" at the same time. Creating opportunities for students to think seriously about school and education may be an unexpected focus for a math and science teacher, but similar to Mr. Hall, Mr. Jackson understood the complex interplay between motivating students to want to learn and teaching mathematics and science. He considered it a critical part of his job to get all students motivated and interested in learning, and he admitted that it was sometimes a struggle to think of creative and relevant ways to do this.

The research literature provides a range of views on the idea that students in urban and highly diverse settings do not find value in learning or education. Some research shows that students of color in these contexts, such as African American or Latinx students, or English language learners, do not value learning, or they see academic achievement and success as "uncool" or as achievements for White students to aspire to.[2] Another line of research counters this position, suggesting that students of color from urban and highly diverse settings *do* value learning and education. This literature stresses that students' interests and what they value depend on their social environment and their interpretations of what is acceptable and expected of them in their space.[3] The research that points to the importance of context in determining student value and interest in learning counters the "acting White" thesis, which has been dangerously used to describe why some students of color do not perform well in school. Either way, there was a power structure among the students at Bridge Middle School that Mr. Jackson came to understand. His grasp of such a power structure was essential for him as he constructed opportunities for his students to learn.

POWER STRUCTURES AMONG STUDENTS

Implicit and overt social and academic power structures exist among students in schools. Some of these power structures are conceptualized by adults and are shared by students. Other power structures are constructed and expressed by and among students themselves. Understanding these power structures and how they operate and are enacted can help educators bridge the space between social and academic facets of the school environment.

In the previous chapter, I discussed how adults at Stevenson High School, a predominantly wealthy and White school, had created an academic power structure in which students were classified into high, middle, and low groups. Indeed, even in social contexts of all White students, social hierarchies exist. A broader context can be seen in a similar social power structure that existed among students in an urban social context, Ballou High School, which was captured by journalist Ron Suskind in an important book: *A Hope in the Unseen: An American Odyssey from the Inner City to the Ivy League*.[4] The book provides an account of Cedric, a high-achieving African American student, who beats the odds and succeeds in one of the poorest inner-city neighborhoods of Washington, DC. Cedric matriculates and transitions from Ballou High School to the Ivy League of Brown University. Suskind describes the social power structure among the students at Ballou in three, perhaps interconnected, levels: (1) those who were high achieving were at the bottom; (2) successful and gifted athletes were in the middle, as there was a level of effort and achievement that converged with playing sports; and (3) drug dealers and gangbangers were at the top.

My experiences as a high school English teacher in a mostly Black, high-poverty school several years ago told a very different story. The valedictorian and salutatorian were usually African American, and while student athletes and those who might be classified as troublemakers certainly were held in some esteem and respect, most of the students did not reject academic success and achievement. Among the students, the valedictorian and salutatorian were praised, not teased, for being academically successful. Moreover, students did not, from my experience, relegate academic success to "acting White." I share my experience as a high school English teacher to reiterate the point that different social contexts will reveal different results related to how students in urban and highly diverse contexts (or any) interpret academic success and achievement. Although I will maintain the integrity of Mr. Jackson's interpretation of his view on student learning and sometimes lack of interest in learning, I must also nuance the narrative to suggest that not all students in urban contexts will devalue academic success and school overall.

At Bridge Middle School, according to Mr. Jackson and based on my observations, the athletes and cheerleaders were often held in the highest esteem among their peers. Because of their respect among the other students and the social power structure, Mr. Jackson worked to get the popular students on his "side" to develop a classroom culture that stressed the importance of learning and doing well in school. He relied on those at the top of the student-constructed social power structure to help "recruit" their classmates to appreciate and value learning in the classroom. He attempted to bridge what it meant to be "cool" and to be smart. Mr. Jackson believed that the majority of students—even those who might not normally be actively engaged in learning—would get connected as well when they witnessed their "cool" classmates involved. Many students did in fact follow their classmates' leads.

In essence, Mr. Jackson encouraged his students to value learning by targeting the socially constructed "most powerful students" to serve as implicit role models. He believed he needed to use such power as an anchor for the engagement and learning he hoped would result from the collective of his students. He said, "I try to target the coolest. I try to target the toughest. I try to target the most popular students, and I get them to understand and follow my vision. And once I get them, the rest of the class usually follows." It is important to note that Mr. Jackson was not trying to manipulate the students but, rather, help them develop a critical understanding about what they were learning and its importance. He could not stress enough the power and influence his students had on each other.

However, because Mr. Jackson felt confident that his students were constructing their own picture of him, especially his decisions related to his being "fair" in the classroom, he constantly referred to the idea that he had to be consistent with his expectations: "I don't care what your [power] status is—you are going to get consequences. I don't care if you are the big linebacker bully in the school or if you are the quiet little girl who is eighty pounds and never does anything. I want you serious about your work [engaging in learning]."

To recap, in many respects, students' peers were *much* more important to them than their teachers or even their parents. Mr. Jackson found that the most popular students at the school possessed a great deal of power and influence, and he believed that he needed to learn the social power structure and get those "powerful" students on his side for the sake of learning and relevance in the classroom. He shared his strategy: "You have to get the people who have the most influence—the peer influence is very big in their [the students'] world, very big. So if you get the toughest kids, the strongest kids, the most powerful kids, you get them to 'buy in,' then you have got it [for the entire class]." In class, it was obvious that Mr. Jackson had gotten this buy-in—even the students who were considered the most popular and/or the toughest seemed to be actively involved with learning. Perhaps Mr. Jackson was successful in this regard because he deliberately and assertively sought out those at the top of the social hierarchy to promote the value and relevance of learning in the classroom community.

CONSTRUCTING IMAGES AND PERCEPTIONS AS REALITY

At times, educators may believe that students are wrong about how they have interpreted and/or constructed the world—particularly about what happens during a classroom episode such as when a teacher corrects some "off-task" behavior. However, educators must realize that our perceptions become our reality and that we rely on our past experiences to help define what becomes real to us.

Throughout my time observing Mr. Jackson's practices, he consistently pointed to image and perception, both among students and between teachers and students. For Mr. Jackson's students at Bridge Middle School, perception *was* reality. He knew that students were watching what happened in the classroom: how he handled interactions and conflicts with his colleagues, whether he called on the same students all the time, whom he asked to help him with tasks in the classroom, or how he handled disruption from one student to another. He needed, in his words, to be "fair, firm, and consistent," and he recognized that students' perceptions of what he did and how would play a critical role in whether they would be willing to attend his class and complete their classwork.

Mr. Jackson wanted his students to have a positive image of him and what was going on in the classroom, and he did not want any of them to feel that one student was more important than any other. They were *all* his students, and he wanted them all to maximize their potential and succeed. Like Mr. Hall, Mr. Jackson believed that he was somewhat of a mentor to his students and therefore always needed to take the high road and do what was right, no matter what occurred. Probably because of his cool demeanor, students seemed to look up to Mr. Jackson; he had earned their respect. But Mr. Jackson tended to operate from a sameness (equality) framework while Mr. Hall adopted more of a responsive (equity) approach. Mr. Jackson was clear that he believed his practices, words, interactions, and overall experiences with his students needed to be "the same." Mr. Hall demonstrated that his work with students would need to be more iterative and would vary based on students' history and the situation.

The fact that Mr. Jackson saw himself as a mentor to his students likely played a role in his decision to wear a shirt and tie each day. He believed that his attire was an important part of his image and power as a teacher and that his students needed to see him in a certain light. In Mr. Jackson's words, "Teachers should dress for where they are going, not necessarily where they are currently." This statement really connected to one of the main missions of his teaching: *he wanted his students to envision life beyond their current situations.* He believed his students sometimes saw their current situations as bleak (lack of material resources, struggles with family members, conflicts with teachers and classmates); however, he wanted his students to realize that they did not have to accept negative circumstances without fighting to change them. Moreover, he wanted his students to see the future possibilities for their lives.

The idea that students visualize themselves beyond their current situation was profound, because many of Mr. Jackson's students' experiences were limited to their local communities and circumstances. One White male student, Jared, who I learned was living below the poverty line, told me that he had never traveled outside his immediate community of Bridge Middle School. When I shared with him during one of my visits to the school that my wife and I had traveled to a mall on the south side of the city over the weekend, he said he had never been to that mall and had never seen other parts of the city—let alone traveled outside the state. I learned, for example, that several of the students at Bridge Middle School had never gone on a vacation with their families and did not know anyone personally who worked in corporate America.

Educational historian Vanessa Siddle Walker explains that before desegregation, teachers taught their students as if they were already living in desegregation.[5] They prepared their students for life beyond what they were currently experiencing. Similarly, the notion of seeing life beyond the present was a central element of Mr. Jackson's teaching and his own professional journey. For instance, he aspired to become a principal and dressed for where he was going in his career, not necessarily, according to him, for where he was. Part of the image Mr. Jackson wanted his students to embrace was of him as a person who was headed for promotion and a higher level of professional success.

Student image and perception were consistent themes of Mr. Jackson's mind-set and practices because he understood that students were both constructing images and perceptions and talking to each other about these images and perceptions (whether Mr. Jackson believed they were accurate or not). Images and perceptions were being constructed, then, both individually and collectively as the students in the school made sense of what Mr. Jackson and other teachers were doing in the school community. Mr. Jackson understood the importance of image and perception construction among his students because he immersed himself in their worlds to more deeply understand them, develop relationships with them, and teach and learn with them.

IMMERSION IN STUDENTS' WORLDS

Getting to know students means that teachers might have to move into a space that capitalizes on what is going on in students' worlds. Through immersion, teachers learn what is happening with students, what their interests are, and how students spend their time outside of school; they then use such knowledge in their classroom decision-making—to build learning connections, connect for relationships, and more deeply understand the social, emotional, psychological, mental health, and academic needs of their students.

By immersing himself in students' experiences both inside and outside of school, Mr. Jackson deepened his connections with his students. It is important to note that, based on my observations and conversations with students, Mr. Jackson was not perceived as intrusive when he pursued information about his students' lives. To the contrary, his queries into what was happening with his students stemmed from his genuine interest and concern for what was important to them and what they were experiencing inside and outside of school. He allowed his students to lead in helping him understand their experiences. Dr. Johnson, portrayed in chapter 3, also stressed how important it was for her to not be too intrusive when she attempted to learn more about, in her words, "Asian American culture" at Stevenson High School. Mr. Jackson's efforts to "remain current" in what was happening in the students' worlds helped him bridge the inevitable cultural divides between him and his students. Although Mr. Jackson and many of his students were African American, there was still ample room for conflict, division, and inconsistency due to a range of variances between them. Ultimately, he believed that he needed to immerse himself in the worlds of his students to design learning environments and develop instructional practices that connected to his students and that did not appear "foreign" to them. I have come to understand that the examples a teacher employs in a lesson, the nature of questions posed, how students are allowed to express themselves, and whose knowledge is validated (or not) in the classroom are all related to cultural practices, identity, and preferences that can have a huge bearing on students.

Where instructional approaches were concerned, Mr. Jackson advised, "implement things from their world into their academic setting. So, if I am doing math problems, I am going to have problems with stuff that comes out of the rap world or the video game world . . . Just recently, our basketball team was doing really well, and I used the players in the math assignments, and that gets them [the students] engaged." It's important to note that Mr. Jackson was not merely talking about incorporating "their world" experiences from time to time in the learning that took place. Rather, he was referring to "keeping their worlds" at the center of the curriculum and teaching. From my observations, his students looked forward to word problems with real-world relevance. They would often correct Mr. Jackson's errors about the number of points a player scored in a game, the number of rebounds a player had, or when and why a player fouled out of the game, which might seem insignificant or irrelevant to others but was a big deal to the students because it was their reality, their world, and they wanted the examples to tell a truth.

I wondered how Mr. Jackson was able to stay so current with what was happening with his middle school students in order to "implement things from their world into their academics." Mr. Jackson was able to recite versions and lyrics of hip-hop songs, list names of the most popular professional athletes, recall who won the NBA championship or Super Bowl in any particular year, and talk about plot, setting, and characters from the latest movies and television shows his students were watching. He was, in a sense, immersed in popular culture. Mr. Jackson explained why he was so connected to the pop culture world of his students: he "lived" in their worlds through his own children and had a sense of where his students were developmentally because of the age range of his children. But there was another reason for his connection to his students' culture and their cultural practices, as he went on to explain: "I am a DJ—I like the rap music myself. I play rap music [outside of school]. I feel like a kid at heart sometimes, so I kind of stay in touch with them in that way too." So Mr. Jackson knew the codes that many of his students were speaking, practicing, and enacting in the hallways or during downtime in the classroom. The language commonality code provided for natural interactions between Mr. Jackson and his students, although the students seemed to transition from speaking in slang or more casual language to more "academic" language without his having to remind them (although I am not confident Mr. Jackson would have in fact reminded them to speak standard English). There was, without question, mutual respect between Mr. Jackson and his students. The students did not take Mr. Jackson's connection to hip-hop or pop culture as an indication that he was a peer. To the contrary, they respected him because in their eyes he had earned it. Part of their respect for him likely emerged from the fact that they could relate to him, and he to them.

One could argue that Mr. Jackson was at an advantage in teaching his students at Bridge Middle School: (1) he was African American, (2) he was male, (3) he had children around the same age as his students, and he enjoyed many of the same interests and practices as his students (listening to hip-hop, playing video games, and watching sports, in particular). It is important to note that Mr. Jackson did not believe that it was impossible for other teachers to immerse themselves in students' worlds, even if they did not share one of these characteristics, practices, or qualities. In fact, Mr. Jackson asserted that it is teachers' responsibility to do so. Mr. Jackson believed that by learning about the worlds of their students, teachers could enhance the learning that took place in the classroom. In his words: "You have to immerse yourself in their world in some form or fashion. I am just lucky to come from the world that I teach in. . . . I truly live in that world, so I am immersed already in my natural life." Mr. Jackson in fact lived in the very community in which he taught. His students saw him in the community (at the supermarket, recreation center, barbershop, church, and so forth). He added, "So if I were in a system where the students came from a different world [community], I would just have to immerse myself in their world." Mr. Jackson advised: "You have to understand their desires, wants, and needs and dislikes . . . You have to implement that in your academics because *if they are not interested, then they are not going to learn*" [emphasis added]. Clearly, there was a direct connection between the immersion of this teacher in the students' world and the learning opportunities available in the classroom. As mentioned, Mr. Jackson had a genuine interest in and affection for music and hip-hop in particular, and he used this asset (music awareness) in his teaching. He believed that all teachers should use what they themselves possess as assets, as well as allow students to use what they have in the classroom as strengths. One asset that Mr. Jackson brought into the classroom, as a DJ and father of three, was a knowledge of and interest in hip-hop music.

MUSIC, HIP-HOP CULTURE, AND LEARNING

Teachers need to understand the music, hip-hop culture, and learning nexus, especially if their students are immersed in practices that require such immersion. Understanding the connections, whether teachers like the genre of music or the hip-hop culture or not, can serve as a tool to understand student interests, build relationships with them, and construct teaching and learning opportunities that connect with students.

Some type of music was almost always playing in Mr. Jackson's classroom, and at times, students from other classes would stop by and look in, just to see what was being played on any particular day and at any particular time. The participation of some youth in what is known as hip-hop culture makes it necessary for teachers to understand it and to build from it in the classroom.[6] There are particular ways of living associated with hip-hop culture that researchers find to be relevant to the knowledge base of teachers if they are interested in deepening their understanding of youth who operate in and through cultural frames associated with hip-hop. Urban teacher education researcher Jason Irizarry explains how drawing from hip-hop culture, rap music, and youth culture can inform teachers about working with students, especially Latinx students, English language learners, and African American students. His study provides "examples of how a group of teachers in urban schools [embodied]" cultural characteristics associated with hip-hop culture that served as a bridge to connect teachers and students.[7] Some teachers reject and consciously resist all forms of hip-hop culture rather than using them as a means to connect with students and to scaffold learning opportunities in different subject-matter domains. Consequently, students are often in opposition to a more mainstream culture. The idea is that teachers and students locate common cultural connections to optimize instructional and learning opportunities in a social context.

When asked about the relevance and reasoning behind his implementation of music in the classroom, Mr. Jackson said: "Well, it's nothing new. It was actually used in ancient Egypt where they used drums and instruments in the classroom. I do it for a couple reasons. Number one reason is kind of selfish—I like it . . . [some] people take smoke breaks or eat chocolate—I like to listen to music. And, it soothes me. It's usually jazz, sometimes some soft rock, [or] some soft R&B, but it's usually jazz, occasionally classical." He had also done some research about music and learning in the classroom. He shared his findings: "The research states that when you play soft music, it calms students down and if you continue to play it, it kind of works as association in learning—when students take tests, and you play the same songs [as what was played when covering the material during instruction], they can remember something about the assignment [or content] through the sound of the song—through association." So, he was adamant about the place, relevance, and appropriateness of music in the classroom, having learned about its benefits through reading as well as his own experiences with his students.

It appeared that the students enjoyed the class, especially the incorporation of music, perhaps because the teacher offered something different from what typically happens in too many classrooms across US society where students come in, sit down, listen to the teacher, are told what to do, have very little voice and input in the classroom, do work sheets, and are dismissed.[8] I would hear students in the hallway or in the cafeteria report that they were ready to "get to Jackson's class." They were eager to find out what was going to happen on any given day, and they especially wanted to hear the music.

One learning opportunity the students really enjoyed was what Mr. Jackson called "Science Feud," a game that served as a form of review for upcoming examinations. During these "feuds," Mr. Jackson would play music that students could dance to—music that was relevant and responsive to students' interests, such as hip-hop. And the students loved it! He explained the structure and relevance of the game, which to me was not that innovative. Like the popular game show *Family Feud*, students would answer questions about some dimension of science that had been covered in class. The hook was the *type* of music being played. It was the kind of music the students wanted to hear—the same music they listened to during their free time at school and outside of school. Of course, the music that he played was free of profanity and vulgarity.

After dividing the class into teams, as the students walked up to the front of the room to answer a question during Science Feud, Mr. Jackson played music that the students enjoyed, typically rhythm and blues or hip-hop. Sadly, many students are forced to sit in classrooms without any real meaning or connection to what they care about, whether that is music or other interests. For Mr. Jackson, the classroom was not a place to be in opposition but one where students could find connections, solidarity with, and relevance to their interests. The popularity of the Science Feud outlasted the students enrolled in Mr. Jackson's class. He described how "the sixth graders I had who are now in seventh or eighth grade . . . still come by when I have it [Science Feud] going on, and they say, 'I wanna play, I wanna play.' They like it." Mr. Jackson told me that while the students enjoyed playing the game because they wanted to listen to the music, they actually studied the material and tried to answer the questions correctly. In essence, the students felt they could relax a bit while still working hard to answer the questions.

POP CULTURE, TEACHING, AND LEARNING

Popular culture informed Mr. Jackson's beliefs, attitude, disposition, mind-set, and practices with his students. Based on my learning with Mr. Jackson, I suggest that other teachers can utilize popular culture in ways that can benefit their classroom instruction and help them build connections with their students. Examples of popular culture that students may be involved with and that teachers should be aware of include the following:

- *Music:* Students enjoy listening to all kinds of music, including rap, hip-hop, rhythm and blues, rock, jazz, country, and classical. At Bridge Middle School, some students are even aspiring (or already successful) musicians and musical artists.
- *Movies:* Students enjoy a range of movies, including comedy, horror, drama, romance, and suspense. Some students even aspire to become professional actors and are consumed by not only the entertainment of watching movies but also the mechanics and technical aspects of moviemaking and/or directing.
- *Sitcoms:* Students also like to watch weekly television shows. They are often faithful to certain sitcoms or dramas that allow them to connect with characters and story lines.
- *Reality shows:* Increasingly, television stations, such as Music Television (MTV), Bravo, Black Entertainment (BET), Oxygen, Oprah Winfrey Network (OWN), and Country Music Television (CMT), feature reality shows that allow students to follow "real" people through authentic experiences, such as dating and competitions of all kinds. Students I spoke to at Bridge Middle School were watching *Love and Hip Hop*, *Basketball Wives*, and the *Atlanta Housewives*.
- *Video games:* Games allow students to engage in competition, either with themselves, the gaming system, or friends. Gaming interactions allow students to connect with local friends and relatives as well as those far away. They also allow students to engage their imaginations

and improve their performance over time, using either a personal computer, a laptop, or other gaming systems connected to their television or computers.

- *Magazines:* Although not as common as in the past, printed magazines such as comic books, *Teen Vogue, Girls' Life, Seventeen*, and *Cosmopolitan* are enjoyed by students. Online sources, such as MTV News (www.mtv.com/news) and www.allure.com, are also becoming popular with young people.

These magazines sometimes provide extra information about other forms of pop culture they are experiencing, such as what is happening on a sitcom or in the life of a reality television star. Adolescents engage these outlets, which help shape their worldview and even their identities.

At a time when students are actively engaged in shifting cultural contexts and social practices experienced through social media—such as Snapchat, Instagram, Facebook, Twitter, and even text messaging—students' ability to handle problems can be a matter of life or death. Consider the growing number of students who report feeling unsafe or depressed because they have been bullied by classmates online. The American Society for the Positive Care of Children reports that 16 percent of high school students (and 55 percent of LGBTQ+ students) have been cyberbullied in the past year—and that students who are bullied are more than twice as likely to consider suicide.[9]

Never before have we experienced the kinds of cultural practices in which students engage through social media, practices that influence both academic and social development. To be sure, information-rich cultural contexts can enhance students' opportunities to learn. However, students' practices in the broader cultural landscape of technology can also be challenging—and dangerous—if students have not developed tools to work through difficult situations such as conflicts with classmates. Even at very young ages, children are now engaging in cultural practices that can lead to serious challenges if they do not have the ability to understand the root of an interpersonal conflict and solve it. Consider these data from Edudemic:[10]

- Eighty-eight percent of teens value social media because it "connects them with friends they rarely see."
- Fifty-one percent of kids say they've been bullied online, and 49 percent say they have been the online bully.
- Eight is the average age when a child begins regularly consuming online media.

Indeed, many students are much more interested in pop culture than in their school subjects. Linguist and language and literacy researcher James Gee reminds us that students will engage with pop culture—music, sitcoms, video games, comic books, and magazines—for hours and hours but will rush to finish their homework or not complete it at all.[11] Moreover, Gee, along with other language and literacy researchers, such as Jeffrey Duncan-Andrade and Ernest Morrell, provide additional insight into the kinds of information that popular culture can provide, which educators can learn from and build on in the classroom.[12] For instance, Gee stresses that video games are complex, and students respond to the challenge as they learn what it takes to play them. Yet in the classroom, students sometimes avoid engaging with difficult learning tasks. So what is it about video games that students are drawn to that can assist educators in designing complex, rigorous learning opportunities in the classroom?

According to Gee, video games give players/students an opportunity to build a strong sense of identity. For example, players can typically choose a game or select a "person" or player to play with during a game. Later a player is allowed to select another "person" or player if the player is not satisfied with the performance of the previous one. In this way, students see identity as fluid and evolving and are allowed to rebuild, reconstruct, or rework their identity when necessary. The opportunity to select another player is also advantageous when players "mess up" or are eliminated from a phase of the game. The idea is that players have multiple chances to succeed and move to higher levels in the gaming world and that the game does not "give up" on players per se (a point that will be explored in more depth later).

While teachers may resist the notion of actually gaming themselves, given their schedules and interests, they may find that the games are a way to relax. Also, teachers may find that when they coach a sport or serve as the faculty sponsor for a club, they are able to develop relationships with students that allow them to challenge students to succeed academically. For instance, Mr. Hall, in particular, demonstrated the power of playing one-on-one basketball with one of his more difficult-to-reach students and how that gesture opened the door to their relationship; the student began to engage more in the classroom and both Mr. Hall and the student benefited.

Gee also shares that video games expect players to produce and create, not just consume, knowledge and information. This requirement is consistent with the philosophical and theoretical ideas of Freire, who insists that learners bring a wealth of knowledge into the classroom that should be used to construct and assemble new knowledge.[13] In this sense, teachers should strive to work *with* students in learning, not adapt a position that they are just pouring knowledge into students. This approach is what Freire refers to as a "banking" approach, where "the scope of action allowed to the students extends only as far as receiving, filing, and storing the deposits" they receive from teachers or other educators, who are considered the depositors of knowledge, while students are those who must be taught, or are the consumers of knowledge.[14] McCutcheon maintains that teachers are not the only, or even the main, arbiters of knowledge. Students, too, are knowledgeable and should be allowed to draw from and showcase their knowledge in schools.[15]

In addition, Gee explains that video games allow players (learners) to engage in deeply complex problem solving. The proposition is that learners must figure out multifaceted layers of complexity in solving problems, which are typically based on what players have learned and been exposed to in previous phases of the game. Students usually enjoy the challenge of trying to figure out complex problems as they build on previous knowledge and experiences. Gee has found that video games allow students to explore and take risks without huge consequences. For example, in many games, players are allowed to start from where their last game ended, and video games always provide players with more than one "life" to live. In other words, once a player is defeated or makes an error in a game, the game does not necessarily end. There are additional opportunities for players to solve the problem or defeat an opponent, for instance. Thus, the lesson here is that students need and deserve multiple opportunities for success in the classroom, and they should be allowed to create, construct, recreate, and reconstruct their identities as they grow, mature, and develop in knowledge, ability, and skill. In short, videogaming advances and rewards the fact that people are developing beings and should get better over time. Students should be encouraged to give their best effort to a task and feel confident that there will be opportunities for them to keep working at it without fearing that they will fail or be considered a failure—note my purposeful distinction between the two (failing versus failure). Students should not be seen as having "arrived" but as those who will develop.

Gee also explains how video games are designed to guide students through various phases and dimensions of life and learning. For instance, preliminary knowledge, opportunities to learn and grow, and experiences come early in the game; more elaborate and sophisticated experiences build on this knowledge and understanding, moving to more complex forms of knowing, expertise, and experience. The importance of building knowledge and scaffolding learning opportunities is obvious; teachers should be mindful of how they construct earlier phases of learning, carefully assessing what students know, then deliberately crafting later learning to build on and from those early phases.

Music is another popular form of expression, and students are able to express their preferences and interests through the type of music they enjoy. The choice that students enjoy is an important principle that is transferable to teaching and learning. By allowing choice, teachers can provide students with opportunities to make some decisions in the learning process. Although the teachers showcased in this book had developed some innovative instructional moves that were drawn mostly from their ability to connect with their students and build relationships with them, they did not provide much of a learning space for student choice. In fact, Dr. Johnson, in her practices, expected students to read aloud even if they did not feel comfortable.

Music allows listeners to locate common identity markers with artists and song lyrics; it can provide relevant real-life lessons by allowing students to fantasize, role play, or empathize with the artist. Music engagement with artists, for instance, creates opportunities for teachers and students to exercise their imagination and creativity—all of which can be transferred in the classroom. For instance, many of the students who engage with music and are drawn to the artists performing have not lived in the same community as the performers. They may not necessarily relate their own lives to what is being spoken or sung. But students can build their creativity, empathize with, or even yearn for the kinds of messages conveyed. These skills are important, and the practices of transferability can be emphasized when teachers are attempting to help students dissect and/or analyze a piece of literature in a classroom.

In listening to the types of music that students listen to, teachers learn what students like. They can use this knowledge to build lessons or just to demonstrate that they have actually heard a particular song or genre of music that is popular with their students. As Duncan-Andrade and Morrell declare: "Turn up that radio, teacher!"[16] Students are often fascinated to learn that teachers have even heard of some of the most mainstream artists, such as Jay Z, Beyonce, Taylor Swift, Lady Gaga, Common, Queen Latifah, Rascal Flatts, Usher, Carrie Underwood, Kanye West, Ariana Grande, Christina Aguilera, Bruno Mars, Drake, Justin Bieber, Trey Songz, and Will Smith.

Similar to video games and music, sitcoms can provide important insights for teaching and learning. They also can provide strong contextual grounding: when a program begins, actors (or teachers) must be prepared to capture the attention of the audience (students). If there is not a profound, or at least interesting, start to the show (or a lesson), students may become disengaged. Immediately capturing the audience's attention is crucial for both television producers and classroom teachers. Sitcoms must contextualize a story or message quickly and keep viewers tuned in because they have only thirty minutes or fewer to set the stage, provide the details, and (most of the time) resolve the story; in other words, they need to hook the audience, much in the way a teacher needs to capture students' attention. As with a sitcom, teachers should also create a guiding narrative that persuasively links the different elements of the lesson covered. If successful, a sitcom will have viewers who want to discuss the story with friends and family members later, and the audience will eagerly await the next episode. Would it not be refreshing if schools were places where students yearned to be and eagerly anticipated what was coming next?

Television shows of interest to students may include sporting events and weekly sitcoms. Teachers may find that they already possess some similar interests in shows, such as pivotal sporting events like the Super Bowl, NBA playoffs, Stanley Cup, March Madness, golf's Masters Tournament, the Olympics, and the World Series. What I have come to learn is that even when teachers have only a marginal interest in or knowledge of a television show, this link can provide a powerful and relevant opportunity for teachers and students to connect.

Engaging in popular culture and learning about ways to bring lessons from popular culture into teaching and learning have potential to assist educators. However, I understand and agree with Duncan-Andrade and Morrell when they remind us that some culture is considered "high" and acceptable while other forms are viewed as "low."[17] Hip-hop and popular culture can be considered as low—culture that is insignificant and irrelevant to the kinds of high cultural experiences traditionally valued in learning environments, such as classical music. Thus, educators may struggle to see the relevance of and possibility for using particular types of music as, for instance, a cultural experience to connect with students through curriculum (what they teach) and instruction (how they teach it). The reality that teachers and others see certain kinds of music and certain types of culture as high or low is infiltrated with -isms and phobias—too many to name. Duncan-Andrade and Morrell queried, as do I: Will schools continue to be places where students do not want to be, where they do not enjoy learning and find relevance, or will they ever be places where students really find value and relevance to their lives and experiences?

LEARNING ABOUT STUDENT INTERESTS

Developing knowledge about student interests can be as essential to teacher learning as learning their subject matter. Learning about student interests means that teachers construct learning opportunities with students that are relevant to them and allow students to express themselves in the classroom.

Teachers may wonder how they can learn about student interests generally, not only in popular culture. It was evident that Mr. Jackson had learned how to gauge his students' interests. Other teachers who are serious about understanding student interests and engagement outside of school should consider the following techniques to build knowledge and perspective that can be used in the design and practice of learning opportunities in the classroom:

- Ask students about their interests by actually engaging in one-on-one and group conversations with them.
- Specifically ask students what they did over the weekend, with whom, for how long, and which aspects of those actions they enjoyed (or not).
- Develop assignments that allow students to share their interests.
- Engage in reciprocity where teachers also talk about their own interests; teacher sharing can increase the likelihood that students will feel comfortable sharing. Moreover, teacher sharing humanizes them.

The preceding four suggestions are excellent examples of how educators learn about student interests or at least what engages them outside of school. It is critical, however, that teachers try not to overtly express their value judgment of student preferences in music and/or movies with questions like, "How in the world could you enjoy listening to *that*?" Although they may not find relevance or connections with the music, the point is for them to build knowledge about and try to make connections (relationally and instructionally) with their students.

Extending what Mr. Jackson learned in his work, teachers might do the following:

- Make explicit connections between student interests in pop culture and their curriculum and instructional practices.
- Demonstrate that they have heard a popular song, have seen a movie of interest, or recognize an artist many students admire. Mentioning the movie or song or engaging in conversation with students about an artist can serve as a conduit for building relationships because students may more readily see a teacher as a real person who actually listens to the radio or watches movies, or perhaps plays video games; some students find it difficult to perceive of their teachers as "real people" who share some of their interests.
- Create opportunities for students to analyze and critique the content of movies, music, and sitcoms through the curriculum. The idea is to shepherd students into building the skills they need to critique and deeply question what they are listening to or watching. Such critique should encourage students to think about the ways in which song lyrics can perpetuate sexism, racism, a myth of meritocracy, cultural conflicts, and so forth. When teachers create opportunities for them to question, critique, and analyze, students are able to see texts in varied forms, as Dr. Johnson stresses. Texts are prevalent through and in people, places, song lyrics, movie scripts, performances, and so on.
- Request and expect students to find "companion" pieces that compare, contrast, connect, and contradict canonical or traditional forms of writing in American or British literature. Or use music or movies to illustrate and expand on content in other disciplines such as science, social studies/history, art, or mathematics. The point is to build synergy between and among students' interests and help students build cognitive and analytic skills to think beyond the obvious.

In the next section, I shift the discussion to Ms. Shaw, who also diligently cultivated relationships with her students—but not through music or other forms of popular culture. She in fact critiqued much of the engagement and practices of her students outside of school. However, she worked to instill a sense of purpose and history with her students to help them understand the role of social activism and change to improve their lives and their communities.

INTRODUCING MS. SHAW

Ms. Shaw was always immaculately dressed. She frequently wore a stylish scarf to accent her attire, which was often a linen suit because it complemented the student uniforms in the Bridge school district. Ms. Shaw was teaching from the moment her classes started until the students walked out the door. Sometimes she would be "teaching" as the students were in line at the door preparing to change classes. Her students were always engaged in some project, discussion, or writing assignment. Furthermore, I never walked into Ms. Shaw's classroom when she was not at the front of the room. She never sat at her desk, which was in the back corner of the room. Her desk looked more like a storage area than a place to work. She was a powerful storyteller, and students seemed to hang on her every word. On a rotation basis, Ms. Shaw taught the following courses: civics, reading in the social studies, and multicultural education in the United States. She had been teaching for thirty-five years, and she had attended Bridge Middle School herself as a child.

TEACHING AS MISSION AND RESPONSIBILITY

Some teachers see their work as involving more than conveying information or facilitating learning opportunities. They perceive their work as educators as what they were "called" to do, and thus they believe they have a responsibility to their students and to the broader profession of teaching.

While Mr. Jackson had a deep passion for popular culture, Ms. Shaw had a much more traditional mind-set and approach to her practice at Bridge

Middle School. She believed it was her responsibility and mission to teach and to help students build a skill set to help their local community after they graduated from Bridge Middle School and eventually high school. She also wanted her students to develop a mission-minded approach to their decisions and actions. By mission-minded, I mean that she wanted her students to think about a broader collective purpose and about their "calling" in life. This mission or calling was not tied to religion or even spirituality per se. Rather, the mission was for them to examine their communities and think about ways to improve them. Ms. Shaw wanted her students to develop skills that would allow them to contribute to something beyond themselves. She made it clear that it was part of her role, responsibility, and "calling" to help her students serve and change their communities. This change that she advanced was linked to her desire for her students to find their "purpose" in life—the "why" of their existence.

Ms. Shaw attempted to facilitate learning opportunities that helped her students develop knowledge and skills about some of the social realities, particularly in the Bridge community, that they were not necessarily aware of. She felt very strongly that there was a need for her students to develop a mind-set to serve their communities and find ways to change and improve it. Part of her focus was due to the fact that she wanted her students to build agency and to become leaders in the community who would protect and preserve their local community. Ms. Shaw, like Dr. Johnson, shared personal narratives throughout her lessons to help the students understand the content she was teaching. In an interview, she shared: "Now I am almost sixty . . . when we were taught in teacher training, we had a mission. Our mission was to go out to serve . . . to reach and to help the generations." She believed that reminding students that they were on earth to make a contribution to humanity and to think about their "purpose" and contribution to society beyond their current situations was essential to their success.

Encouraging students to think outside their present mind-set and experiences became a major feature of what she perceived as her responsibility to her students. Helping students see life beyond themselves and the present was also a consistent theme of Mr. Jackson's mind-set and practices.

In essence, Ms. Shaw wanted her students to recognize that they were part of a larger community (inclusive of but also beyond Bridge Middle School) and she wanted them to think beyond themselves when making decisions.

It was clear from my observations that Ms. Shaw believed that she was "called" to the work of teaching, and she attempted to cultivate relationships with all the students at Bridge Middle School. Such a calling meant that she was proud of her decision to become a teacher, and she believed as a social studies teacher in particular she could help her students build the knowledge and skills necessary to contribute to society.

To be successful at teaching her subject matter, similar to Mr. Hall, Dr. Johnson, and Mr. Jackson, Ms. Shaw recognized the importance of building relationships with her students and also treating them as human beings worthy of empathy and compassion. For instance, during a class period I observed, Christine, a student in Ms. Shaw's fifth period, walked into Ms. Shaw's second period with an "assignment sheet" from in-school suspension (ISS). Christine looked perplexed and sad, and it was obvious that she had been crying. Consider the following interaction I observed between Ms. Shaw and Christine:

Christine: Ms. Shaw, fill this [the assignment sheet] out. They [the administration, assistant principal] put me in ISS. [Tears started to flow.]

Ms. Shaw: Christine, what's going on?

Christine: I just don't like her [referring to one of her other teachers].

Ms. Shaw: Well, Christine, you will meet a lot of folks in your life you don't like. You've got to learn to work with people you don't like. It's going to be all right, though, because you are smart, and you've got to let that situation roll off your back.

Christine: I knew you were going to say that, but I still don't like her.

At this point, Christine still looked like she was deeply troubled and hurt either by being sent to ISS or by the situation she experienced with the teacher, whom she declared that she "does not like." As Ms. Shaw was gathering "assignments" for Christine to occupy her time in ISS, it appeared that she noticed the troubled look on Christine's face. It seemed that Christine was taking the situation very seriously and that it was causing her emotional distress.

Ms. Shaw: OK, Christine, sit down. Just hang out in here with me for a while. You don't need to go to ISS in this state. How is your sister doing? You know I have taught all your older sisters, and you all are smart girls. What would your sister Tonya say if she saw you all upset like this?

Christine: She would tell me to calm down.

Ms. Shaw: Exactly. Just shake this situation off, Christine. It is so not the end of the world. You will bounce back from this. How is Tonya doing?

Christine: She is fine. She just got married.

By the time Ms. Shaw finished posing questions to Christine about her sister and reassuring her that she was indeed "all right," Christine had calmed down. In fact, by the end of their exchange, Christine looked like a completely different person. She was now ready to move forward with her punishment in ISS.

Later, when I talked with Ms. Shaw about the interaction, she said she worried that, had she allowed Christine to leave the classroom in the state she was in, she would have run into even more problems. She felt responsible for Christine and invited her to hang out in her room until Christine was in a space to move forward. In addition, as students made decisions and as she taught them, she reflected on the intricate and complex nature of race and its role.

REMEMBERING RACE

Although we have made significant strides in US society (and consequently in schools), race is still a salient issue in society and in education that must be addressed if we are to have a fighting chance at educational equity, justice, and diversity. Remembering race, pre-desegregation, allows teachers the opportunity to gauge how far we have come but also reminds us how far we need to go in education.

Ms. Shaw also talked explicitly about race and its relevance in her practices at Bridge Middle School. In the classroom and during interviews, she reflected often on her own experiences as a student and teacher pre-desegregation, and she discussed how her mind-set had been shaped by the "Black community." She explained that "Black culture" had fostered a sense of community commitment, and she was taught that she should use her increasing individual influence and success in ways that contributed to the collective society. This broader emphasis on community and change was evident in the kinds of experiences she wanted to construct for her students. Ms. Shaw's ability to think deeply about herself and her own experiences, and about how her identity construction helped ground her desires and instructional designs for her students, was consistent with the ideas Dr. Johnson emphasized.

As she related, "In the Black culture, that has also been our mission [to serve and to change/improve communities]. It was our mission and responsibility in our families and our churches and our homes . . . [When I was in grade school] we heard that in different ways . . . we heard that in sermons, [at church and] we heard it at home." Ms. Shaw regretted that a community-focused discourse did not necessarily still permeate the various spaces and institutions her students frequented: school, churches, homes, and so forth. As an ideal, she desired that her students would be focused on human and community improvement rather than on materialism and individualism (a point I will address in more depth later).

Moreover, Ms. Shaw said her decision to design and promote a community-based orientation in her work was precipitated by the fact that she had been helped throughout her life, especially in the Black community: "And so, as I became a teacher, somebody helped me along the way; somebody showed me, and then they corrected me." As a teacher who had spent many years at Bridge, Ms. Shaw perceived all the students in the school as "my kids." She would "correct" students in the hallway or the stairwell if necessary. When I observed her correct students not in her classes, the students, who all knew her name, modified their behavior immediately. For instance, one day I saw some students wrestling near the stairs and Ms. Shaw walked over and said firmly, "Are you serious?" But rather than send the group of students to the office, she directed them to move on to their class. On another day, some students were throwing a football from the landing to the top of the stairs. Ms. Shaw walked over and told the students "to get it together." In both cases, the students smiled, apologized, and moved forward. In her words, she had taught most of the boys before, so the relationship was already established. It appeared that she had gained respect from students in the Bridge school community, not only those in her classes.

Ms. Shaw seemed to have a recurrent view that as a Black person, her goal was to serve and improve the situations that were "unfair" and "unjust" and to help her students work toward such commitments. This community emphasis was consistently reinforced in her classroom. For example, she would ask the students to think about what could have been done to improve people's situations in the past and what could be done in the present. Her class discussions were very focused on aspects of history that guided students to make explicit links to current-day situations, rather than on remembering a host of dates, "facts," and names. Her focus seemed to be on conceptual development (such as the theme of community change and improvement) and skill development (such as pushing students to critically analyze a current event or an historical set of circumstances). These historical and current social ills often focused on the fact that "our students are mostly African American." Overall, though, she seemed to worry that her students had forgotten about the historical role of race in society and how racism could still manifest in their experiences. She wondered if the students were prepared for the racialized experiences they would inevitably face in society, especially as they moved into adulthood. She explained that many of her Black students seemed to take a "race is not important" position in many of their discussions, and this seemed to be of concern to her. Still, she did not force her own view—that race was in fact important—on them. In addition to thinking seriously about race, she wanted her students to move beyond a focus on materialism to one more connected with service for and to humanity.

MOVING BEYOND MATERIALISM

Society's intense and relentless focus on material possessions can complicate priorities and create a desire for personal wealth, distracting students from more germane and important goals, such as using their resources and assets to assist others.

Ms. Shaw believed that all of her students needed to be more community focused, and she drew from her experiences as an African American woman to discuss why community was so important. It is important to note that she felt all her students needed to be more community focused, not just her Black students. Her references to race, though, allowed her to reflect on her own experiences growing up during a time when you "had to be" concerned about aspects of life greater than self. In addition, it was evident that her commitment to service and her efforts to promote it through her teaching were so prevalent in her work because she had attended Bridge Middle School herself and had at one time lived in her students' community. Combined with her emphasis on community and what she called her "African American culture" was her concern that students were interested in material possessions, not necessarily the knowledge and skills that could improve and impact something greater than themselves as individuals.

Ms. Shaw was committed to helping her students realize that life was about more than what one could acquire materially. She felt it was her mission and responsibility to help her students realize that they too were "responsible for their communities," and she challenged them to make changes in their communities when they witnessed something that was "unfair, unjust, or simply wrong." Through the many stories she shared, her students came to realize that because Ms. Shaw had experienced life before desegregation and had experienced racism firsthand, she did not want them to take for granted all the sacrifices people before them had made on their behalf. She explained that people had died for the privileges that they currently enjoyed, and she believed that some of her students did not realize how close we as a country still are to segregation and to broader, more systemic forms of discrimination, racism, and sexism. Thus, her decision to highlight community over material possessions was often couched in her reflections about times when she had substandard materials as a student and even a teacher, such as "Black-only facilities and resources, used textbooks," and dilapidated educational facilities. When students did not handle their educational materials properly, she would remind them that at one point in US history, Black students had only "hand-me-down" and out-of-date books.

Ms. Shaw was also deliberate in introducing her students to people from the Bridge County area and beyond who had made tremendous strides forward in their careers and communities. In other words, Ms. Shaw believed that life not only was about succeeding personally but also should have "purpose for the masses." She shared the experiences of then senator Barack Obama, Ruby Dee, Dr. Bobby Lovett, Reverend Andrew Young, and others. Her sharing tended to be juxtaposed to current celebrities who were "quick" to share their big houses and fancy cars yet not necessarily contribute to community service and uplift. Thus, while Mr. Jackson made explicit links to celebrities and pop culture "icons," Ms. Shaw actually attempted to disrupt such admiration, pointing her students to historical individuals and institutions (such as the Southern Christian Leadership Conference) that worked to improve society and end discrimination.

Ms. Shaw wanted her students to learn about these individuals and institutions so they could recognize how their own journeys were inextricably tied to those they discussed of others in the classroom. She believed, similar to Mr. Hall, that students sometimes see the end result without recognizing that many people we celebrate have gone through hardships (including "deep-rooted poverty, racism, discrimination, and abuse") to get to where they are currently. Material possessions, she would explain, are the rewards of hard work and dedication, but many of the African American people she exposed her students to had service as their mission, not things. What seemed particularly insightful through her practices was her sharing of local "servants" in the Bridge community who continued to attend "council meetings, run for office, or speak at a community event about crime in the community."

Like the other teachers in this book, Ms. Shaw saw it as her responsibility and mission to accept and serve in multiple roles inside of the school to support her students. Thus, she was concerned that her students cared more about what some called "bling" than about issues related to the human condition. She believed that the media and popular culture had actually "harmed" students and seduced them into concentrating on the "wrong things." Indeed, such a position ran counter to Mr. Jackson's view of the role, influence, and relevance of popular culture for sure.

ACCEPTING AND SERVING IN MULTIPLE ROLES

Although they may not yet realize it in teacher education programs, whether traditional or alternative, teachers will assume and serve in multiple roles—beyond a content-area teacher—to connect with students and meet their many and varied needs. In their practices, teachers learn that they either accept the multiple roles that students need and come to expect, or they work to circumvent them. Successful teachers, though, seem to understand that effective teaching involves much more than classroom instruction, requiring them to serve students in myriad ways and in a range of meaningful roles.

When thinking about her role in the school, Ms. Shaw embraced the idea of assuming many roles in working with her students: "There are some teachers who are saying, 'That's [serving in multiple roles] not our job,' but it becomes your job because somebody's got to take on that role [the different roles required to support students] for the students. A lot of things I didn't understand either . . . when people told us when I started teaching that you are going to be the social worker; you are going to be the parent; you are going to be the friend . . . when they said all that stuff I said 'sure,' . . . but I see that I've become that. And I can either take that role, or I can say . . . I am out of here." Thus, students enter the learning context with needs to be met, many of which teachers must address and fill in order to be successful and support students.

Mr. Hall held a similar orientation when he started teaching. He simply wanted to "teach science" and for his students to "fall in love with science." But he, similar to Ms. Shaw, discovered the multiple roles teachers play in working with young people in schools. These teachers started where they were, but did not stay there. As a teacher whom one of her students referred to as her "mama," Ms. Shaw had come to assume multiple roles in her practices in order to bridge opportunity gaps, although she did not understand the multitude of these needs as a student or early-career teacher, learning and building skills to teach. In her practice with students over the years, she explained that she has taken on roles that she never thought she would need to assume as a classroom teacher. In this way, the students showed her what they needed and expected, and she responded.

Similar to all the teachers showcased in these case studies, Ms. Shaw understood that relationships were critical to her success as a teacher. When students see a teacher in a role that "fits" or is responsive to one of their needs, they are willing to trust enough to learn from the teacher—to push themselves to engage in materials that may have seemed difficult otherwise. Thus, the fact that Ms. Shaw performed roles that filled voids in some students' lives propelled students to open up to her and enabled her to build relationships with her students that might not have been possible otherwise. Based on my observations, Ms. Shaw taught the students life lessons—lessons that often emerged from her own story. She made explicit connections to her students' lives outside of the school context—connections not only to their current circumstances but also to their lives in the future. For instance, Ms. Shaw explained to the students the importance of honesty, what was necessary to secure a good-paying job, and the importance of building and "securing" social security. In an interview she explained: "I do want them to work, so they can get some Social Security money in the system . . . [I ask them] who is going to take care of you for the rest of your life? And who wants to?"

She spoke candidly with students about what happens when people do not develop knowledge and skills, and in many ways she assumed roles that allowed her to teach life lessons beyond the stated and expected curriculum. She shared real consequences with her students, which encouraged them to think about realities they might not have considered without her insight. Because she was at an age where she could retire, she was attempting to provide a window for her students that allowed them to visualize what was possible as well as what the challenges could be if they were not conscious and conscientious about the decisions they made. In this sense, Ms. Shaw assumed the role of mentor or counselor because she wanted her students to think beyond their current situations and to imagine life when they could receive Social Security in retirement.

It is important to note that Ms. Shaw attempted to demystify and break down some of the anxiety many of the students may have felt about preparing for their futures. However, she was unyielding about sharing information that could impact students' current and future lives. She refused to present everything as "easy," and she explained to students that they would experience difficulties in their lives, some of which would be the consequences of matters far beyond their control. For instance, she shared with her girl students that they could possibly earn less than their male counterparts in their professions. By presenting data on the overhead projector, Ms. Shaw prompted her students to react and ultimately construct proposals for changing or disrupting such a sexist reality. Moreover, she expressed to students that they were not immortal and that life would bring challenges that they would need to be prepared to work through by building necessary knowledge, skills, and attitudes. As Ms. Shaw shared with me, she worried that her students could become involved in gang activity or even be murdered in their very own community. She said that she watched and read the news carefully over the weekend and was always especially grateful when she would see all her "babies" arrive at school on Monday. She said that the fact that her students were living in a tough neighborhood made it necessary for her to be a bit "tough" with her students, and she often expressed to them that one wrong move, and they could end up in serious trouble.

In short, Ms. Shaw wanted her students to take their learning and lives seriously, and she was very direct with how life could be if the students did not engage, work hard, and serve. But Ms. Shaw did not embrace a meritocratic way of seeing the world. To the contrary, she wanted her students to work hard but was quick to tell them that they were living in an unjust society—where wages and benefits would be paid and rewarded inequitably, for instance. In this sense, she was no-nonsense. During my entire time studying at Bridge Middle School, I never saw Ms. Shaw send a student out of the classroom, and I never observed a student being rude, noncompliant, or disrespectful. Importantly, in like form, I never observed Ms. Shaw being rude or disrespectful to her students. That is, the students reacted to Ms. Shaw in a way that mirrored how she treated them. Ms. Shaw expected her students to produce high-quality work. She would insist that they redo assignments that did not meet her high expectations. I am not sure how many middle school teachers would focus their students to think about Social Security as a priority, but Ms. Shaw attempted to paint pictures for students that could help them think about where they were potentially headed, demonstrating multiple options and pathways that could end with personal and community success or failure. In this way, Ms. Shaw acted as an "other mother" (see the important work of Foster and Irvine), a point that will be taken up later in this chapter.[18]

While Ms. Shaw provided concrete examples of how life could be for students in the real world, she was also careful to explain that they would not have all the answers: "They understand what their purpose here is. 'I am not here to entertain you. I am here to help you and direct learning and guide your learning.' I keep telling them I don't know everything because now there is so much information that we'll never know. So, they understand. But, I'll tell you what, I know how to learn the answer, and I'll show you how [to find the answers to problems]. So I make that clear. So I'm not all-knowing."

In her role as an "other mother," she helped her students understand that they must become lifelong learners and work to build knowledge needed to succeed and solve problems. Such learning opportunities are important for students who may struggle to understand why they are on earth and what they are supposed to be doing here.

Consistently, Ms. Shaw also encouraged her students to take pride in themselves and in their school. She particularly urged her girl students to honor their bodies as young women and to think about their futures, as she wanted them to become independent and to reach their goals. She stressed to all her students the importance of attire and appearance, and urged them to pay careful attention to how they dressed and carried themselves because they were representing not only themselves but also their school, their parents, their ancestry, and her as their teacher and other mother.

SELF AND SCHOOL PRIDE

When educators invest in students, encouraging them to believe that they are important contributors to the broader school social context, students may be more willing to build pride in their school while simultaneously enhancing pride in themselves.

Ms. Shaw was committed to building school pride at Bridge Middle School and to helping students build a sense of personal pride. This was important to her because many of the teachers and students in the school saw themselves as family. One recurrent question in Ms. Shaw's classes was, "What is good citizenship at this middle school?" She wanted her students to treat others well and to reflect the positive attributes of the school when they went out in the community. Ms. Shaw believed that as a community, they needed to revive and return to some of the core values that were evident before desegregation, when she was a student at Bridge Middle School: "In urban schools, we are going to have to go back—you know, in the sixties we were making so many gains, and there was so much self-pride—why? *Because we were proud of what was on the inside and not on the outside.*

We have to go back to our core values. Love and respect for one another, integrity, humility, self-discipline, honesty. *And it's not that they don't have that, it's just that it can be lost in a world where 'stuff' matters more than people.*" [emphasis added]

To be clear, Ms. Shaw was not criticizing or blaming her students for a lack of character or integrity. Rather, she pointed to a society that often pushes and rewards materialism and "stuff" over people's hearts and minds. Indeed, Ms. Shaw stressed that school and self-pride were essential, and conveying this belief was one of the primary goals in her teaching. Her students seemed to buy into these ideas, as Ms. Shaw regularly reminded them of the importance of doing what's right, even when others do not. She stressed to students who were having disagreements with one another that they must not allow the conflicts to define who they were and who they were becoming. For her, doing what was "right" mattered more than retaliating against someone who had in their view "mistreated" or "disrespected" them. Ms. Shaw clearly assumed roles and shared insights with students far beyond what was expected of her because she believed that part of her role was to help students build pride in themselves as well as in the Bridge Middle School community. School pride, in her opinion, would translate into student pride in their home communities.

BLACK TEACHERS AND TEACHING

Mr. Jackson and Ms. Shaw attempted to address opportunity gaps among their students at Bridge Middle School, although they did not discuss their efforts using "opportunity gap" language. As a Black teacher, Dr. Johnson, too, was addressing opportunity gaps, although her setting, a predominantly White and affluent community, was very different from the context that Mr. Jackson and Ms. Shaw experienced, a space with large numbers of students of color living below the poverty line. Their mind-sets and practices were consistent with and extend an established body of research about Black teachers and their teaching practices. Much has been written about Black teachers—their experiences, their curriculum development, and their teaching in public school and higher education classrooms, both pre- and post-desegregation.[19] For example, Siddle Walker makes the following observation in her analysis of African American teachers during segregation: "Consistently remembered for their high expectations for student success, for their dedication, and for their demanding teaching style, these [Black] teachers appear to have worked with the assumption that their job was to be certain that children learned the material presented."[20]

The Black teachers presented in the research literature worked overtime to help their students learn. Although teaching during segregation, the teachers in Siddle Walker's study reported that they were preparing their students for a world of desegregation.[21] Siddle Walker's findings are consistent with the mind-set and approaches of Mr. Jackson, Dr. Johnson, and Ms. Shaw. They were preparing students for experiences they currently could not even imagine they would encounter. Moreover, as educational leadership researcher Linda Tillman explains, "These Black teachers saw potential in their Black students, considered them to be intelligent, and were committed to their success."[22] They saw their roles and responsibilities as reaching far beyond the hallways of their schools, and the teachers had a mission to teach their students because they realized the possible consequences for their students if they did not teach them and if the students did not learn.

Research suggests that "Black educators are far more than physical role models, and they bring diverse family histories, value orientations, and experiences to students in the classroom, attributes often not found in textbooks or viewpoints often omitted."[23] Thus, Black teachers (like teachers from other racial and ethnic backgrounds) are texts themselves, and the pages of the texts for many Black teachers are filled with histories of racism, sexism, and oppression, as well as strength, perseverance, and success. These "texts" are rich and possibly transformative, and they have the potential to help students understand the world and work to change it.[24] This is evident in Ms. Shaw's unyielding goal to have her students change and improve the world. Historically, Black teachers have had a meaningful impact on Black students' academic and social success because they deeply understood their students' situations and their needs, both inside and outside of the classroom, in no small part because they lived in the same communities. However, it is important to note that Black teachers have not only shown success with students of African descent but with those from other racial and ethnic backgrounds as well. Research shows that students from all racial backgrounds actually prefer Black teachers.[25] Using data from the Measure of Effective Teaching study, researchers found that students "perceive minority teachers more favorably than White teachers."[26] The point here is not to suggest that White teachers cannot and do not elicit favorability among students. The point is that we have the potential to learn much from teachers of color and Black teachers in particular.

In terms of Black teachers, research suggests that Black teachers maintain high expectations for their students,[27] and they empathize with rather than pity the students who are not succeeding academically and socially.[28] Also, the research literature explains that many Black teachers do not accept mediocrity, and they *insist* that their students reach their full capacity. Having such high expectations gives students the best chance to mobilize themselves and their families and communities. Moreover, these teachers understand that allowing students to just get by could be devastating for them in the long term.

The care and concern of Black teachers has been described as "other mothering" or "other parenting" in that teachers take on a parental role, as did Mr. Jackson, Dr. Johnson, and Ms. Shaw.[29] In other words, as fictive kinship, the teachers want the best for their students—just as they would want for their own biological children. In my own research, I found there is a strong level of advocacy among Black teachers with Black students.[30] Students can sense teachers' commitment and care for them. I found that students recognize when there is unnecessary distance between them and their teachers. Students may question: "Why should I adhere to this teacher's requests and desires when the teacher does not really care about me?" Students often act defiantly in order to distance themselves from what they perceive as uncaring and disrespectful teachers. This conflict may continue until teachers and students negotiate the level of care, connectedness, and commitment necessary for all to succeed in an academic environment.

In figure 4.1, I provide a summary of some of the major features of Mr. Jackson and Ms. Shaw's mind-sets and practices as they attempted to address and close opportunity gaps at Bridge Middle School. Moreover, the figure captures some of the findings regarding effective teaching already established in the research literature. These principles should be read as potential practices that might be transferable and adaptable to other situations and settings.

FIGURE 4.1

Summary of teachers' mind-sets and practices to address opportunity gaps

To address opportunity gaps, the teachers in this and previous chapters:

Built and sustained relationships: Perhaps most important, teachers understood that students needed to get to know them and that they needed to get to know their students. They saw their students as members of their family. In other words, they engaged in "other mothering" and "other parenting" with their students.

Stressed the value and importance of learning: Teachers explicitly conveyed the importance and value of education and learning to students. They helped students understand and embrace the reality that one can be smart and intelligent and, at the same time, cool and hip.

Immersed themselves in students' lifeworlds: One of the teachers, Mr. Jackson, attempted to understand what it meant to live in the world of his students through music, sports, film, and pop culture. He incorporated this knowledge and understanding into the learning opportunities in the classroom.

Incorporated pop culture: Mr. Jackson understood the multiple layers of popular culture that his students were interested in outside of school. He built on and incorporated this knowledge, insight, and understanding in developing relevant and responsive lessons and activities for students in the math and science classroom.

Did more with fewer resources: Teachers did not allow what they did not have to hinder their efforts, goals, visions, and rigorous expectations for their students. Mr. Hall pushed his students to see themselves as scientists capable of academic success despite meager science lab materials. They did whatever it took to succeed and for their students to succeed; they never gave up, even when resources were scarce.

Rejected deficit notions: Teachers concentrated on and connected to the assets that students brought into the classroom and built on those assets in the learning contexts. They also understood their own assets as teachers and used those as a foundation to bridge opportunity gaps in the classroom. For instance, Dr. Johnson and Ms. Shaw were powerful, engaging storytellers, so they used this asset in their instructional practices.

Understood equity in practice: Mr. Hall understood the difference between equality and equity. He worked to meet the needs of individual students and realized that their curriculum and instruction practices as well as their disciplinary practices might not be exactly the same between, among, or across all students at all times. Rather, he realized that he should practice equity and respond to students depending on the particular needs of each student at a particular time. Mr. Jackson, on the other hand, adopted a consistent sameness approach to his practices.

(continued)

FIGURE 4.1 *(continued)*

Summary of teachers' mind-sets and practices to address opportunity gaps

Understood power structures among students: Teachers understood that there were implicit and overt power structures among the students. Mr. Jackson recruited the most socially constructed "popular students" to embrace the vision of learning and engagement in the classroom in order to get other students motivated to learn.

Understood the self in relation to others: Teachers co-assembled knowledge and understood points of intersection and convergence between themselves and their students. They used this knowledge and understanding to build and sustain relationships in the classroom. Dr. Johnson, Mr. Jackson, Mr. Hall, and Ms. Shaw were consistently thinking about themselves and their own role and responsibilities in supporting their students' learning and development.

Granted students entry into teachers' worlds: Teachers allowed students to learn things about them and made connections to demonstrate the commonalities that existed between them. Mr. Hall, for instance, shared how he grew up in poverty, and as a result many of his students were able to relate to him. All the teachers profiled in this book shared personal stories with their students and allowed students to share theirs in order to build community, collective knowledge, relationships, and points of reference.

Conceived of school as a community with family: Teachers conceived of school as a community that was established by all those in the environment. They celebrated and embraced students' voice and perspectives in how the community would be defined. Teachers respected and cared about those in the community as they would family members.

Dealt with the presence of race and culture: Teachers rejected color-blind, culture-blind, and diversity-blind ideologies. They saw themselves and their students as racial and cultural beings and used that knowledge in working with students and in teaching them.

Perceived teaching as mission and responsibility: Ms. Shaw and the other teachers cared deeply about their students and developed mission-minded approaches that allowed students to reach their potential. Ms. Shaw saw teaching as her calling and took it personally when students did not succeed academically. She did not promote religion or spirituality. She simply wanted them to find deep meaning for life.

5

White Teachers Learning to Teach

Roles and Relevance of Teacher Preparation

IN THIS CHAPTER, I focus on a group of White teachers who were in a traditional teacher education program learning to teach. Teacher education researcher Christine Sleeter poignantly declares that we who work in teacher education should "research backwards" to gain insight about supporting and equipping teachers with what they need to be successful in any classroom across the nation.[1] By "researching backwards," Sleeter stresses that those learning to teach and teacher educators should focus on promising and successful teacher practices and teaching in preK–12 classrooms, and design teacher education curriculum, pedagogy, and related learning experiences (such as student teaching) accordingly. A persistent challenge in addressing and hopefully closing opportunity gaps in preK–12 classrooms concerns how teachers are prepared, regardless of whether in traditional or nontraditional teacher education programs.

Teacher education—where teachers are prepared to build knowledge, attitudes, mind-sets, paradigms, perspectives, beliefs, skills, and actions essential to meet the instructional needs of all students—should be thought of as an ongoing imperative.[2] Like educational experiences and professional learning and development in other fields, such as social work, medicine, or engineering, teachers' learning does not (and should not) end when they graduate from a teacher education program.[3] Learning continues in-service, while teachers are actually working in preK–12 classrooms. The cases presented in the preceding chapters have provided what I hope are useful insights into the complexities that real teachers and students face in addressing opportunity gaps. In this chapter, I turn to challenges teacher education programs face in preparing teachers to develop (1) the mind-set to understand opportunity gaps and (2) practices that will address them. Of course, the opportunity gaps that I have discussed and consider so important for all students are those related to diversity, equity, justice, and teaching.

In the first part of this chapter, I draw insights from six White teachers who are learning to teach. Based on my work over the last two decades, I believe these teachers provide a representative sample of the kinds of challenges and promise that teacher education must engage, with a focus on the diversity-opportunity connection. As I share voices and implications from these six White teachers, I concurrently discuss roles and relevance of teacher preparation programs across the United States and beyond. I then discuss the complex roles that teacher educators—those who support the learning and development of teachers—play. I assert that we need to look carefully at *who* teaches in teacher education, *how* these teacher educators were trained, *to what degree* these teacher educators have the knowledge and skill to advance a diversity-opportunity agenda in the preparation of teachers, and *whether* teacher educators are willing and committed to supporting teachers with what they need to maximize preK–12 students' opportunity to learn. I also outline some structural and systemic challenges that we in teacher education sometimes face, and how those challenges can block efforts to implement, advance, and transform teacher education programs.

CHALLENGES IN TEACHER EDUCATION

Both traditional and nontraditional teacher education programs face numerous challenges, some of which are substantiated while others are not. Criticisms of teacher education include the following:

- Teacher education programs are not rigorous enough.
- Teacher education programs do not provide enough subject-matter knowledge for teachers to convey that content successfully in the classroom.
- Teacher education programs have not shown sufficient evidence that teacher "training" actually correlates with preK–12 student outcomes (mainly scores on standardized tests).
- There is too much variation among teacher education programs in their coverage of content and their expectations for teacher learning and development.

A recurrent national debate among many in teacher education concerns the type and structure of programs that prepare teachers for preK–12 teaching—traditional or nontraditional. For instance, studies suggest that particular teacher education programs (university-based versus alternative) are better than others, based on preK–12 students' performance on standardized tests, teacher persistence and attrition rates, and teachers' self-efficacy (see, for instance, Darling-Hammond, Chung, and Frelow).[4] This debate is serious, but it is clear that neither structure (university-based or alternative) is going to vanish. Thus, because teachers will be educated through different teacher education program types and structures (traditional and nontraditional), I stress that our energies should be focused on developing these different structural types regardless of their orientation. The point of ensuring optimal quality of these programs regardless of their structure is linked to my desire to support preK–12 student academic, social, emotional, and overall success.

INTRODUCING THE TEACHERS

The six White women teacher candidates (hereafter *teachers*) provide insights about roles and relevance of teacher preparation. Through their lived experiences, learning, and interactions, these teachers demonstrate challenges and successes we might draw from in thinking about how we center equity, justice, diversity, and opportunity in the preparation of teachers. These teachers' backgrounds and experiences are representative of the kinds of teachers that I have come to know as a teacher educator across other situations, having worked in different teacher education programs over the last twenty years. For instance, I have taught in at least three traditional teacher education programs and have conducted hundreds of professional development workshops for practicing in-service teachers; most of these workshops centered on issues related to opportunity and diversity. My point here is not to suggest that the stories of these teachers, or of any teachers in this book, should be generalized. I hope that readers, preservice and those already teaching, will improve their work after reading this book—that they will start where they are but not stay there. Some of the data I share emerged from a course I coplanned and cotaught with a colleague, Margaret Smithey, several years ago.[5] While my colleague and I engaged in some research regarding our teaching experience in the course about diversity, I alone conducted and analyzed the interviews with teachers that I share in this chapter.

Although all identified as White, the teachers showcased in this chapter represent an important range of diversity. Laughter has warned us against a monolithic narrative about White teachers.[6] Thus, I realize that it is essential to consider factors beyond race related to identity and demographic characteristics when sharing the stories of other people. Rather than providing individual characteristics of each teacher and focusing on a separate case for each of the six teachers, I instead present a collective case study. I focus on common themes that emerged among, across, and between these teachers.

TROUBLING THE RELEVANCE OF DIVERSITY AND MAKING SOMETHING OUT OF NOTHING

Although teachers may read in textbooks or hear in lectures that teaching involves developing a conceptual toolkit related to understanding diversity, many of them still do not believe it will matter much in their particular classroom. Many White teachers who attended largely racially and ethnically homogeneous (predominantly White) schools, for instance, aspire to and believe that they will return to their hometowns and teach in very similar schools in terms of demographics. While they accept the reality that diversity matters for some teachers or even understand changes we see in society related to diversity, they may still struggle to see how diversity will matter for them. Consequently, teachers sometimes believe that emphasizing diversity is disadvantageous because it forces them to think about issues that really do not or will not exist in their particular situations, including their contexts and conditions. They may fear that they are "making something out of nothing" if they think deeply about how what they teach will impact the diverse population of students they teach. Unfortunately, these teachers sometimes do not realize that they may not be able to return to their "dream" job or school. They may indeed teach in one of "those" highly diverse or urban schools for which they may feel grossly underprepared.

Fundamentally, many of the White teachers did not understand the relevance of diversity and teaching because they attended what they believed to be pretty homogeneous schools themselves (whether public or private).[7] In fact, my experience working to prepare these teachers revealed that many of them did not see themselves as racial or cultural beings. They saw other groups of people as having a race or a culture, and they used themselves as the (White) racial and cultural norm or standard by which others were and should be compared. That is, some saw (1) themselves, particularly White middle-class people, as the norm, (2) others as "diverse" or having a distinctive culture or race, and (3) a focus on diversity and teaching as mostly irrelevant. Some teachers found it annoying, to a degree, that an emphasis would be placed on diversity because their worldview and frames of reference had not required such an emphasis, and they struggled to envision how diversity would play any real role or purpose in their professional lives as teachers. Similar to Mr. Hall, these teachers wanted to focus on practices related to teaching their subject matter—"What does this mean for how I teach science, math, or English language arts?" many of them queried. Some of the teachers did aspire to learn more "classroom management" strategies that they mostly wanted in order to "control" their students and their classrooms. Of course, I stressed to these teachers that they should not work to control the bodies and minds of other people.[8]

It was difficult for some of the teachers to shift from mind-sets and ideas they had developed when they were students themselves—that is, to shift from thinking as a preK–12 student to thinking as a teacher. Like Mr. Hall, teachers with whom I have worked over the years found it troubling that they would need to expend any energy thinking about diversity and teaching. As noted, one persistent problem regarding our need to address opportunity gaps is teachers' beliefs that it is not necessary or appropriate for them to see race, recognize how diversity matters, or understand the salience of diversity for teaching in the preK–12 classroom. I have argued throughout this book that such avoidance in fact *contributes* to opportunity gaps. Many of these teachers had a "prove to me that diversity is worth my time" mentality. When teachers have such a mind-set, too much time can be spent in a teacher education course trying to make a case for *why* diversity matters, rather than focusing on *what teachers can do* in their practices to address diversity and opportunity.

The discourse among teachers in many courses I have taught over the years begins with why diversity really matters and why teachers should be concerned about it. This initial focus is logical. However, even after several weeks of relevant learning opportunities on the importance of diversity for preK–12 teaching, as conveyed through intense curriculum and instructional practices, most of these teachers still exercised their privilege to keep questioning why they needed to think about diversity just as much as the subject matter. In essence, these teachers wanted to "just teach math" or "just teach reading," and help their students "become good at it." It is true that when these teachers observed or taught in diverse and/or urban schools (through student teaching or practicum experiences, for instance), the emphasis on diversity in their teacher education program became more logical to them. However, there remained a recurrent wonder and frustration about how a focus on diversity would really matter in the grand scheme of teaching and learning. Perhaps it is this mind-set—a failure to recognize the role of diversity in their practices—that exacerbates opportunity gaps.

When asked during an interview how diversity mattered or would matter in her teaching, one teacher explained, "I don't think it did [matter] as much the first part of the semester because of the population I was with. I was teaching in [Oxford County] and the population was very much White. I had a class of twenty-two. I had two African American students and one from Vietnam. Everyone else was White. So I think I was thinking about it but again, that was part of my frustration at the beginning of the course where I felt like I had a lot more going on besides talking about diversity and cultures, and different cultures and how to consider that when you're teaching. But now my current . . . fifth-grade placement at [Jonesboro County is] about fifty-fifty [Black-White]. So it really is much more evident to me—the different cultures that are in my classroom. And I have thought about it."

The field experiences of the six teachers showcased in this chapter played a substantive role in how they thought about the diversity focus in the teacher-education classroom. Similar to Dr. Johnson's experiences at Stevenson High School in a predominantly White social context, the six White teachers all seemed to feel that focusing on aspects of diversity and opportunity was irrelevant, inconsequential, and useless in their mostly White teaching and observation [practica] contexts. In many ways, the teachers in this chapter perceived the White students as "normal," and when they changed field sites to more racially "diverse" spaces, they began to see more clearly why we would be discussing anything beyond how to teach a particular subject matter in preK–12. Teachers continued to point to firsthand experiences, whether through student teaching, practicum, or personal experiences in contexts with an enormous range of diversity, as essential to their mind-sets and willingness to try different pedagogical and curriculum strategies in the preK–12 classroom. One teacher reported, "[One of my teaching experiences] had English language learners from nine different countries. So, I've really had the opportunity to test out a lot of things we've been talking about in class and try and formulate my own opinions on them."

Not only was there a pervasive theme of "prove to me that diversity matters," there was also a concern that emphases on diversity may have been making them paranoid or, as one teacher explained, "unnecessarily suspicious" and "obsessed" about it. Teachers worried that focusing "so much attention" on diversity would force them to see and think about issues that were not "really" there but were constructed through images that were painted in the teacher education classroom. One teacher maintained that she was concerned we were "making something out of nothing" by focusing on matters of race in particular. In her words, "I thought if you spend too much time on it—I think that maybe sometimes you can make things an issue that aren't an issue. And I don't know if that's just ignorance and my own lack of awareness or whatever." I discovered several of the teachers felt that attention to race and diversity meant that they would start "seeing things" and making up diversity-related issues that did not really exist or would not exist in the classroom when they began teaching.

For example, the same teacher stated: "Like I had a group of boys . . . they were all African American, and they all hung out together, but they were never hostile or mean or exclusive to anybody else. And nobody felt threatened by them. I wouldn't have thought anything of it. But now that we've talked about race and all that 'stuff,' I was trying to figure out, why are they doing that [hanging out together]?" Never mind the question of why the teacher might believe this group of African American boys would be "hostile," "mean," or threatening; this teacher was concerned that my attempt to disrupt a color-blind mind-set now caused her to wonder if she was recognizing things that she would not have in the past.

This teacher's concern has been echoed by others I have taught over the years. Rather than perceiving her experience of questioning color blindness in a positive light, as one that allowed her to push herself to think about the underlying meaning of the "boys hanging out together," she was a bit suspicious and questioned why she was being guided to think about something that might not be a real issue or that she would not have thought about otherwise. Frustrated, she explained further: "I don't know if it was anything that I even needed to think about because it didn't seem to cause any problems."

The tendency for racial and ethnic groups of students to hang out together to the exclusion of others is not a trivial social, psychological, or emotional phenomenon. In her important book, *"Why Are All the Black Kids Sitting Together in the Cafeteria?" and Other Conversations About Race*, psychologist Beverly Tatum poses this very question and then offers important insights into the kinds of support such groups provided for each other.[9] In other words, students rely on each other and find strength through their same-race interactions across different contexts. However, a group of Black students I approached with the same question at one school wondered why anyone would pose such a question to Black students. They then posed a different question: "Why are all the White kids sitting together in the cafeteria?"

Another teacher remarked that it was important "not [to] specifically [make] problems where they didn't exist" and not "to make a big deal about it [race and diversity]." These six teachers often reflected back on their experiences as preK–12 students and how similar they were to their classmates'. While observing a "diverse" classroom, they were open to discussing race and diversity as they related to their mind-set, classroom practices, and the kinds of learning opportunities they would be able to construct in their own preK–12 classrooms, but they still were not convinced that diversity and opportunity were linked. As one teacher declared, "If a problem does come up, I don't want to automatically think it's something that I need to encourage and bring up . . . I've definitely learned how to relate to different people . . . to try to figure out what method works for each student . . . but I worry that I'm going to make a big deal . . . If there is a problem, if there is a conflict, then I'm just going to automatically attribute it to [issues of diversity]."

The fact that at least some of these six teachers did not understand how schools are set up to maintain the worldviews, norms, expectations, and overall cultural practices of the White majority is a problem. Still, another teacher promised me in her interview that she certainly refused to "make problems where they didn't exist," and it seemed that, in many of their responses, the six White teachers showcased in this chapter were actually looking for reasons why a diversity or race-centered rationale for what they experienced was inappropriate and incorrect.

FEARFUL TO JUST SAY IT

Some societal wisdom would suggest that the best way to address difficult issues is to ignore them—and certainly not to talk about them. Such a position—to avoid using particular words or to avoid certain topics—can actually result in unexamined mind-sets and practices that can leave teachers feeling hopeless and that can be harmful to young people. Teachers may question the degree to which there is any hope of addressing certain topics because they feel unprepared to use specific words or phrases in a teacher education course or program, or even in a faculty meeting once they have begun teaching. Teachers can be fearful that they will be ostracized or judged for their positions on difficult topics that are sometimes politically charged.

For many of the six teachers, it was difficult to even say the word *race* or to use terms like *Black*, *Latino/a*, *African American*, or *White*—especially early in a course. I have also observed teachers struggle to use words such as *immigration*, *President Obama*, *power*, *privilege*, and *oppression*. In class one day, I used the word *nigger*, explaining what I heard from a high school student as he was reciting the lyrics to a popular hip-hop song. Several teachers expressed how surprised they were that I felt comfortable using "that word," even in the context of quoting another. One teacher declared that he was never allowed to use such language growing up in his home and that he felt completely uncomfortable voicing the word, even when quoting. Ironically, this same teacher, adamant that he never used the word, admitted that his friends sometimes used the word *nigger* when sharing jokes. This teacher rationalized that it was acceptable for his friends because they were "just joking around," but he would never do so personally. That this teacher did not believe it was necessary for him to question his "friends" to disrupt their language is problematic. But this teacher did not view it this way.

Clearly, we socially construct words and phrases and give them power and meaning. I am not suggesting that teachers and teacher educators should not be mindful in how they engage in discourse or how they select words. However, when teachers are afraid to use certain words or phrases, they are often demonstrating their own biases and belief systems. Not being able to call the former president by his title, President Obama, reveals deep-rooted issues that these teachers could not necessarily recognize. When they referred to other past presidents, they called them "president": President Reagan, President Bush. But in the very same sentence they referred to President Obama as "Obama." Even after I brought the omission of *president* to their attention, the teachers continued in this practice. One teacher stated that she called other presidents by their full name or last name without the "president" handle and accordingly rationalized that I was making a big deal out of nothing.

However, I attempted to stress the power and potential of talk in our teacher education program. I wanted teachers to feel comfortable expressing what they thought and felt through talk. Indeed, I have learned that teachers grow when they talk, and part of the talk necessary for the kind of work we must do to address opportunity gaps in preK–12 requires teachers to be vulnerable. Teachers can serve as critical partners in helping each other work through lingering issues when they express their beliefs and thoughts about pertinent dimensions of teaching and learning. In short, I believe it is a disadvantage in teacher education when we hold White teachers' language hostage because of some power we have given to words. We should be focusing instead on the particular intention behind the words being used and then help educate teachers about how some words perpetuate inequality or inequity while others are more emancipatory. People become more precise with their language when they deepen their knowledge. But when teachers do not talk, they make it difficult to understand what they think and believe.

These teachers were also concerned that they would be considered politically incorrect if they used particular words. As White teachers new to the discourse of diversity, the six teachers seemed to be talking more in code out of fear than expressing what they really felt or believed. I have found that this fear has stifled important conversations that have the potential to expand teachers' mind-sets, particularly regarding diversity and opportunity gaps in preK–12 classrooms. My observations suggest that teachers worry they will say something that will offend others, and they consciously avoid conversations about the very issues they are grappling with in their heads and should be discussing with their colleagues—ways to improve their teaching practices. Over time, teachers started to reveal that they were struggling with, for instance, how their parents had called lesbians "dykes" when they were younger or how family members had called families in rural communities "poor white trash." Fear, in this sense, can halt progression toward educational justice and equity when we do not create spaces where any of us might feel free and safe enough to say what we really mean.

RACE AND RACISM—HISTORICAL AND FAMILIAL ROOTS

Much of what we learn about race and racism in the early years of our development comes from family members (and our parents and caregivers in particular). Attempting to gauge the roots of educators' deeply ingrained implicit racist beliefs can help them work through them. While teachers may admit that their parents have held racist beliefs and views about others and have used racist language, they often fail to equate that language with actions. Inappropriately, teachers may separate the racist language they have heard from their parents from their racist acts. They fail to understand that language is indeed action, and they may not grasp how their implicit beliefs and perceptions manifest in what they do, albeit unknowingly.

While one teacher, as described in the previous section, expressed that he was never allowed to use what he called the "*n*-word" growing up, some teachers in this study confirmed what I have suspected and what the research literature has substantiated: teachers' views on race, racism, and other forms of prejudice are often rooted in their historical experiences, particularly within their families. Several of the six teachers showcased in this chapter reported that they had heard racist, sexist, xenophobic, and homophobic comments from their parents growing up. Rarely, though, did they report instances when they actually witnessed some acts of racism or sexism by their parents. Perhaps it is this disconnect—the fact that these teachers did not equate words or mind-sets with action—that made it difficult for them to understand how their mind-sets, beliefs, and language could and would shape their practices.

In speaking of her familial roots, one teacher explained that her mother would express "racist" and "prejudiced" views about different groups of people, such as African Americans. The potency of parental views can have a lingering influence. Take, for instance, the number of people who continue to vote a parent's political party or who follow a parent's religious preferences long into adulthood. One teacher remarked how her mother would have "lost it" if she had decided to date a "Black guy" during high school. When asked if it would have mattered if the "Black guy" had been an honor student, she did not hesitate in her reply: "No."

Another teacher explained that she had come to believe that her mother was racist when she was growing up: "I [have been] worried by what I learned and understood about racial injustice and equality . . . [because of] my own mother's racial prejudice." Interestingly, it appeared that two teachers' reflections about their mothers' "racial prejudice" seemed to have resulted in a desire to fight it. In short, for a few teachers, reflection on some negative, insensitive, or inappropriate statement, action, experience, or mind-set, such as sexism, resulted in their wanting to do and be the opposite. This same teacher expressed: "I want my children to grow up in an integrated environment rather than the racial isolation I experienced growing up . . . I don't want my children to be racist, and they will not hear me talk in this [racist] way."

Promising experiences that seemed to disrupt deep-rooted familial issues related to race were those that placed teachers in real-life situations and required them to confront diversity personally, head-on. For instance, as explained previously, these teachers appeared to open up a bit when they observed a highly diverse teaching context. Experiences that placed White teachers in spaces they were unaccustomed to or where they were the racial minority gave them opportunities to think about and question the roots of their beliefs and how their lives had been shaped by particular norms and expectations not necessarily shared by all. One teacher explained that she had to be placed in a situation where she was the racial "minority" to recognize the kind of person and teacher she wanted to become: "I think very early on I was confronted with [racism], particularly from my mother . . . She was a very prejudiced lady, and I know that that influenced me early on." She went on to relate a real-life experience she had in the Peace Corps: "Right before I came to this program, I was with the Peace Corps for a while, and that was my first opportunity of being a [racial] minority [in a sustained context]. And that probably was the main push to where I feel that I am today. Without that experience I would probably be a lot closer to the way I was raised, my background . . . So I think that that [experience in the Peace Corps] helped me to where I am today."

It is difficult to understand the struggles teachers have in making the diversity-opportunity connection without understanding their personal historical, developmental trajectory and also how their familial experiences molded their thinking and practices. Several teachers I worked with over the years have pointed explicitly to the negative "racist" and "prejudiced" experiences they had with their parents over the years, and examining these roots seems critical to understanding how to prepare White teachers (and all teachers) to address opportunity and diversity in the preK–12 classroom.

I turn in the next several sections to the kinds of mind-sets and practices exhibited by some of the six White teachers that illustrated the potential of addressing the diversity-opportunity connection. Like the exemplary teachers discussed in the previous chapters, many of the teachers with whom I worked over the years demonstrated the kinds of understanding, commitment, and development that I believe would prove essential in their becoming successful teachers of all students. Several teachers with whom I worked began their teacher education programs with some of the problematic issues described earlier in the chapter, but they progressed to build mind-sets that provide a foundation for their successful teaching practices.

CULTURAL CONNECTIONS AND ROLE MODELS

There is pedagogical promise when educators recognize the value in preK–12 students being taught by teachers of the same background. When students interact with and are taught by someone from the same racial, ethnic, and cultural background, they are more likely to see themselves reflected in the curriculum, to develop understandings of complex learning opportunities because of examples used, and to be more willing to take risks in a classroom setting.

Although I recognize there is no such thing as a distinct African American culture, European American culture, or Asian American culture, and so forth, the six teachers showcased in this chapter conflated race and ethnicity with culture when they discussed their positions. These teachers struggled to understand that there was no single African American culture. Similarly, Ms. Shaw, in the previous chapter, talked explicitly about her experiences in an "African American culture." However, the term

African American denotes an ethnic group of people, not a singular, static cultural group; there is a wide range of diversity among African American people and communities, although there are some consistencies. African American people share a history of slavery, Jim Crow, and other forms of systemic discrimination, oppression, and racism that binds the group. They also possess a shared history of spiritual grounding, strength, intellect, and resilience through some of the most horrific situations that any group of human beings has had to endure.

However, while there are shared experiences, there are also many differences among people of the same race and ethnicity. It is critical that readers of this book do not essentialize or generalize the points discussed about any one racial or ethnic group. Readers should not consider the ideas discussed about any group to be static and pejorative.

When these teachers more deeply understood the opportunity-diversity convergence, they started to understand micro (classroom), meso (institutional), and macro (societal) level issues that had some influence over what happened to students and what they experienced. One teacher reported her concern about the low number of African American role models available for African American students in her school. She explained that she had developed a deeper understanding of what it meant to students to have role models of the same race or ethnicity in school. In her practicum site, she began to consider the enormous void of same-ethnicity mentors available to African American students in her school. She explained: "I worry that my African American students see so few positive role models that are their race in school. After our discussions in seminar, I have really begun to wonder what kind of message it is sending to our African American students." The teacher went on to explain that many of the African American adults in her school were there in "service roles"—custodial and cafeteria jobs in particular. The low numbers of African American people in teaching positions in the school began to "worry" her because she was concerned about her Black students' ability to relate and connect to Black adults in professional roles. I did not interpret this teacher's view and explanation of Black people in "service roles" as a slight or insult. Rather, I interpret her comment as a genuine one: What happens when Black students, other students of color, and White students only see Black adults in their school in service, rather than professional, roles?

The teacher maintained how important role models had been in her own experiences as a "White girl" in school and how her teachers had even inspired her to become a teacher. In her words: "Growing up, I never had an African American teacher or principal. Actually, all of my principals and teachers were White. I never had an Asian or Hispanic teacher or principal either." However, she did make important connections with her White teachers and principals, and she believed that many of her Black students lacked this opportunity, which was problematic in her view. While her critique and concern appeared initially on the micro level as she reflected on the classroom environment, a broader look at her concerns suggested that the school and district might consider working to increase the numbers of African American teachers and other potential professional role models in her school. She questioned: "What are they [the district] going to do about this void for these kids?" Through empathy for her students, this teacher had developed the type of mind-set that I believe has potential for how she might approach her work in the future—how she would work to close opportunity gaps. She put herself in her African American students' shoes, a cognitive, conceptual, and affective shift that was not easy for many of the teachers with whom I worked.

POWER AND PROMISE OF TEACHING A BILINGUAL TEXT

There appears to be power and promise when students engage bilingual texts. Bilingual texts can enhance learning opportunities for English language learners as well as native English speakers in a classroom.

One teacher actually incorporated what she referred to as "Mexican culture" into her lessons in the classroom. She explained: "I just recently did this project with my kids. It was like Cinderella stories from different countries, and one of the stories was a Mexican Cinderella, and my girls from Mexico really wanted to have that story. So it was something that they could relate to." The teacher discovered firsthand that her Latina students could "relate to" the story; they got excited about reading it in their first language, Spanish. She explained that the Latina students "had a bunch of other people in their group as well . . . Part of the book was written in Spanish, and so they said they liked learning in Spanish along with the book, too. So that kind of opened my eyes as well. It was something that the girls from Mexico could relate to."

The teacher reported that the Mexican students felt very confident about reading the sections of the book written in Spanish, and they seemed to appreciate the opportunity to learn from a bilingual text. The teacher continued: "It made them [the Latina students] feel a little bit more comfortable, I think. It was also kind of an eye-opening experience for other people [students] . . . We talked a lot about how they're similar to the story that they know and how they're different. And we also talked about why those differences are there." Furthermore, the Latina students were able to be the authority on the text, and it provided them space to showcase some of their expertise with their classmates, such as knowing how to speak and read Spanish fluently. This experience suggests that the teacher started to see the promise in incorporating some bilingual texts in her classroom for the benefit of her students, especially her Latina students. Particularly in a context—a district—that promotes "English-only" policies related to teaching and learning, this teacher (and others) will have to negotiate what they come to know from and do in their practice with policies that do not necessarily align with good teaching.

DANGERS OF STEREOTYPING AND LOW EXPECTATIONS

Teachers can have good intentions about instructional and curricular needs of students but actually do more harm than good if they begin to stereotype certain groups and lower their expectations such that these students are not meeting and exceeding the broader school, district, and state standards. To be clear, being opportunity-centered does not mean that teachers water down the curriculum. Rather, being opportunity-centered means that teachers build rigorous expectations with the students in front of them.

Although I was always concerned that teachers could develop generalizations and stereotypes about students from any gender, racial, ethnic, or cultural background or group, I learned that at least four of the six teachers showcased in this chapter began to develop the heart and mind to teach all students effectively. These teachers mostly had good intentions, and although all of them seemed to struggle to understand how to meet the needs of all their students, their efforts and energy seemed to be in a place that would allow them to build the skills and practices necessary to support their students' success. Unfortunately, good intentions gone wrong can dangerously affect students' academic, intellectual, and social success, in both the short and long term.[10] For instance, one teacher shared with me an experience related to assessment that I believe was potentially harmful for her students: "I learned in my last teaching placement with a majority of African American students [that] they're very much more towards verbal learning. A couple of times I gave them a choice of assessments, written or verbal, and they almost always chose to tell me verbally."

The promising aspect of this teacher's words and conceptions about her African American students and assessment was that she attempted to recognize her students' strengths and preferences. Accordingly, she was responsive to them. Many teachers would likely have continued with business as usual, failing to recognize how assessments should be used to track student learning and development over time. In particular, teachers should use formative assessment data to alter their instruction. Moreover, some assessments may measure only one dimension of what students know. While her realization was problematic, the teacher above learned from her students that they performed better on verbal assessments than on written ones. However, given the myopic ways many of those in power in education think about assessment, it is reasonable to ask whether this teacher was setting the African American students she worked with up for failure by not expecting them to follow the written assessment norm. In this way, teachers have to reasonably alter and respond to students within broader community expectations. Unfortunately, preK–12 schools shortchange students who fall outside the realm of what educators and others in power believe to be acceptable, normal, and appropriate forms of assessment: pencil and paper tests (and too often Scantron tests that require bubbling in multiple-choice items).

Moreover, was this teacher stereotyping the African American students she described as "very much more towards verbal learning?" Could it be that her African American students preferred to complete the verbal assessment because it required less effort and not because they were not capable of completing the written assessment? This teacher summed up the reality for many teachers when she stated, "If you're not paying attention to those things [how students learn and are assessed], then you're shortchanging that student if you're not looking at how they learn [and demonstrate that learning] the best." I would add to her position that if teachers are not paying attention to broader, more systemic, and structural guidelines, such as the ways in which students are expected to demonstrate their learning, then they could potentially do more harm than good—even though the teachers have good intentions. For teachers to understand the complexities just described, teacher educators themselves must know what issues to address with teachers, how, when (developmentally), and why. I address the role of teacher educators in teacher education in the next section.

ROLE OF TEACHER EDUCATORS IN TEACHER EDUCATION

While teacher educators have made important strides in preparing teachers for the diversity and opportunity gaps they may encounter in preK–12 schools, we cannot assume that teacher educators, many of whom were practicing preK–12 teachers themselves, are committed

> *to equitable practices. Like teachers, teacher educators are diverse themselves and have varying positions on what the focus of teacher education courses and programs should be. In other words, as we focus on the learning and development of preK–12 teachers, how do we build a cadre of teacher educators across program types who have (and build) knowledge and experiences that push opportunity-centered practices?*

Thus far, I have shared some of the challenges and the promise demonstrated by six White teachers. My work with them is representative of the kinds of experiences and insights I have had during my time working with other teachers on developing mind-sets and practices necessary to support students too often placed on the margins of teaching and learning. I turn now to discuss teacher educators. Preparing teachers to address the opportunity-diversity nexus is difficult work, and there is no script (nor should there be). While it may seem easy to critique teachers learning to teach, those of us preparing teachers also need to examine ourselves in our quest to educate and support teachers. Teacher educator and researcher Cochran-Smith stresses the importance of teacher educators investigating themselves and their own practices as they attempt to understand the teachers with whom they work.[11] For instance, she examined her own work and her teachers' constructions of race and was able to shed light on complexities inherent in the teaching and examination of race in teacher education.

Preparing teachers to teach can indeed be vexingly complicated work in general. Teacher educators should support teachers in building knowledge and skill to teach for diversity. Teaching for diversity means that we embrace, celebrate, and sustain difference—not simply tolerate or accept it. Because people enter teacher education programs with a range of needs, there is no one-size-fits-all program or practice. Cochran-Smith maintains that she had "become *certain only of uncertainty* [emphasis added] about how and what to say, whom and what to have student teachers read and write, and about who can teach whom, who can speak for or to whom, and who has the right to speak at all about the possibilities and pitfalls of promoting a discourse about race and teaching."[12]

Much of Cochran-Smith's concern focuses on how to develop a teacher education curriculum and related experiences that will successfully prepare teachers for life in the preK–12 classroom. As discussed earlier, teachers' responses to racialized and diversity-centered curricula in teacher education vary. For instance, in my own work, which is consistent with Cochran-Smith's research, teachers' responses to diversity/race-central discussions, assignments, and activities on the classroom level ranged widely: some were receptive and reported new insights and consciousness relative to their preK–12 students' needs; others were resentful and did not understand why such topics are necessary. When teachers' responses follow the latter—frustration due to a focus on diversity or race—research suggests that resentment can overshadow the effort put forth by teacher educators. Brown wrote: "Resentment is frequently reflected on teacher evaluations, whereas resistance is apparent in inadequate pre-class preparation, reluctance to engage in class discussions and activities, and a lack of commitment to required cross-cultural interactions and research."[13]

However, teachers alone cannot be blamed for their development and their experience in a teacher education program or course. Teacher educators themselves must be prepared to structure teacher education programs in ways that allow teachers to develop. For instance, teachers' resistance can result in their silence in the face of important discussions and related learning opportunities about racism, injustice, diversity, and inequity. This silence can manifest because teachers believe they are being forced to think in a certain way, which counters the idea that all in a teacher education classroom should feel free to voice their positions and to construct knowledge and ways of knowing—even when they are inconsistent with those of the teacher educators or others in a classroom setting.[14] When such forced thinking occurs in the teacher education classroom, it reflects how preK–12 classroom environments tend to function when teachers orchestrate how students think and function.

Still, the racial backgrounds, knowledge, experiences, and mind-sets of teacher educators and how they understand and position themselves pedagogically and philosophically in the education of teachers should be considered. In other words, it is wrong to assume that teacher educators are automatically committed to preparing teachers to meet the complex and diverse needs of preK–12 students, and it certainly cannot be assumed that they are committed philosophically, theoretically, practically, or empirically to such a focus. In chapter 1, embedded in my discussion of color blindness, I shared student and teacher racial demographics and suggested that we needed to be mindful of these data when discussing what researchers have called a demographic divide. In a similar way, I believe we need to pay more attention to the racial demographics of teacher educators. Figures 5.1 and 5.2 summarize these racial demographic trends.

These figures display racial demographic information for both tenure-track and non-tenure-track faculty in teacher education programs. These demographic data suggest that we should be concerned about increasing the numbers of teachers of color not only in preK–12 social contexts but in teacher education as well. My point is not to suggest that White teacher educators cannot provide optimal learning opportunities for students but that teacher educators of color can add an important layer of diversity that can help teachers develop mind-sets necessary to teach equitably in preK–12.

Teacher educators' own experiences with race-related matters are sometimes remote and vicarious.[15] Accordingly, as teacher educator and researcher Merry Merryfield writes: "We know very little about the ability of college and university faculty and other teacher educators to prepare teachers in multicultural and global education. Do today's teacher educators have the knowledge, skills and commitment to teach for equity and diversity either locally or globally?"[16]

Thus, the racial identity of teacher educators themselves and their commitment to diversity can have a huge bearing on teachers and on the kinds of learning opportunities available to them as they learn how to teach for diversity and close opportunity gaps that exist throughout US school communities and beyond.

FIGURE 5.1

An emerging picture of the teacher preparation pipeline: Race and ethnicity of full-time faculty in professional education programs by rank, 2018

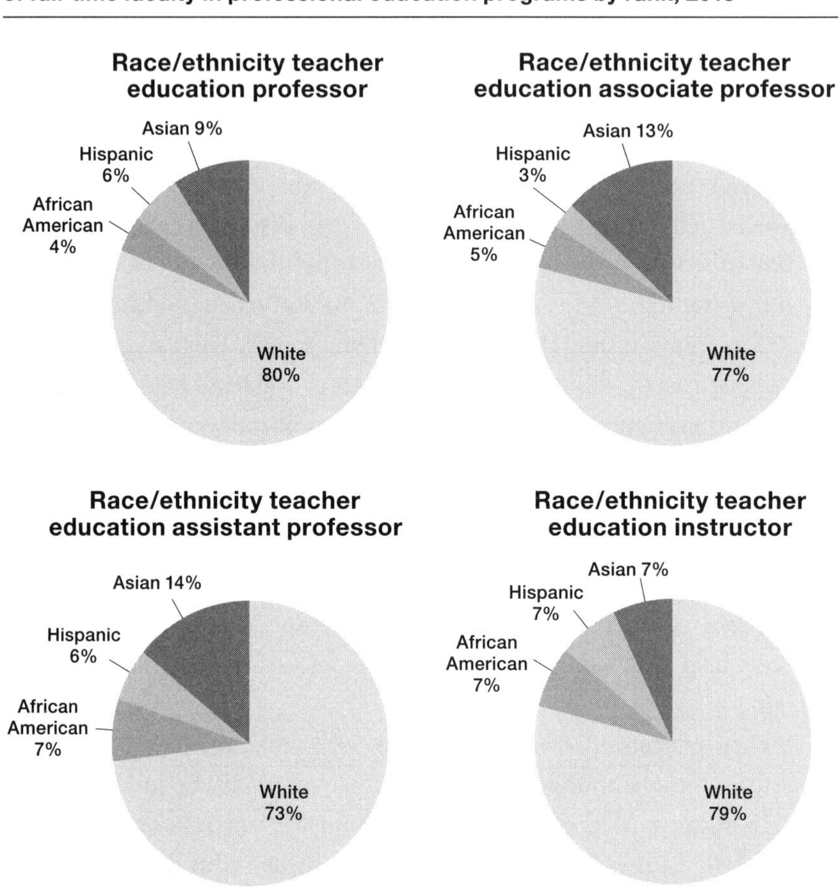

Note: Some totals do not add to 100 due to rounding.

Source: Adapted from J. E. King and R. Hampel, *Colleges of Education: A National Portrait* (Washington, DC: American Association of Colleges for Teacher Education, 2018).

FIGURE 5.2

An emerging picture of the teacher preparation pipeline: Race and ethnicity of full-time faculty in professional education programs, tenure and non-tenure track, 2018

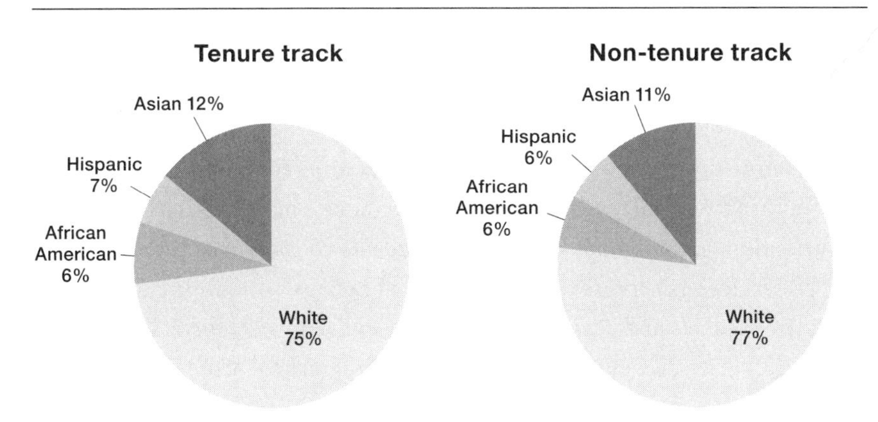

Source: Adapted from J. E. King and R. Hampel, *Colleges of Education: A National Portrait* (Washington, DC: American Association of Colleges for Teacher Education, 2018).

STRUCTURAL AND SYSTEMIC CONCERNS IN TEACHER EDUCATION

Because individuals create systems and structures, what teacher education programs emphasize will vary quite substantially depending on the views of those in the program. This variation can lead to uneven learning opportunities for teachers.

My analyses have revealed that there are no specified standard curriculum or instructional practices for teacher education programs, although the programs usually follow some specific standards and guidelines for accreditation through different associations. From a broader curricular and instructional perspective, research suggests that it is not enough to have one stand-alone course on race, diversity, urban education, or equity in a teacher education program.[17] I believe the goals of understanding *all* students and their experiences, developing racialized knowledge, and understanding trends and issues relative to diversity and opportunity should be at the core of teacher education programs. Ideally, opportunity-centered practices would be deeply integrated into the fabric and structure of a teacher education program. As a group of researchers observed:

> As instructors of one class in a large, complex program, we realize we can go only so far on our own. Our foundations course is marginalized from the curriculum and methods courses that students consider most important. If preservice teachers are to become more efficacious in teaching culturally diverse students and preparing all students to live in a democratic, multicultural society, we must work together as a program toward these ends.[18]

Curricular and instructional opportunities and experiences in teacher education, as well as the structure of teacher education programs, may need to change. Ladson-Billings found that "most [teacher education] programs were satisfied with adding 'multicultural content' rather than changing the philosophy and structure of the teacher education programs."[19] The core of teacher education programs—the nature and focus of the programs, the emphasis on certain issues over others—can be considered microlevel policy matters that need to be reexamined.

Where there is not a structural and systemic focus on opportunity and diversity in teacher education programs, the few isolated and marginalized courses that endeavor to prepare teachers can fail. At the core of those structural issues is (1) who teaches in these programs, (2) what they believe to be central to the curriculum, (3) who enrolls in the programs, (4) the kinds of historical experiences these teachers and teacher educators alike have had to contribute to the curriculum, and (5) the nature of their core commitments to opportunity-centered practices.

Teacher educator and researcher Kenneth Zeichner explains that "it has come to the point that the term social justice teacher education is so commonly used now by college and university teacher educators that it is difficult to find a teacher education program in the United States that does not claim to have a program that prepares teachers for social justice."[20] The question is, are all these programs really *practicing* a social justice teacher education mission? If so, how can we build knowledge about what these programs are actually doing in order to construct a broad curriculum base from which others can create and learn? Some faculty members in teacher education programs claim to have a social justice orientation. However, they may not practice their professed ideology in terms of decision-making. With only one or two courses that offer a few sessions on race and racism, for example, it is no wonder many teachers commence from teacher education programs unprepared, or underprepared, to teach students of color, those whose first language is not English, those who live below the poverty line, and those who do not fall within a White, mainstream, middle- to upper-class socioeconomic status, heterosexual, socially constructed norm. These preK–12 students and their families can then become the victims whom society, the media, politicians, teachers, principals, board members, and other adults in and out of schools blame for all the problems in preK–12 education.

In short, reshaping curricular and instructional emphasis related to diversity and opportunity gaps is especially important in teacher education if (a) there is not a range of courses focusing on opportunity-centered mind-sets and practices embedded in the program, and/or (b) programs have difficulty recruiting teacher candidates who have a desire to teach in contexts with diverse groups of students, and/or (c) students do not come into the program with some understanding of and affinity toward teaching for social justice. Again, even where opportunity-centered classes exist, teachers may not be open to such ideas, issues, and practices. Teachers may resist a curriculum and instruction that diverge from what they believe to be important. Thus, I am suggesting that teacher education programs become more coherent in their focus and mission in preparing teachers to meet the complex needs of preK–12 students. As teacher education programs are restructured, teacher educators should remember that their programs should be designed to address the needs of *all* teachers enrolled in teacher education programs, not just White teachers.

PREPARING ALL, NOT JUST WHITE, TEACHERS FOR DIVERSITY

Teachers of color do not necessarily enter teacher education programs with a deep understanding of what it means to teach for diversity. Teacher education programs (including courses and related experiences) need to be structured to address the developmental needs of all teachers, not just White teachers. My point holds consistent even as the majority of teachers are White. All teachers must build knowledge, attitudes, dispositions, and consequently opportunity-centered practices that can more effectively support preK–12 students.

Teacher education policy makers (including professors involved in the process of accepting students into teacher education) sometimes embrace a more racially diverse population for one of several (selfish) interests. When admission policies and practices are adopted to increase racial diversity, they are sometimes justified as "benefiting" the interests and needs of White teachers.[21] In this line of reasoning, a diverse student/teacher population is important because White teachers can learn from non-White teachers.

This mind-set is rarely reciprocal; what about opportunities for nonmainstream teachers to learn from White teachers? *All* teachers need and deserve preparation that can help them meet the challenges they will face in the preK–12 classroom. Clearly, nonmainstream teachers learn from their White counterparts and vice versa, yet the intention and vision of recruiting teachers are sometimes one-sided. It is critical that teacher educators remember that nonmainstream teachers may come into a teacher education program unequipped to meet the needs of preK–12 students. Further, as I have come to understand, nonmainstream teachers may have been brainwashed into believing that they (and students from nondominant groups) are inferior, and thus they may consciously or subconsciously concentrate on the negative attributes and characteristics of their preK–12 students and communities of color. As Tatum writes:

> In a race-conscious society, the development of a positive sense of racial/ethnic identity not based on assumed superiority or inferiority is an important task for *both* White people and people of color. The development of this positive identity is a lifelong process that often requires *unlearning the misinformation and stereotypes* [emphasis added] we have internalized not only about others, but also about ourselves.[22]

Course syllabi and related instructional and curriculum practices can imply that teacher educators are concerned about the needs of their White teachers and that racially diverse teachers should simply learn "by default" or come into the learning environment with what they already need to succeed. To the contrary, teachers—all of them—need support to get better.

Thus, in some instances, teachers of color have to learn from curricula and related experiences that are tailored to meet their White counterparts' needs.[23] Published curriculum materials such as textbooks used in teacher education programs often make recommendations "based on the assumption that preservice teachers are White." This approach could alienate preservice teachers of color—for instance, what about the curricular and instructional needs of Asian or Latinx teachers? As teacher education researcher Adrienne Dixson observes, the teacher education curriculum can look very much like the preK–12 curriculum. It can privilege the positions, norms, needs, worldviews, and expectations of White people.

Many volumes are published to address the developmental, conceptual, pedagogical, philosophical, and curricular needs of White teachers, while the needs of other groups of teachers are considered far less often. In addition, teachers of color are sometimes recruited to be a "spokesperson" for their race. For example, during class discussions, they are asked to address every issue facing their race in education. I have observed that such an expectation can cause these teachers to retreat from the teaching and learning exchange because they cannot—and, more importantly, *should not*—be asked to speak on behalf of their entire race or ethnicity.

BENEFITS TO DIVERSIFYING THE TEACHING FORCE

There appear to be benefits to the teacher education curriculum and contextual discourse when teachers and teacher educators are culturally and racially diverse. Of course, this diversity can and should include White teachers who have lived in different parts of the United States and world as well as those who possess other diverse experiences and characteristics.

One of the six teachers showcased in this chapter explained to me in an interview how during one of our seminar/class discussions, "She [the Asian teacher] shared how she felt . . . And I think that's what has helped me the most, just taking that stance [of the Asian teacher]." She found the Asian American teacher's perspectives especially insightful, and she was able to link them to what she described as a "tangible reality."

Another teacher explained that the racialized experiences I shared as a Black man teacher educator contributed to her new perspectives on "others." During a class discussion, this teacher kept questioning me about whether I always perceive myself as a "Black man"; that is, whether there are times when I forget that I am Black and do not think about it or prioritize it in terms of my identity. She referenced this class discussion in an interview and explained that this exchange made a powerful difference in how she thought about others, particularly African Americans, and she linked it to her practice:

Teacher: Are there not times when you forget that you are Black? Are there not times when you forget that you are a Black male?

Milner: No, I always see myself as Black, and I always see myself as a Black male.

Teacher: Do you always feel the pressure of being Black?

Milner: I am always aware of the stereotypes and assumptions that surround my racial and gender identity.

Teacher: Do you ever wish that you could just be "Dr. Milner the person" and not "Dr. Milner the Black person"?

Milner: I see my professional identity as importantly intertwined with my racial and gender identity.

In our interview, the teacher explained: "I kept pushing you to speak whether . . . there were times when you could forget who you are in the sense that you didn't wonder, worry, it wasn't in the back of your mind that someone was seeing you as a Black man . . . to me the greatest impact [from our course] was you being [sic] able to just state without any wavering on it at all that [you always] see yourself as Black." The gist of this argument is that having teachers as classmates and as teacher educators of color can potentially have a meaningful impact on the White teachers' learning and development in a course or teacher education program. The question is, what about the benefits for and needs of teachers of color?

CHALLENGES FACING TEACHER EDUCATORS OF COLOR

Similar to teachers of color in a teacher education program or preK–12 context, teacher educators of color sometimes face added pressure to represent their racial and ethnic group. While their representation may be seen as an asset, their voice and perspective can be marginalized or silenced because they are outnumbered in philosophical and conceptual discussions and debates. Ironically, White people can become the expert on everything and teacher educators of color are expected to just default to silence and defer to the White majority. While teacher educators of color may not have power and influence over aspects of the program that really matter, they are still expected to serve on committees to represent "minority issues," and teachers and colleagues often look to them to solve complex problems related to diversity. Moreover, teacher educators of color are expected to teach diversity-related courses even when these courses may not be well aligned with their interests and expertise.

While I have argued for the need to increase diversity among both preK–12 teachers and teacher educators, such diversity can bring challenges as well. During class discussions and related assignments, clashes sometimes ensue between teachers and teacher educators, especially when the teacher educator is African American and the teachers are White. As Ladson-Billings explains, teachers in the teacher education classroom may refuse to participate in discussions about race and culture when they disagree with what is being covered in the course. The result can be what she calls "silence as weapons." For an African American teacher educator, discussions about race and culture can be silently interpreted as the professor's "putting forth a particular political agenda."[24] Students may shut down when uncomfortable issues related to diversity and opportunities are discussed.

In my own teaching and research, despite my best efforts to provide spaces where race, diversity, and opportunity were at the top of the instructional agenda, I have observed teachers disengaging during class discussions, particularly when the topic was race and racism in the preK–12 classroom. This counterproductive silence can leave teacher educators and their students perplexed about *what* should be covered related to race, *where* (in what contexts) race can be addressed, and, perhaps most important, *how* the issue might be explored.[25] What do teachers really think about discussions of diversity in teacher education? What is the nature of their silenced dialogue?[26] Moreover, in what ways are they silenced? Why are they silent? And, most critically, how might teachers' unstated concerns and positions show up in their preK–12 practices?

Coupled with the concerns that can emerge when teacher educators of color work with mostly White teachers is the added pressure to assume what I have come to call a diversity-savior role. Teacher educators of color are sometimes expected to represent diversity in many situations and facets of a program. This means, for instance, that teachers from different racial and ethnic backgrounds consistently meet with teacher educators of color and expect them to help them solve diversity dilemmas from a range of perspectives. Furthermore, teacher educators of color are also often delegated to the one or two diversity courses in a program regardless of their subject-matter expertise or area of interest. They are often expected to serve on committees in order to have "diverse" representation. But when these teacher educators of color do serve on committees, they are too often not listened to because they are outnumbered in terms of their cultural and racial background and belief system. Teacher educators of color are often invited to do diversity guest lectures in classes and to be the go-to person for teachers in programs on diversity matters that White teacher educators cannot address. Teacher educators of color are also expected to speak on behalf of their cultural and racial group for the benefit or interest of their colleagues. For example, these teacher educators are asked to explain a behavioral pattern that they have observed in a teacher or student of color. White teacher educators bring their critiques to what is shared and may still go about their business without serious attention to what the teacher educator of color has shared. And ultimately, unfortunately, White allies may be few and far between when teacher educators of color need support and advocacy.[27]

SUMMARY

Unlike other disciplines where there is an accepted, standard, and understood body of knowledge, teacher education is much more dynamic, and perhaps it needs to be. There are, of course, positives and negatives to this reality that bring about bittersweet outcomes for both teacher educators and teachers. This chapter demonstrates some of the pervasive problems and promising possibilities that teacher education programs face in preparing teachers for opportunity-centered mind-sets and practices. What is clear is that teacher education remains relevant and important to the preparation of teachers, whether traditional or nontraditional. While the field of teacher education has improved in providing teachers with curriculum and related experiences that address diversity, there are lingering broad issues to consider in the field:

- Increased external pressure to provide evidence of programs' effectiveness

- Structural incoherence between programs, where there is perhaps too much variation in terms of the level of curricular and instructional emphasis on opportunity and diversity
- Lack of consistency and commitment among teacher educators to address diversity
- Increasing the numbers of teachers and teacher educators of color and from diverse backgrounds (such as men) in the field
- Constructing and deconstructing curriculum and instructional experiences that meet the needs of all students, not just White students
- Addressing the uneven stress and burdens as well as invisible work placed on teacher educators and teachers of color to be the diversity go-to person in teacher education programs

The six White teachers demonstrated some consistent themes that teacher educators should consider:

1. Early in their program, most of the White teachers had difficulty understanding the relevance of diversity for their own work, and they worried that they may have been making an issue out of diversity when it really did not matter.
2. Most of the White teachers were fearful of offending those in the teacher education classroom, so they avoided using particular words, and even avoided particular politically charged topics for fear of saying the "wrong" thing.
3. Overall, the White teachers' positions (beliefs and mind-sets) were guided by and grounded in their familial history, especially their experiences with their parents and caregivers. These histories helped shape the White teachers' views on diversity (especially race).
4. Most of the White teachers were sometimes in danger of stereotyping their students and lowering their expectations of them, although this may not have been their intention.

Although many of these challenges emerged especially early in the learning and development of these White teachers, four of the six showed promising growth throughout their program, building opportunity-centered mind-sets that hopefully will result in their preK–12 practices.

Indeed, concurrent with problems and tensions that emerged among the White teachers showcased in this chapter were promising dimensions of their thinking and mind-sets. For instance, White teachers in my study

- started to make sense of the importance of cultural connections and role models for students. A teacher explained that the underrepresentation of teachers of color in her particular school was problematic, and they even started to look beyond their school, viewing the shortage of teachers of color as a "district" issue—moving from a microlevel critique to a more systemic problem.
- had good intentions and attempted to empathize with their students. Their commitment to think about their work with students with both head and heart, I have found, can be the foundation for them to develop the mind-sets and practices that meet their preK–12 students' needs.
- began to incorporate aspects of diversity into their decision-making, and they began to witness for themselves the benefits of, for instance, using bilingual texts in the classroom.
- in some cases wanted to disrupt and fight against the racist or homophobic language that they had heard growing up.

These aspects of preparing teachers to address diversity and opportunities underscore the importance, salience, role, and relevance of teacher education as we continue to support teachers who dare to teach and support every child, every day. But the learning and development of these six teachers and other teachers do not end when they graduate from teacher education. These teachers need to be supported in service as they work to get better. In this regard, teacher education needs to not "stay there" in terms of how we support teacher learning and development in practice.

6

Opportunity-Centered Teaching

IN THIS CHAPTER, I focus on what I am calling and conceptualizing as opportunity-centered teaching (OCT). OCT provides a counterforce to multilayered opportunity gaps that exist in classroom, district, and community practices and policies. So far, throughout this book, I have demonstrated what opportunity gaps are, why they are sustained, and, through case studies, how real teachers have addressed them. Here, I pull together central features of OCT that can advance our conversations away from focusing solely on opportunity gaps and the practices of teachers toward a unifying framework that helps teachers think about how to address gaps in opportunity. To be clear, I am advancing through the framework that when mechanisms are in place, guided by educators' deep reflections, belief systems, and practices, students have a better chance for positive outputs. However, the framework is focused mostly on inputs that can lead to desired outcomes. As educational researchers come to observe and understand OCT, I hope the framework provides language to explain and make sense of OCT.

OCT addresses gaps in opportunity by prioritizing structural, systemic, and practical tools, strategies, and mechanisms to support student success inside of school. Four key tenets shape OCT. OCT begins with and is grounded in the premise and foundation that relationship building and cultivation are essential to co-constructing a classroom ethos that builds on students' assets, honors and draws from their identity, and brings out students' capacity. Developing knowledge and practices to assemble authentic relationships is viewed as necessary and exemplary of good teaching across grade span, subject-matter areas, and geographical locations. Relationship building is seen as central to good teaching and learning, not peripheral.

A second tenet of OCT concerns community knowledge and learning. Communities have important spaces of expertise that can help shed light on what is happening with students and what should happen inside of schools and classrooms. Thus, OCT requires that educators intentionally build community knowledge, understanding, and insights that allow them to deepen and align curriculum and instructional practices with the community. Such alignment means that *community* and *curriculum* are seen as complementary, iterative, dynamic, grounded, and guided by mutual understanding of both. Curriculum informed by community knowledge honors, addresses, and draws from community history, wisdom, preferences, needs, and practices. In short, community knowledge allows teachers to shape, reconstruct, and build their practices in more informed, relevant, and meaningful ways.

Related to building community knowledge, a third tenet of OCT, curriculum convergence, designs outside-of-school practices in tandem with those inside of school. Educators come to understand that learning opportunities conceptualized as an "extra" form of the curriculum for students can be merged and purposely developed to make connections to a formal curriculum. Students experience curriculum and pedagogical practices outside of school that are too often not understood or connected inside of school.

In addition to designing learning opportunities that align with students' outside-of-school practices through curriculum convergence, educators must understand that the psychological, social, emotional, and mental health of adults and young people is necessary for teaching and learning success. Thus, the fourth tenet of OCT is psychological and emotional health. Educators, other adults in students' lives, and young people *all* need to be psychologically and mentally stable and healthy in order to maximize interactions, practices, and experiences.

TENET #1

OPPORTUNITY-CENTERED TEACHING IS ABOUT RELATIONSHIP CULTIVATION

In theory and rhetoric, the notion that teachers must build relationships with students is logical and well accepted. For instance, I rarely, if ever, hear practicing educators contest the idea that constructing relationships is a critical aspect of their success with students in any classroom or school. The question, however, is, How do teachers and other educators build those relationships to maximize OCT? Further, how do educators sustain relationships, when conflicts are looming, in order to maximize learning opportunities? How might relationships be extended beyond teacher-student to consider other connections, which can be essential to student success?

Clearly, building relationships with students is about meeting students where they are, attempting to understand them, and developing connections with them that go far beyond the immediate classroom setting. A forerunner to such an exchange requires that teachers are *willing to find the good* and the worth in students. All students possess positive characteristics and attributes, but these are sometimes overlooked and undervalued—especially if they fall outside of teachers' own worldviews and experience in their own lives as students or even with their own children. Thus, relationship cultivation might require that teachers refocus and sharpen their lenses when considering and centralizing student strengths and assets.

OCT means that every single student, even those who may not have a strong academic, social, or relational history, has a fair and equitable chance to build and connect in a school and classroom. Indeed, relationships are foundational to student development among those whose teachers have known them only in a negative light or those who have not well experienced education. This negative view of students might have been passed down from one generation of teachers to another. In elementary schools, teachers talk to each other about their views on particular students rather than allowing their colleagues to build their own impressions. In middle and high school, teachers still talk among themselves about students, but teachers also garner information based on records other teachers have constructed. Or teachers may have personally experienced negative interactions with students in the past. Regardless of the source of the negative perception, when teachers do not have a positive frame or an appropriate developmental lens to view particular students, it can be difficult to recognize that all students, despite their differences and challenges, are worth investing in. Relationships cannot be established if teachers do not see assets and positivity among students. Further, it is difficult to build relationships with students if teachers are not willing to give students a chance.

Are teachers prepared and willing to build relationships with students whose life realities are very different from theirs? Are teachers prepared and willing to build relationships with students who look, act, and interpret the world differently from their teachers? Are teachers willing to relax their egos and view students—all students—as young people worth fighting for? Relationship cultivation as a foundation to OCT requires teachers to see students as young people who deserve adults in their lives willing to work on their behalf, advocate for them, recognize them as capable of success, and push agendas that benefit them.

Educators have to recognize and remember that students have sometimes internalized negative words and perceptions about themselves, which can make it difficult for them to identify their own potential or to trust and give teachers a chance to help them develop their talents and strengths. Teachers may find that they need to bridge gaps of self-doubt and worthlessness to help students acknowledge their own potential and promise. For instance, at home, students sometimes hear and may internalize and believe only what their parents and siblings say is "wrong" with them. Students may hear all kinds of negative messages from different adults or other family members that can have a lasting negative impact on them:

- You will never amount to anything.
- You're ugly.
- You are worthless and should be ashamed.
- I regret the day you were born.
- You're too loud.
- You are getting too fat—you need to lose weight.
- You're not smart.
- You don't work hard enough.
- You have a bad attitude.
- You're not athletic enough! No wonder you never start in any games.
- You remind me of your "no-good" mother or your "no-good" father.

Although students may hear and experience this type of language in a literal sense, they also "hear" teachers and other educators degrade them through implicit language, codes, and actions. Black and Brown children, beginning at an early age, hear and interpret negative messages when educators talk about gaps in their achievement in comparison to other groups. Students discern these negative messages when they overhear educators talk about particular groups of students as "so aggressive" and "violent," or refer to them as "kids these days." These statements can have lasting negative influence on students, which may consequently have significant impact on the lives of young people. Moreover, negative words and perspectives that have been *spoken into students' lives* can make it difficult for them to become motivated to engage in the academic curriculum and/or in social or athletic opportunities at school. When students believe adults only see the challenges or negative aspects about them or their situations, it can be difficult to build, cultivate, and sustain relationships with them. To combat negative experiences students may have had, OCT means that educators (1) deliberately and consciously counter and disrupt destructive language students may have heard inside and outside of the classroom, and

(2) help students visualize themselves as different from the negative ideas and language they have heard and have come to believe and accept.

Indeed, language is perhaps the most important mechanism we have to construct relationships, for these reasons:

1. Talk is a form of action and doing.
2. Talk is a good iterative step in working through conflicts and addressing challenges before, while, and after issues emerge.
3. Sustained talk allows people to triangulate responses, connect deeply with people, and move beyond surface-level interactions.
4. Talk requires educators and students to build trust over time.
5. Talk allows people (especially adults) to explicitly express their empathy for and support of students. It also allows them to apologize to students and build long-term relationships.

But what specific practices can teachers develop and enact in their classrooms to build and cultivate relationships?

Classroom Relationship Practices

There are many micro- or classroom-level practices that can help teachers mold relationships with their students. Consider the following practices that teachers can engage in to deepen their knowledge of students.

- *Student interviews:* Educators have a chance to talk to and with their students, both formally and informally, to learn about them. Teachers sometimes spend infinite amounts of time talking *about* students to their colleagues or to students' families but minimal amounts of time actually talking *to* students themselves. Interviewing students prompts teachers to think about some questions before interacting with students and build probative questions over time. The practice of interviewing students allows teachers to engage in conversations with students themselves to learn from and about them. Teachers can then incorporate this learning into the class curriculum and teaching in ways that honor privacy but build on student interests and needs.

Over the years, in my university classroom, I have used the practice of interviewing to gain deeper insights into the students in front of me. The idea here is that building and sustaining relationships is essential not only in preK–12 classrooms but in all classrooms. OCT shepherds teachers and students into places of humanity where relationships are core to what happens in the classroom; all teachers, working with the youngest to the oldest, learn to develop skill sets to build the kinds of relationships that support all. For instance, when I conducted interviews and learned of a student's interest in a particular aspect of education, I remained mindful of that area of interest and attempted to make explicit linkages to those interests in my own practices. When I read journal articles and books, or when I was engaged in research projects, I often made copies and shared writing or related materials that might be of interest to that student. I have found that opportunities to engage in interview-like interactions were essential throughout a course—as early as possible and consistently throughout a semester, term, or year. While the interview may seem too formal, it provides opportunity for teachers to pose useful and relevant questions that may not emerge organically through day-to-day interactions.

- *Connected assignments:* Another practice that can help educators build their knowledge and understanding of their students' lifeworlds is the deliberate assignment of projects and tasks for students to share experiences and interests with teachers. In language arts, assignments might include journal or essay writing that focus not only on particular subject matter but also content that centers students' interests, motivations, challenges, successes, and objectives for the course and life beyond it. In social studies, assignments might include family history projects or local community-studies projects that have a real connection to the subject matter being covered. In mathematics or science courses, assignments might include student-constructed word problems or family- or community-based inquiry projects where students investigate the effects of environmental patterns related to health, crime, and/or poverty in a community. The point is to co-construct assignments that are connected to student interests and also their community, homes, and lives outside of the school context.

- *Classroom talk and dynamic discourse:* Teachers have an excellent opportunity to construct classroom learning time in ways that allow and foster classroom discussions that place students front and center. In other words, subject matter being covered is and should be viewed as tangential to the important point that subject matter is being taught and learned by and with human beings. Learning about students to build insights about them allows teachers to more deeply understand what is happening inside and outside of school. Classroom discussions give students opportunities to share aspects of their experiences that they find appropriate, relevant, and meaningful. For instance, when I taught high school English, I used to facilitate what I came to call "rap sessions" that allowed students to have conversations with each other and me about what was happening in their lives (inside and outside of school). The students in my classes would develop categories/topics of interest that they wanted to discuss, and we selected topics out of a hat so students could debate issues or just share their perspectives on a particular theme. The experience was inundated with learning opportunities: (1) it allowed students to think about and construct a position; (2) it helped students develop counterpositions and counterpoints to debate classmates when they disagreed; (3) it encouraged students to learn how to substantiate their positions, listen to others, and build coherent narratives and arguments; and (4) it provided students space for voice, perspective, and authority in the classroom. The discussion sessions with students enabled them to develop voice and perspective, and they allowed me to gain knowledge about the students. When discussing her pedagogical approach and voice, hooks wrote:

> As a teacher, I recognize that students . . . enter classrooms within institutions where their voices have been neither heard nor welcomed, whether these students discuss facts—those that any of us might know—or personal experience. My pedagogy has been shaped to respond to this reality. If I do

not wish to see these students use the "authority of experience" as a means of asserting voice, I can circumvent this possible misuse of power by bringing to the classroom pedagogical strategies that affirm their presence, their right to speak, in multiple ways on diverse topics.[1]

Thus, classroom discussion to build relationships should be dynamic and occur at different times. In classroom settings where such discourse might seem inconsistent with how knowledge is co-constructed, discussion and classroom talk are still essential to help build cross-person knowledge and understanding. Once students build the capacity to talk with and among others, we have a better chance of knowing who they are and what they know.

- *Attend an extracurricular activity of a student:* Another important way for educators to build classroom-level knowledge and concurrently relationships with students is to attend students' activities before or after school. Engagements might include sporting events such as a football, lacrosse, or basketball game, a band or chorus concert, or a play/theatrical production. Attendance at such extracurricular events is potentially powerful, even when the teacher is not on duty. Such attendance is something that teachers on the elementary through high school level can do (even when elementary students participate in extracurricular activities through community recreation centers, for instance). Students consistently report that it means something special to them when teachers take time out of their schedules to attend an activity they are involved in.
- *Visit a community site in students' communities:* In addition to attending an extracurricular activity, deliberately visiting, patronizing, and otherwise engaging in the community where teachers teach and also where students live (note these two locations may be different) can be a powerful way for teachers to learn about their students and build relationships with them. Locations that may help build insight include supermarkets, gas stations, libraries, hair salons (including beauty and barbershops), community centers, and churches,

synagogues, or other worship sites. In essence, when teachers immerse themselves in students' communities, they are able to learn what is happening in students' neighborhoods and their worlds outside of a learning environment.

Practices that have real implications for the classroom like the ones I describe above have the potential to help teachers build important knowledge essential for relationships as a core feature of OCT (see the summary of these recommendations in table 6.1). There are also broader school-related practices that have the potential to assist educators in building relationships—again, with the ultimate goal of building OCT.

Schoolwide Practices to Build Relationships

In addition to classroom-level practices that help teachers build and cultivate relationships, schools can also initiate, develop, and expand broader, school-level programs to establish relationships and simultaneously

TABLE 6.1
Classroom relationship practices

Nature of practice	Description
Student interviews	Educators have a chance to talk to their students, both formally and informally, to learn about them. Teachers sometimes spend infinite amounts of time talking about students to their colleagues or to students' parents but minimal time talking to students themselves.
Connected assignments	A practice that can help educators build their knowledge and understanding of their students' lifeworlds is the assigning of projects and tasks that allow students to share experiences and interests with teachers.
Classroom talk and dynamic discourse	Teachers have an excellent opportunity to construct classroom learning time in ways that allow and foster classroom discussions that place students front and center.
Attendance at extracurricular activity of a student	An important way for educators to build classroom-level relationships with students is to consistently attend students' activities before or after school.
Site visits in students' communities	Deliberately visiting, patronizing, and otherwise engaging in the community where teachers teach and also where students live (note these two locations may be different) can be a powerful way for teachers to learn about their students and build relationships with them.

address aspects of diversity and opportunity. The following examples (summarized in table 6.2) outline recommendations and practices that educators in schools might consider:

- *Language-learning resource program for parents and families:* Such a program can provide families in a school community with opportunities to acquire a new or second language that can assist them in the school community and beyond. Moreover, the chance to learn English, Spanish, Arabic, French, Chinese, and other languages, particularly languages represented in a school community, can also help those in the community build relationships at the same time. I learned from a parent in Ohio that a school was planning to provide child care for parents interested in the language program. Indeed, families

TABLE 6.2
Schoolwide practices to build relationships

Nature of practice	Description
Language-learning resource program for parents and families	Such a program can provide families in a school community with chances to acquire a new or second language that can assist them in the school community and beyond.
Parenting/family workshops	Because parents sometimes do not understand all that is expected of them to help their children achieve success, the workshops could be structured to assist parents to be active participants in their students' education.
Diversity-related theme for the semester or year	The development and implementation of a theme for the academic school year or semester can allow those in a community to build common knowledge about the theme.
Schoolwide movie viewing	Schools can consider holding periodic, annual, semiannual, or quarterly movie showings and invite the school community (parents, teachers, students, community members) into the school to address dimensions of diversity and opportunity.
Community-centered dinner	Quarterly, semiannually, and/or annually, schools could host a dinner for parents (and other caregivers) and community members along with teachers, staff members, administrators/principals, and students.
Schoolwide book reading	Schools might also consider adopting a schoolwide yearly reading selection that showcases some aspect of diversity or opportunity. The book should be read by all those in the community—students, teachers, community members, parents, and staff—and teachers can use the reading as a site for discussion and curriculum construction across different age spans.

should maintain, embrace, and showcase their own first language, and this program can provide opportunities for them to expand.

- *Parenting and family workshops:* Because children do not come with a manual when they are born, parents—particularly new parents—could benefit from the knowledge, insights, recommendations, and expertise of others. Such workshops and learning opportunities can help parents understand what Delpit describes as the "culture of power" and encourage them to partner with the school to maximize student learning opportunities.[2] Because parents and families sometimes do not understand all that is expected of them to help their young people achieve social and academic success, the workshops could be structured to assist parents in being active participants in education. It is important that these workshops be designed to allow parents and families to have voice and perspective in the design and implementation of the workshop. Parents and families should not be told how to parent but should be provided information on strategies to support their families. Parents and families participating in the workshops can also provide insights from which others can learn. Parents and families may not parent the way educators do, but this does not mean they do not care about their children. Moreover, parents and families may not be aware of how to support their children in a school culture. Some parents and families, for instance, may see their role primarily as an economic resource, not an educational one. They may need additional resources, suggestions, and recommendations on ways to support their children academically. Some families and parents, as students, vowed that they would never return to school after graduating (or being pushed out of school) because of the negative experiences they had as students.[3] Also, some parents may be intimidated by the discourse of a school, especially if they were not educated in a Eurocentric, traditional academic environment. Some families and parents work long hours, which can make it difficult for them to be physically present at school as well as academically and psychologically available for their children at home. These realities are not a consequence of parents' not caring about their children but a function of the social world in which they live. All these factors may be related to why parents and families are not showing up at schools. But family and parental involvement and engagement go far beyyond showing up at school. The question is: What role might/should schools play in reversing parents' lack of perceived involvement? Moreover, if families and parents did start showing up at school, would educators know what to ask them to do in order to support their children? Are educators prepared to see the value in parents and what they bring into the school? How do educators build on families' and parents' assets to support student learning? Moreover, family and community involvement happens not only when they show up at school but in other ways as well. Underrecognized family involvement includes homework help, fund-raising for the school, and showing up to support sporting events—even running the concession stands.

- *Diversity-related theme for the semester or year:* The development and implementation of a theme for the academic school year or semester can allow those in a community to build common knowledge about the theme. Teachers can incorporate aspects of the theme into curriculum and instructional practices throughout the year.[4] Students themselves could suggest a diversity theme, and the entire student body could vote on the top three ideas, eventually selecting one. Possible themes include *opportunity, diversity, poverty, justice, equity, equality,* and *injustice.* Such a schoolwide focus can allow for synergistic aims, enabling students and educators to learn and build knowledge about the importance and essence of the theme from multiple vantage points through multiple subject-matter areas. Parents and families, of course, should be involved and informed about the theme, and community members (such as professional athletes, community organizers, business executives, or entrepreneurs) might be invited to school to provide narratives about their experience with a particular theme.
- *Schoolwide movie viewing:* Another event that builds school-level relationships among students, educators, parents, and community members is movie days or movie nights. Schools might hold periodic,

annual, semiannual, or quarterly movie showings, inviting the whole school community (including parents, family members, teachers, students, and community members) to the school to address dimensions of diversity and opportunity. The movies can be used as "sites" for curriculum connections that support students in grappling with complex matters, which can assist them in building knowledge, skills, and mind-sets transferable to other areas of their work and lives. There is a litany of teacher-centered movies that display White teachers as "saviors" of students living in poverty, students of color, and students whose first language is not English. It is critical for those in a learning context to remember that movies that paint a White educator as the protagonist to students "in need" convey messages that may perpetuate unintended stereotypes. Moreover, movies such as *Lean on Me* can showcase an African American school principal in a light of rage and hostility, presenting a picture that is one-sided.[5] Indeed, Black school principals are far more than upset, mean, and frustrated administrators who must carry around baseball bats to keep law and order. Thus, by way of caution, I encourage movie selections that are balanced in perspective and that show marginalized people in a light of success, not only in roles of servitude, need, or hostility. In addition, I encourage those viewing the movies to use them as a site for discussion, and in particular as an opportunity to critique and analyze major themes in the movies without accepting the themes as simplistic, static, literal, necessarily accurate, or pejorative.

- *Community-centered dinner:* Quarterly, semiannually, and/or annually, schools could host a dinner for parents (and other caregivers) and community members along with teachers, staff members, administrators/principals, and students. I was mindful in my decision to include "other caregivers" in my list of those who should be invited. Educators must expand their notions of "parental" involvement to include extended family and community members. Indeed, students tend to have a range of people in their lives who help shape and mold them for success. For instance, older siblings might need to be involved if parents work late hours. Students' grandparents, aunts, uncles, and "other mothers and fathers," those who serve as surrogate parents, might also need to be considered. During the dinners, there might be a keynote address, or students might organize and plan the program's focus as they showcase their talents. I know of several schools in Tennessee that have adopted very different approaches to this idea of family/community dinner. One suburban school actually has an annual formal dinner and auction. An urban school in the same city holds a fish fry each year. Both events have standing room only. Food, perhaps, is the draw, but the goal is for families and students to talk to each other and to educators about educational, community, and social issues that can benefit the interests of all.

- *Schoolwide book reading:* In their journey to build community, schools might also consider adopting a schoolwide yearly reading selection that showcases some aspect of diversity or opportunity. The book should be read by all those in the community—students, teachers, community members, parents, and staff—and teachers can use the reading as a site for discussion and curriculum construction across different grades. Where possible, schools might select a reading that expands on the theme chosen for the year, or they might choose a book that has a complementary movie. In both cases, students and others in the learning community can use the reading as an opportunity to share knowledge around a particular issue or theme and to voice their views of the major ideas in the book. Where possible, parents should be invited into the school to engage with their children in discussions about particular aspects and themes of the books.

Having established both classroom- and school-level suggestions (see table 6.2 for a summative visual), strategies, and insights that teachers and schools can consider to build relationships with students (their families and parents) through OCT, I turn now to discuss important insights about community knowledge as central to OCT. Community knowledge is important for relationship-centered practices as well as curriculum and instructional practices.

TENET #2

OPPORTUNITY-CENTERED TEACHING IS ABOUT BUILDING COMMUNITY KNOWLEDGE TO INFORM PRACTICE

Communities are deeply rich in human capital—regardless of the zip code, whether rural, suburban, or urban. But educators in some schools may struggle to understand how to build on the many talents and assets of community—perhaps because in order to recognize and acknowledge expertise in a community we, as educators, must see the brilliance of the students with whom we work. In other words, it can be tough to recognize what communities possess and can offer when we cannot or refuse to acknowledge the assets of students who come from those communities. Over the years, I have heard teachers, counselors, coaches, social workers, school psychologists, and principals in schools with large populations of Black and Brown students, those who live below the poverty line, Muslim students, those whose first language is not English, and those who have a learning disability talk about their students, parents, and communities in disheartening ways. Some common examples:

- "These students' parents do not care about or value education—they don't even show up for parent-teacher conferences."
- "These students' families do not help them with their homework or school projects."
- "There is so much violence in their communities—they don't even care about each other."

But every single student in our schools, including those who are often placed on the margins of learning, should be viewed as a vessel of knowledge and knowing: all of these young people come to schools with significant intellectual and cultural gifts and talents. Because our educational system has been relentless in "schooling" students to become less of themselves, rejecting important features of their identity, we miss out on what "education" can actually be and can mean for advancing a truly democratic, pluralistic society. Mwalimu J. Shujaa and his colleagues stressed that we should be advancing educational practices over schooling practices.[6] Education over schooling honors and builds on students' strengths. Education helps students build skills to question, critique, and improve situations inside and outside of schools. Schooling is a process of business-as-usual practices where particular White normative structures are reproduced. Students outside of the White norm are expected to assimilate and "melt" into preexisting, oppressive cultures and cultural practices that undervalue their humanity. Building community knowledge involves educators deliberately learning about their community and building relationships, not only with students and their families but also with other community members to enhance teaching and learning opportunities.

By community relationships, I mean not only that educators work to learn about and build relationships with people in a community but also that as educators we build knowledge about and relationships with community in the abstract: What do we know about the history of the communities in which we teach and our students live? From what sources do we build this knowledge? What geographical opportunities are there for students in a particular community (parks, recreation centers, libraries, transportation mechanisms, and so forth)? What material resources are available in the community? What human capital and social identities are present in the community?

It is well established that educators' knowledge informs what they do.[7] So a pressing question is how educators can build their knowledge of community to inform their instruction and support for students in their classrooms. I observed a White teacher (Mr. Hall, introduced in chapter 2) over a period of two years who initially informed me that his main focus and "job" were to "just teach science" to his racially, socioeconomically diverse students. But eventually he realized that understanding his students and their communities was essential to the teaching and learning process. In other words, as an outsider to the community of his students and school, he could not "just teach science" effectively until he developed tools to understand his students and their broader ecological reality and systems. Students, families, and community members, this teacher came to understand, are the experts on their experience, and educators should intentionally listen to the wisdom and insights of those people who know them best. These learning opportunities to build knowledge should focus not only on people but also on the broader ethos of a community.

Below, I outline strategies and tools that can help educators build this knowledge essential to closing opportunity gaps and that address challenges some teachers face related to diversity (see table 6.3 for a summary).

- *Community immersion—live in the community:* One obvious way for educators to build knowledge about a community is to actually live where their students live and attend school. In their research on culture, community, and segregated schools, Linda Tillman and Vanessa Siddle Walker have highlighted the value of teachers actually living in the communities in which they teach.[8] Such residential arrangements can provide for powerful trusting relationships as a foundation to establishing layers of knowledge through experience that educators are able to merge in teaching and learning. Community immersion also may enable educators to provide other types of support for students, such as social welfare services that might go undetected otherwise. Moreover, when they live in students' communities, teachers are able to build lessons and come up with meaningful examples that bridge content, instruction, and learning. Living in the community also gives educators opportunities to deepen their understanding of a place and the nuance that might seem simple, obvious, or mundane. Nuancing, deepening, and aligning community knowledge with academic and social development provide for better professional judgments among educators.
- *Community engagement—engage in community affairs:* Even when they are not able to or simply do not live in the same neighborhood as their school, educators can build knowledge about a community by reading and talking about the goings-on in students' lives and by

TABLE 6.3
Community knowledge to inform practice

Nature of practice	Description
Community immersion	The most ideal form of community learning, where educators actually live in the community of students and schools.
Community engagement	Requires educators to read and study aspects of the community as well as engage in community affairs such as education councils and board meetings to support schools and classrooms.
Community attendance	When educators consistently attend student events in their communities, they can build relationships with their students and learn about them as well as other features of the community as they observe and talk to community members.
Community investment	Requires educators to deliberately spend and offer their financial and other resources in the community of their students and schools.

immersing themselves in the fabric of the community. This form of engagement is varied; some of the practices are more vicarious while others are lived. For instance, educators can attend community meetings, council meetings, religious ceremonies, and community events and reflect on their own lived experiences as educators in relation to those of their students and their families. Moreover, community engagement means educators actively read newspaper articles, blogs, and other materials that help tell a complex story of community. It is important for educators to read widely and to triangulate (engage other information sources) to draw logical conclusions about what is actually happening in a community. *Engagement* in the life of a community, as opposed to mere *participation* or *observation*, is the key. Engagement means that there is real commitment—long term, persistent, and consistent—in the actual affairs of a community for learning, understanding, and development.

- *Community attendance—attend students' extracurricular activities:* In a previous section, I described the role of community attendance as a valuable practice among teachers building relationships with students.

This level of community knowledge requires educators to expand their focal area to include but not be limited to what is happening with a particular student or group of students. When teachers regularly attend community activities for and/or with their students, they have a chance to learn not only about their students but also about the communities in which the activities are taking place. I have learned in my work with teachers that some of them believe their involvement with students should end after the school day (or perhaps after they have coached basketball or lacrosse or directed a band concert or a school play). But attending students' extracurricular activities outside of school in their communities—from baptisms or bar mitzvahs to Little League events or even a pickup basketball game—is a necessary aspect of learning for teachers at all grade levels. Such attendance allows educators to learn about students' interests and talents outside of school, demonstrates a level of care and interest to families and students, builds trust from students and families, and gives educators an opportunity to engage in informal conversations with people that can enhance knowledge.

- *Community investment—invest in the community:* Educators can also build community knowledge and show real commitment by advocating for business and economic development in their schools' and/or students' neighborhoods. In addition to their time, educators should spend some of their economic resources in the community—at grocery stores, gyms, and gas stations. I recall that my mother, who owned a beauty salon in my community, styled several of my teachers' hair when I was a student. Of course, I am confident there were conversations about my academic performance during those appointments but that investment showed a real level of commitment on the part of my teachers. They were building knowledge about me, the community, and other students in the community because my friends' parents also visited my mother's shop for services. Table 6.3 provides a summary of those recommendations.

TENET #3

OPPORTUNITY-CENTERED TEACHING IS ABOUT CURRICULUM CONVERGENCE

As my nine-year-old daughters get older, it is becoming increasingly clear that they will be inundated with outside-of-school activities. These include piano lessons, swimming and gymnastics lessons, and theater classes. And high school students are especially busy. They are participating in afterschool activities sponsored by their schools as well as outside organizations (such as religious organizations and recreation and arts-based centers). Students' school-related activities tend to be classified by schools as *extracurricular*: art, band, theater, and sports. Extracurricular activities also cover many club and social opportunities such as drama, community service, agriculture, and forestry. But such engagement is rarely honored, considered, or linked as a central part of the formal curriculum of schools. These activities tend to be seen as tangential to what really counts as students' learning opportunities. OCT requires that the various curriculum experiences of students converge with the formal school curriculum.

High school students are also starting to date, and they are hanging out with friends. Also, I have met students in different types of environments (suburban, rural, and urban) who were working part-time jobs. But the students in part-time positions in suburban schools tended to be working to "build responsibility," or to "pay for prom" or graduation expenses. Others held part-time jobs (babysitting, clerking at Walmart or a convenience store, or working at a fast-food restaurant) in order to have money for clothes, gas for their "starter" cars, and so forth. Students I have met in rural and urban communities tended to work part-time jobs for different reasons. The most extreme reason has been to support their families. In Pittsburgh, students' work included everything from shoveling snow to tutoring younger students. Regardless of the reason for working part time, those students may struggle to complete extensive homework assignments.

Expanding Lenses

What we sometimes forget is that adolescents' outside-of-school interactions and involvement can be viewed as part of a curriculum, albeit "extra." What if schools better constructed inside-of-school curriculum and learning opportunities with those that are outside of the regular curriculum? How could we build stronger synergy between the formal curriculum practices of school and students' practices and engagement outside of the regular school day? If we understood that students learn outside a formal curriculum, then how could we build curriculum convergence between and among those learning opportunities? If we could build those connections—between the formal in-school curriculum and the informal outside-of-school curriculum—we could potentially decrease the number of hours students spend on redundant learning opportunities that do not add much value to their overall learning and development portfolios.

Students in all types of schools are also charged with what can be described as mountains of homework. I talked with a high school student in a suburban school a few weeks ago who said that he sometimes spends two to three consecutive hours on homework at least twice per week. This student also explained that he was busy with other afterschool initiatives: he was playing sports; he was involved with his school's upcoming play; he was tutoring his younger brother in math. I was anxious for him as he revealed that he sometimes fell asleep during his morning classes because he was exhausted. But the student did not seem concerned. For him, this was a normal part of what it meant to be in high school, and this normalizing began as early as middle school when he became most active in sports.

Homework

But for what purposes are students expected to complete "mountains" of homework each night? Why do schools continue assigning large amounts of homework, including challenging tasks that students or their families do not necessarily understand? Returning to the heart of the intentionality of homework assignments is essential. Clearly, when teachers assign homework, we must ask ourselves just whose work is being developed and evaluated? For instance, a student whose mother is a chemist probably has the ability to help her child with chemistry homework in ways that someone outside of the domain does not. Moreover, even if that parent is too busy to help with homework, this same parent may have the financial resources to hire a tutor to help the student complete a homework task. In both scenarios, the student is at an advantage because of access and opportunity that too many children do not have. These advantages are a direct result of affordances—frankly privileges—that are far beyond the control of students themselves. The assigning of, expectations for, and assessment of homework, then, are equity issues that are not trivial by any means.

What happens when students decide to, need to, or must work a part-time job after school? How do schools account for the hours these students spend at work outside of school? Thus, it is unacceptable, unrealistic, unfair, and inequitable for students to experience the exact same homework requirements. The point is for educators to carefully attend to students' experiences outside of school and design learning opportunities in school that account for those outside-of-school practices. I have learned that a reasonable number of middle and high school students living below the poverty line work part-time jobs (babysitting, mowing lawns, working at fast-food restaurants) to support their families.[9] Many of these students are indeed good students, are motivated to learn, and aspire to earn good grades. A large number of them plan to attend either a two- or four-year institution of higher education. However, they struggle to concentrate on and complete homework tasks after working long hours after-school and on weekends (some closing restaurants and getting home close to midnight or later). One student shared with me that the restaurant where she works as a cashier sometimes requires that she remain for an hour or two to complete closing tasks after the store closes at 10:00 p.m.

Thus, the serious question we should be posing is, In what ways can homework further perpetuate inequity? Although I agree that homework tasks could potentially enhance in-class/in-school learning opportunities, questions regarding uneven access to resources outside of school to assist students should be at the very heart of our philosophies and practices in deciding on homework assignments. These decisions should be made with our heads and our hearts and made to align with students' other outside-of-school practices. Teachers and those responsible for making decisions about homework assignments should be mindful that not all students have access to people and resources necessary for them to reach their full learning capacity through homework tasks.

As educators work to more deeply understand students' outside-of-school experiences and practices and to reconstruct learning opportunities to support them with these practices in mind, I recommend the following:

1. Perhaps more than anything, listen to what students are saying about how they are spending their time before and after school and why.
2. Recognize learning opportunities and skills students might be experiencing in their activities outside of the regular school day (sports, part-time work). This means that educators adjust their practices to better align with students' engagements by not giving as much homework when needed.
3. Coordinate with coaches, directors, club sponsors, and, where possible, employers to construct projects that can be completed over an extended period of time and that connect with subject matter/work inside of school.
4. Recognize broader forms of student effort and engagement as assets to the regular school curriculum.
5. Acknowledge and provide emotional, social, and psychological support for and with students who may be working to support their families. Awareness of this strain can help educators understand why students are tired, disengaged, or overall frustrated by traditional school expectations—such as the completion of homework on a nightly basis.

Students are busy, and their out-of-school time should allow them to experience joy without being penalized. Students who live below the poverty line may be forced to work a part-time job or even to babysit and/

or care for younger siblings or family members after school. Educators must not be dismissive of but should empathize with their students. Educators who practice OCT understand that it takes knowledge, skill, and maturation for any student to balance school and work. However, when there is added pressure for students to work to support their family out of need, OCT would design experiences that rally around these students and families. Indeed, working and taking part in extra activities for pleasure are psychologically different from such engagement out of necessity. Thus, OCT is about curriculum convergence, where the extra, informal, outside of school, and nontraditional forms of curriculum are well aligned with the formal curriculum.

TENET #4

OPPORTUNITY-CENTERED TEACHING IS ABOUT PSYCHOLOGICAL AND MENTAL HEALTH

OCT means that educators understand their own and their students' psychological and emotional health as essential to performance. Although many recommendations regarding teaching and learning center on student learning and development, OCT demands that educators themselves constantly reflect on their own mental and psychological well-being. To be clear, teaching is challenging work that requires educators to engage in practices that cause them to think seriously about how they are really doing in their profession. Teachers are sometimes struggling themselves with psychological strain that may or may not be a consequence of their work in schools. Regardless of the source of the psychological issue, educators across racial, ethnic, gender, socioeconomic, and class lines must be vigilant in building skills to address challenges and strain for their own and their students' well-being.

I have been conducting professional development with teachers in schools for about sixteen years. Most of that professional development has taken place in urban and rural communities—places where students and their families may live below the poverty line; where they are seeing increasing racial, ethnic, and religious diversity; or where students' first language may not be English. Most of my professional development sessions focus on curriculum and instructional practices teachers might consider to more closely align with students' cultures, cultural practices, preferences, interests, and needs.

Although many of the issues educators (and students) identify are similar to those I heard years ago, what I hear and observe among teachers now points more to their psychological and emotional strain. In other words, many teachers appear emotionally drained in their work with students. These teachers are both new and more seasoned in the profession. They teach in the core academic areas as well as elective areas. They are racially and ethnically diverse, and they represent a range of gender identities.

During a recent professional development session in the northeast, a teacher expressed that his/her/their high school students were "unmotivated" about their schoolwork and did not "care" about school. Another teacher countered this view with a more nuanced picture. This teacher talked about the local factory that had recently closed, resulting in unemployment of parents. She talked about the strain the families felt to make ends meet and how many of their students were working part-time jobs, caring for their younger siblings, and helping to support their families financially. This teacher, passionate about her students, was resolute in her desire to offer a more complex story of the students they both taught. The teacher began to cry during her account of what was happening with students. Other teachers, including the teacher who related that students and their parents were disinterested in school, also began weeping. Other teachers chimed in too, sharing what they observed among their students and their families, and wept.

I listened intently and keenly observed. The teachers seemed to struggle with "classroom management." They talked about academic "gaps" students had from elementary and middle school that they were expected to address now that the students were in high school. They talked about social media challenges—how students were misusing technology and, in particular, how some students were being bullied by their classmates. They talked about feeling undersupported, forgotten, and/or misunderstood by the central board of education. But they also talked about how "tired" and "frustrated" they were. The common theme I heard among the teachers' many different views of what was happening in their school was a real sense of emotional drain and strain. The teachers—likely similar to their students—were hurting.

Thus, as teachers are working to meet the needs of their students, who is taking care of them? Who is ensuring teachers have what they need to remain whole and emotionally and psychologically healthy? Of course, teachers' emotional struggles likely have a direct influence on their practices and interactions with students.

Although not the focus of my professional development session, it was clear that I needed to provide some concrete examples of ways teachers could take care of themselves and support each other: (1) exercise; (2) check in with each other on a regular basis; (3) retreat—have regular opportunities to rest and recharge; (4) talk with a nonevaluator (someone who does not have the power to punish them for what they share) about what they are experiencing; and (5) journal about their feelings. Indeed, we should (and must) care about our teachers. People who are hurting tend to hurt others, whether consciously or unconsciously. Moreover, we cannot expect teachers or other educators to solve these challenges on their own. We need to build school systems that recognize the hard work of teachers and support their mental and psychological well-being.

Racism and Mental Health

Too many educators—across the political spectrum—covertly or tacitly believe racism has ended in schools and society. Educators may inaccurately believe that racism is solely a function of individual acts, and because they do not believe they (as individuals) commit racist acts, they fail to understand that racism exists on individual, systemic, institutional, and structural levels.[10] Effects of racism likely influence students' social, affective, and psychological well-being.[11] But when we think of student mental health in schools, some may not consider insidious effects of racism that students of color experience. Indeed, because students' experiences of racism can influence their outcomes, it is essential that we explicitly help educators build tools to address issues of racism and discrimination and avoid color blindness.[12]

As described previously in this book, race is about far more than skin color. Race is constructed physically,[13] contextually,[14] socially,[15] legally,[16] and historically.[17] The meanings, messages, results, and consequences of race are developed and constructed by human beings in society, not by some predetermined set of scientific laws or genetics. Genetically and biologically, individuals are more the same than they are different. Racism and racist acts can and do occur both intentionally and unintentionally, but the effects can be devastating in either case. I have found in my research that White teachers tend to develop and enact curriculum and instructional practices in the classroom with the best of intentions but may still be promoting inequity, whiteness, and racism.[18]

Some students experience what is known in the literature as racial *microaggressions*, which are "brief and commonplace daily verbal, behavioral, or environmental indignities, whether intentional or unintentional, that communicate hostile, derogatory, or negative racial slights and insults toward people of color."[19] Students may experience these events inside or outside of school, but the effects can linger, disrupting their daily thoughts and mental well-being inside of school. In their research of the higher education context, McGee and Stovall found that uncomfortable, unwelcoming, stressful, mentally straining, and hostile campus climates can take a toll on students of color and result in health challenges that can ultimately influence their academic performance.[20] Moreover, these researchers identified disturbing instances of anxiety, frustration, stress, depression, uncertainty, thoughts of suicide, and a host of physical ailments like hair loss, diabetes, and heart disease that they linked to issues of racism and discrimination.

The effects of racism take a toll not only on college students, but also on students in preK–12 classrooms, who may experience racism that shapes their mental and psychological health. One high school student shared the following with me:

> That shit gets on my nerves. These damn White people follow me around the store like I'm going to steal the clothes off their backs. The white boys are in the store and nobody's checking them. It's the brothers they follow around, you know? The shit gets old. I'm sick of it. I've been working since I was twelve and saving. I can buy whatever I want in those damn stores . . . but you know it's because I'm a brother that they checking every move I make.[21]

This student was extremely frustrated and visibly upset because he believed his being followed around the store was a direct consequence of his race. And this outside-of-school, societal experience was referenced during a conversation inside of school, which means that the situation was still impacting his thoughts about what it means to be Black. Yet influences of racism that students experience are rarely addressed inside the school building or in teacher education programs, where teachers are developing the knowledge, skills, and attitudes necessary to meet the needs of all learners.[22]

Another student described this experience with a microaggression: "It's like whenever I say something in class she [the teacher] is like 'that's interesting.' But when a White student says the same thing or makes the same point, she's like 'that's a great point.' I'm thinking, that's exactly what I just said. She always does that so I just stop talking."[23]

Although not always as extreme, some students, as was the case in this example, will decide to disengage and retreat from the discourse of the classroom. Students' withdrawal may be consciously deliberate or subconscious. These two examples from students may be seen from those not experiencing a microaggression as minor or potentially inconsequential. But the accumulation of these microlevel occurrences can take a toll on students of color and become significant over time.[24]

Smith, Hung, and Franklin discuss the possible psychological and mental effects of racial microaggressions and suggest that the persistent experiences of microaggressions can lead to *racial battle fatigue*.[25] In other words, students of color can become psychologically and socioemotionally exhausted from experiencing microaggressions, especially as they persist over time. The student quoted above who decides to stop participating in class—"so I just stop talking"—is suggesting fatigue as a consequence of being targeted (intentionally or unintentionally), and her contributions being devalued. In short, in the powerful words of civil rights leader Fannie Lou Hamer, this student appears to be "sick and tired of being sick and tired" and eventually stops taking part in the classroom discourse.

Addressing Racism and Potential Mental Health Effects

Teachers—regardless of their racial and ethnic background—can successfully teach across racial and ethnic differences if they develop the knowledge and skills to do so.[26] This means that the mostly White teaching force can develop skills to recognize the ways in which their racist acts can have real consequences for students' mental, emotional, and psychological health. Also, teachers can develop tools to help disrupt practices that play a role in incidents of racism experienced by students of color in the classroom. Thus, teachers should develop the skills to identify the ways in which they perpetuate inequity and racism and how they contribute—albeit unintentionally—to students' socioemotional and psychological strain.

Teacher education programs need to better prepare teachers and other educators in schools to identify the ways in which students are experiencing racism. As discussed previously, students may be experiencing microaggressions—being followed around a department store, feeling as if their contributions to discussions are devalued—and consequently may become depressed and frustrated, and eventually stop participating in the classroom. It is unlikely that counselors and psychologists will be able to address these challenges alone and without assistance from other educators, such as teachers. Thus, building on the research of Rowe[27] and Kohli and Solórzano,[28] Howard outlined several powerful suggestions to combat microaggressions and other forms of racism through what is known as microaffirmations.[29] For instance, teachers can affirm and communicate to students a space of solidarity with statements such as "I see you. I value you. I appreciate your differences. I am committed to understanding your needs. I believe in your potential. I want to support you."[30]

Students' mental and psychological well-being is essential to their ability to reach their full capacity in classrooms, schools, and society. Mental health support is needed in schools to expose and respond to the pervasiveness of racism that students still experience every day across this nation. The time is now.

In this chapter, I have defined and outlined four essential elements of what I am calling opportunity-centered teaching. OCT is a collective, not a sole, movement that guides educators to consciously address gaps in opportunity to support student learning and development. The framework places front and center those students who, because of a range of diverse characteristics, are most grossly misunderstood, marginalized, and consequently underserved in classrooms and schools across the United States and beyond. Ultimately, for educators, OCT is about connecting with and caring about the students in front of them. OCT is not static; the practices demonstrate conscious and deep agility as educators stretch their teaching practices in ways that disrupt White supremacy, question the status quo, and shed light on the roots and consequences of inequity and discrimination. OCT complements the knowledge and expertise educators develop about teaching their content and draws from the interests and motivations of students to keep them connected in the classroom.

KEEPING STUDENTS CONNECTED

Recently, I overheard a group of three students talking about school as they walked toward a corner store after leaving their bus stop after school. The gist of their conversation as I listened in, at least for two of them, was that they were "waiting on [their] sixteenth" birthday so they could "quit" school: "Man," one of the students shared, "I'm just waiting on sixteen." Although their discourse suggested that they were going to "quit" school, a more careful analysis of their rationales for leaving school suggested that school had quit on them. In other words, from what they described, they perhaps were being "pushed out," as Monique Morris describes in *Pushout: The Criminalization of Black Girls in Schools*.[31] The third student shared that he was going to just "graduate" and then get a job, and suggested to the other two students that they should not give up when they turned sixteen. But the other two students seemed to be conveying that school was not "for" them—they said that they weren't "school" people.

In retrospect, I wish now that I had been bold enough to walk up to the group of three and engage them. I wish I had asked for more detail about their rationales for either (1) wanting to leave school or perhaps succumbing to being pushed out of school or (2) showing up at school to graduate and get a job. But although I did not talk to the group of students, what I heard was enough for me to be reminded that all over the country, some students are "waiting on sixteen"—a time when they can leave formal schooling.

What is it about how schools are structured that causes some students to believe they are not "school" people? How do we create the types of conditions where students—every single one of them—find the value of education and develop a love for learning? I want to suggest that for students like the three I overheard, educators must do more to help them see themselves as "school" and, more importantly, education people.

But my point is not that schools need to do more to help students conform to the regular normative ways in which schools are organized. My point is that schools need to change so that students (1) see themselves, their identity spaces, goals, and aspirations reflected in the school; (2) are able to build insights about how they can improve their local communities, including situations they are grappling with at home; and (3) understand the multiple layers of their brilliance inside and outside of schools. But to accomplish these three interconnected aims, educators—school leaders, policy makers, school counselors, teachers, and social workers—must resist the urge to necessarily teach the way they were taught. Educators must resist the desire to follow curriculum and instructional practices that do not connect with students and ultimately do not help them learn. And educators must resist the propensity to see the lived experiences of their students as tangential to their very own needs to be seen as human.

It is important to note that educators are able to create conditions where preK–12 students stay connected when they build on the tenets of the OCT Framework:

- Opportunity-centered teaching is about relationships.
- Opportunity-centered teaching is about building community knowledge to inform practice.
- Opportunity-centered teaching is about curriculum convergence.
- Opportunity-centered teaching is about psychological and mental health.

FROM OPPORTUNITY GAPS TO OPPORTUNITY-CENTERED TEACHING

In the final section of this chapter, I stress that OCT can counter, nuance, and disrupt gaps in opportunity in ways that can have a lasting impact on students, their families, and their communities (see the summary in table 6.4). For instance, OCT means that educators reject *color blindness* and consciously construct instructional practices that draw from the racial backgrounds and identities of students. Moreover, OCT insists that teachers carefully and consistently examine micro- (classroom), meso- (school), and macro- (district/society) level policies that perpetually punish, "push out," leave out, stereotype, compare to the White norm, and undervalue students of color.

In addition, through OCT, educators deeply understand that it is their responsibility to study and respond to *cultural conflicts* as they emerge. Educators are reminded that we all have cultural histories and experiences that influence how we see, interpret, and approach the world. This means that educators understand that students and their families will have particular ways of perceiving and valuing what gets covered in a classroom, how it is covered, and why. But their cultural preferences should

TABLE 6.4
From Opportunity Gaps to Opportunity-Centered Teaching

Tenet	Instructional consequences	Opportunity-centered teaching
Color blindness (conceptions of race matter)	Educators teach their students in a myopic manner; they do not consider how racially diverse students experience the world inside the classroom, inside the school, and in society. Curriculum and instructional decisions are grounded in a "White norm" that students of color have to just "deal with" and adapt to.	Instructional practices center, build on and from, and contextualize students' racial identity in and through learning opportunities. Curriculum practices deliberately speak from the point of view of students and communities of color (Black, Brown, Yellow).
	Race is seen as a marginal, not central, aspect of developing lessons and enacting those lessons (teaching).	Racial justice practices are seen as central to decision-making as well as to social and academic success among students.
Cultural conflicts (conceptions of culture matter)	Educators refer students of color to the office when they "misbehave."	Practices are developed and maintained to keep students inside of the classroom and to honor multiple ways of "being" and behaving in a classroom context.
	Students are expected to assimilate into cultural norms that do not take into consideration students' cultural experiences and cultural practices. Educators' cultural ways of knowing are viewed as a normative expectation.	Students' cultural experiences and cultural practices are valued and viewed as assets in the teaching and learning context. Educators view their own beliefs and values as fluid and not always "right." Students are able to voice their views, which may be inconsistent with educators'.

Construct	Instructional consequences	Opportunity-centered teaching
Myth of meritocracy (conceptions of socioeconomic status matter)	Educators do not give students multiple chances for success because they believe students are not working hard enough. Educators do not delve deeply into the reasons behind students' lack of engagement or why students do not complete their homework. The reality that performance may be a consequence of students' financial problems is not considered as a source of "problems" in the classroom.	Educators see students' learning and development as a consequence of multiple factors, including but not limited to "hard work." Educators recognize the many outside-of-school realities and practices among students and their families. They work to demystify the myth that students' lack of progress is a function of their students' own volition. Educators reject a "beat the odds," "no-excuses" orientation to student experience. They see students as whole beings and recognize what they bring to the classroom. They understand that financial challenges must be understood, and accordingly their practices shift to address matters outside of student control that can hinder teaching and learning.

(*continued*)

TABLE 6.4 *(continued)*

From Opportunity Gaps to Opportunity-Centered Teaching

Construct	Instructional consequences	Opportunity-centered teaching
Deficit mind-sets and low expectations (belief systems matter)	Educators spend their time remediating students instead of building on the knowledge students actually bring into the classroom.	Educators draw from multiple data points and assessments to determine student potential and capacity for success.
	Educators refuse to allow students to develop their own thinking skills. Students are expected to regurgitate a right answer that the educator has provided. Very little discussion and creative learning opportunities are available. Students are given busywork in hopes that they will not talk; the classroom is viewed as the educators' space, and students are expected to conform and to be quiet. Educators water down the curriculum and have only minimal curricular expectations.	Educators are innovative and develop creative and powerfully constructed learning opportunities that build students' capacity to think for themselves. Educators co-construct with students the learning environment to encourage students to engage in the learning process and build knowledge in ways that align with what motivates and sustains them. Educators build relevant and responsive rigor. They recognize that students meet expectations that are set and established. Expectations are designed to align with students' capacity.
	Educators focus on basic skills only and push students to get a "right" answer in all academic subjects.	Educators push excellence and reject predetermined notions of "right" and "wrong" answers. They focus on student thinking, and on instructional and curriculum practices (inputs) over test scores (outputs).
	Students are not allowed to think outside the box, to develop critical and analytic thinking skills, or to question power structures in order to improve unfair, inequitable realities.	Students are expected to think critically and analytically. The classroom ethos is designed to be a space of inquiry and critique.
Context-neutral mind-sets (social contexts matter)	Educators do not build on or draw from the knowledge or established resources of the local community. Rather than constructing knowledge with the community, educators act as if they are omniscient and miss or possibly consciously avoid opportunities to build substantive partnerships in the social context.	Educators build on local and broader community knowledge as a foundation to curriculum and instructional practices inside of school. Educators consider the community as a dynamic site for learning (people, places, history).

not be viewed as inferior to others. Indeed, OCT requires that educators understand the cultural practices of students, families, and communities and build on those practices in the classroom in ways that shed light on learning opportunities that may or may not seem foreign to students. OCT, thus, demands that educators approach cultural conflicts between themselves and students as opportunities for educators to grow, adapt, and think deeply about why conflicts, mismatches, and inconsistencies may be emerging. Perhaps more than anything, OCT embraces the idea that students are not to be controlled. An essential element of OCT is for educators to co-construct classroom spaces with students where everyone wants to be.

OCT also rejects the *myth of meritocracy.* Educators see students' learning and development as a consequence of multiple factors, including but not limited to "hard work." OCT demands that students work hard but also that educators understand that hard work is not the only, or the main, factor contributing to the perceived success of students. Rather, OCT advances the notion that student success is often a result and function of material and other resources that fall far beyond students' locus of control. Similarly, OCT pushes for and demands rigor among students because teachers understand their students' capacity as well as the broader expectations for them to succeed.

In addition, OCT rejects *deficit mind-sets and low expectations* because it appropriately responds to the humanity and skill set of students in a particular space. This means that teachers recognize student needs and push their thinking and skills to the next level. The goal of such pushing is not for students to memorize information or meet some White norm but to build a strong repository of skills from which they can draw and learn over time. These skills include but are not limited to problem solving, critical thinking, analytical thinking, questioning, and creativity.

Finally, OCT disrupts and rejects practices of context neutrality. Educators understand that they are teaching and working with particular students at a particular time, with specific needs and assets, and in a particular place. In other words, OCT insists that educators build tools to study and learn about a place (inside and outside of a school). This learning allows them to consider opportunity structures and systems that have historically and contemporarily underserved groups of people through, outside of, and as a result of education. OCT means that teachers see the geography of a school as germane to the types of resources available to all (students and educators alike).

Indeed, OCT requires educators to deeply understand outside-of-school realities that shape what happens inside of school, and OCT means that educators draw on and from the expertise, standpoints, and insights of families, parents, and community members as they work to co-construct learning inside of the classroom and school.

NO NEUTRAL SPACES

Education is a political act and teaching is political work.[32] Opportunity-centered teachers understand that there are no neutral spaces in the work of transformative teaching—educators are either working for diversity and opportunity or they are working against it.

Conclusions and Recommendations for Practice

THROUGHOUT THIS BOOK, I have showcased teachers from two different preK–12 learning environments, one high school and one middle school, who have worked to address diversity and opportunity gaps. Also, I have showcased teachers who teach different subject matter: science, language arts, mathematics, and social studies. I have demonstrated that although these teachers attempted to maximize student potential, they had very different approaches and practices in doing so. I have stressed that all students—not just students of color—possess and contribute layers of diversity to the core of education and society, so emphases related to opportunity and diversity should be incorporated in the educational experiences of all students (including spaces with mostly White students), in a range of different educational contexts. In chapter 5, I wrote about some of the challenges and possibilities regarding diversity and opportunity gaps in preK–12 classrooms that teacher educators must work through, drawing from my own research and work in different teacher education programs. I focused on persistent roles and responsibilities that teacher preparation programs, traditional and nontraditional, have in building opportunity-centered practices necessary for teachers committed to building equitable opportunities for students to learn. While I have outlined some of the challenges that the field of teacher education faces on micro-, macro-, individual, and collective levels, I have additionally provided snapshots of the kinds of mind-sets and practices that demonstrate promise for teaching in preK–12 social contexts. I have made it clear that teaching and preparing teachers to teach can be concomitantly bitter and sweet, and that it is complex, difficult, and multifaceted work—especially when teachers are being prepared to address opportunity gaps.

Teaching inherently brings rewards and challenges. There were times when the teachers I worked with and showcased in this book were at their best, and consequently, according to teachers' reports and my observations and interviews, students seemed to benefit. There were times, too, when teachers encountered difficulties as they worked to design and implement learning and related opportunities for students to build social and academic skills, knowledge, and ability. I have attempted to provide portraits of teachers and teaching that demonstrate the complex, yet promising, dimensions of what it means to teach in different contexts: urban and suburban schools as well as high, middle, and elementary school. These schools enrolled students of varying backgrounds—some living below the poverty line, others who were materially wealthy. Some students were English language learners while others were native English speakers. I have deliberately chosen varied portraits to avoid a propensity to look at any teacher, instructional practice, or teacher education program as a panacea, capable of "curing" deeply ingrained structural problems that educators may face in their classrooms and schools. To be clear, a major message of this book is the need for teachers to build opportunity-centered teaching (OCT) that is transferable to different sociopolitical contexts.

A FINAL LOOK AT THE DIVERSITY AND OPPORTUNITY GAP EXPLANATORY FRAMEWORK

In concluding, I hope it is useful to readers to make explicit links between the mind-sets and practices of the teachers presented here and the five tenets of the Opportunity Gap Framework as introduced and discussed in chapter 1. Mr. Hall, Dr. Johnson, Mr. Jackson, and Ms. Shaw all understood how particular mind-sets could stifle opportunity as they designed curriculum and instructional practices for all their students. In their own relevant and responsive ways, each teacher rejected *color blindness* (and diversity blindness) and understood the salience, relevance, and permanence of race and racism in the fabric of society and therefore in schools.

It is important to note that this book demonstrates educators learning to improve their practices. The idea is that these teachers started where they were but did not stay there. For instance, Mr. Hall did not initially believe race would be a critical component of his work as a science teacher at Bridge Middle School, but early in his career, the experience of being called "racist" by some students intensified his reflection on and centering of race and racial influences in the science classroom. Dr. Johnson, too, was called racist for focusing too much—according to some of her freshman students—on issues of race in curriculum practices. Interestingly, in the cases of both Mr. Hall and Dr. Johnson, it was students who expressed the role and salience of race and racism that helped these teachers reject color blindness as essential to how they thought about their work. Dr. Johnson was clearly not color-blind initially when being called racist by White students, but their words did cause her to think more deeply about how race potentially impacted what students learned. Ms. Shaw also grasped how important it was to understand race in her work because she reflected on her historical reality, having grown up during segregation in the same school district where she now taught.

Additionally, as evident in all four case studies, the teachers understood that *cultural conflicts* were inevitable, and they developed practices through the building and cultivation of relationships to address and work through them. However, the teachers did not always see cultural conflicts as a detriment to their success but as opportunities for them to learn, develop, and mature in the classroom. They started where they were but did not stay there by using student feedback, interactions, and experiences to alter their mind-sets and consequently practices. They used cultural conflicts as opportunities to learn from and with their students, and they recognized that cultural conflicts extended beyond race. The conflicts these teachers learned from included a range of inconsistencies that could exist between themselves and their students, such as generational (age) differences that manifested through different cultural practices.

Ms. Shaw, for instance, was more traditional in how she thought about materialism. She did not engage in many of the cultural practices of her students. She did not listen to the music they listened to. She did not watch the same television shows or spend her outside-of-school time engaged in the same practices as her students. She blamed these inconsistencies on generational divides. However, she did not allow these differences to serve as roadblocks to meaningful relationships with her students. In other words, cultural conflicts were inevitable between a teacher who held such strong beliefs about what was important and students who spent lots of time playing video games and/or listening to music (that she did not necessarily approve of). Still, because she was able to learn from and work through the cultural conflicts, Ms. Shaw built opportunity-centered mind-sets and practices.

Dr. Johnson, in particular, was deliberate in her decision to help her wealthy, mostly White students understand and question a merit-based worldview that many of them brought into the classroom. She focused her instructional and curriculum practices on diversity, culture, and race in a predominantly White social context, where such issues were often completely ignored because people believed they were irrelevant. Through the construction of a safe, unintimidating, and what she described as non-threatening environment, Dr. Johnson helped her students think through the *myths of meritocracy* because she understood them as myths—a point that too many teachers fail to recognize. Dr. Johnson provided space for her students to think about how people in society earn resources and are positioned for success in life. She used her own life experiences of marginalization, inside and outside the classroom, to illustrate to her students that success in society and education is not fully determined by the merits of hard work and ability.

Also, the teachers that I have showcased in the case studies refused to hold *low expectations* for *and deficit mind-sets* of their students. Mr. Jackson astutely used student interests in hip-hop to "hook" his students and build relationships with them. He recognized the rich array of intellect, experience, and know-how that his students possessed and brought into the classroom, and he perceived their appreciation for and interest in hip-hop and popular culture as strengths from which he was able to draw and build. Mr. Jackson did not dismiss his students' interests but attempted to find value in what was of interest to them while simultaneously encouraging students to analyze and critique aspects of hip-hop and pop culture that were disadvantageous and even harmful, such as some of the language used to describe women. Also, Mr. Hall had high expectations of his students, and he refused to allow them to get away with mediocrity—even when they got upset with him for correcting them. He would confront his students when they were not reaching their potential or were acting out because he held his students in high esteem. However, Mr. Hall's high expectations far exceeded academic goals. He also held his students accountable for excellence in other areas of their learning and development, such as how they behaved with their friends and other teachers, not only in his classroom but in the broader school context.

In addition, the teachers highlighted in this book seemed to understand that they conducted their work in a particular social context and refused to adopt *context-neutral mind-sets* (and consequently practices). They recognized that their practices had to be tailored to be responsive to the needs of students (and other adults such as colleagues, administrators, and parents) in real school contexts. The teachers understood that knowing a subject matter such as mathematics, language arts, or science, while certainly necessary, was insufficient to successfully address the diversity-opportunity gaps that existed in their different spaces. All the teachers seemed to understand that people—a unique collection of adults and students—created the contexts in which they taught and learned, and their challenge was to deepen their knowledge and skill about the idiosyncrasies inherent in their teaching situations in order to provide effective learning opportunities for all their students. General strategies and principles that teachers develop to build their conceptual and practical knowledge are important; however, the skills and ability to translate, adapt, and implement those strategies and principles at the appropriate times, with particular people, and with meaningful intent and rationale are more critical.

The six White teachers learning to teach in chapter 5 provided what I believe to be essential insight into the kinds of challenges that we face in preparing teachers to address diversity and close opportunity gaps. While the White teachers grappled with understanding the role of diversity in their teaching, four of them seemed to build the kinds of opportunity-centered mind-sets and practices that I believe were necessary to teach all students well.

Collectively, the teachers in this book represent an important range of diversity: a White man, two Black women, one Black man, and six White women. I realize, though, that the perspectives of teachers from other racial and ethnic backgrounds (such as Latinx and Asian) are not represented in this book. I am mindful of and sensitive to this void. Still, I am hopeful that readers can acquire a range of different insights and perspectives from the educators presented here. Perhaps more important, I am hopeful that readers learn from the practices of these teachers. To conclude, I share some troubling stories about diversity and opportunity. Although Latinx and Asian American teachers are not showcased in this book, I provide snapshots of Latinx students and Asian American students throughout this book.

It is important for readers to focus on the opportunity-centered practices of these teachers rather than the teachers themselves. Focusing on these teachers might send the message that the power of the transformative practices as described is a result of these individuals who carry within them something extraordinary that not all teachers can accomplish. To the contrary, although these teachers developed the mind-sets and world-views necessary to look inwardly and improve, other teachers can adjust their practices through opportunity-centered framing and approaches.

TROUBLING STORIES OF OPPORTUNITY AND DIVERSITY

The first story I share below is about English language learners and opportunity structures; the second is about societal perceptions that an emphasis on diversity and opportunity is not necessary.

Short Story 1: English Language Learners Can Benefit "Our Children"

Several years ago, I was invited to give a talk in a moderately large city in the northern United States. During the visit, I was driven around and shown several local schools. My tour guide explained, quite proudly, that the district had begun busing immigrant "non-English-speaking" students to one of the "best" local schools in the district. Even more intriguing for my tour guide was the reality that the district had developed policies that would "pour dollar after dollar" into the school over the next five years so that the "non-English-speaking" students would "learn to speak English." What seemed to excite the tour guide more than anything was the reality that "our English-speaking students [mostly White, upper-class English speakers] in the school were also learning to speak different languages as well, mostly Spanish." It is also important to note that the tour guide did not stress how important it would be for the "non-English speakers" to maintain their native language and build or add to their first language. The emphasis was on the opportunity for those speaking Spanish as their first language to learn English, and for native English speakers to learn Spanish.

What appeared obvious from the guide's description and responses to my questions about the policies and practices in the district and the school where the English language learners would be bused was his interest in the fact that the mostly White, upper-middle-class students were acquiring language and becoming bi- or trilingual. My tour guide and the policy and decision-making body on the district board realized how important it would be for children from higher socioeconomic backgrounds (and perhaps those from lower socioeconomic backgrounds as well) to speak multiple languages in this increasingly diverse country (and world). The district and school were willing to negotiate and provide the resources necessary for the "non-English speakers" to "learn English" because they had figured out that the majority White and wealthy students would of course benefit from the various racial, ethnic, cultural, and linguistic backgrounds that would be represented in the school. There was a convergence of interests between those in power and the "non-English speakers."[1]

I share this story because it is representative of the mind-set and commitments that some have regarding opportunity and diversity. My tour guide was resolute in his position that "our children get to learn Spanish." Sadly, opportunity structures for some groups of students are contingent upon the opportunities and benefits of those in power. In this sense, it is when those in power determine that there is some benefit to them that they are willing to negotiate and do what is right. From an equitable perspective, where we provide students and communities with what they need to succeed and move away from the idea that all should receive the exact same, our goal should be to support students—all of them—as "our" children. And we should do what is right because that is what we are supposed to do as educators and citizenry—not because we are expecting something in return for our own interests. Opportunity-centered practices and policies for all our students should be designed so they can reach their full capacity, even when the benefits for those in power are not so obvious. What my tour guide seemed to forget was that all students must be considered "our children," and that we should always be mindful of and committed to providing optimal opportunities for every student in our schools and districts, not just when we find compelling benefits for another group of students.

Still, when we work toward opportunity-centered practices and address and center diversity, the benefits far exceed a targeted group. As Hilliard explained, "Any reform that benefits those students who are poorly served always works to the benefit of all."[2]

Short Story 2:
Diversity Is What's Wrong with Our School Systems

The second story I share here is one that I experienced after providing professional development on "diversity and education" for a US school district. After my presentation, I was interviewed by the news media, and below are some comments I received regarding my work with the district (note: the statements are taken directly from a public blogging website regarding my visit to the district):

> Paid for Propaganda, nothing less. In the beginning, Immigrants to America came here to learn our culture and to be assimilated into AMERICAN culture. The idea today is to forcefully insert your ideology upon Americans who do not agree with changing what has taken centuries to perfect. At least as near perfection as man is ever likely to achieve. The handwriting is on the wall, America, the writing began immediately after WW2 with the importation of masses of refugees totally different in culture. And values. What kind of idiots worked to bring in people who had just yesterday been conquered by America in War? Many bring a dagger to place in our backs. A nation must have a common language, familiar culture, and true LACK of the very thing you are hyping.

When I shared these comments with one of my colleagues, a White man, he was furious. I was not angry, however, because I was not surprised. The mind-set, belief system, and position of the writer projects ideological dissonance—true variation in the ways in which people think, talk, and write about diversity—in the United States. But the view of the blogger is not distinct, isolated, or an outlier in the grand narrative of how people view the role and salience of diversity in the US. I have worked for many years with teachers in professional development across the country who share this respondent's position and view, though their thoughts might not be expressed in the exact language above. The real question is: How do teachers with such mind-sets and positions teach and provide opportunities for all students? How do we provide educative opportunities for people to realize they are in fact immigrants themselves—that the United States is a nation of immigrants? How do we help people recognize the flaws and imperfections of this country—particularly practices that continue to divide and undermine a true democracy? How do students fare when educators and others in society believe that they should just assimilate into a one-dimensional "American culture" that rejects other important cultural markers and features? How do we encourage educators to use blogs like those above to help students build critical and interrogative skills to question what they read and believe?

Similar comments came from another person who expressed disdain for my presentation to teachers about "diversity and education" and also with the district for inviting me. Consider the statement below, again copied directly from the blogging site:

> Diversity is what is wrong with our school system now. this is still america teach [h]ow to be american and think for themselves. the schools have become indoctrination centers. they can't read are right are think for themselves. miseducated is what you get out of Vanderbilt and miller they all live of tax dollars.

Again, some in society and consequently in education believe that matters of diversity are "what is wrong" in school systems all over the United States. Based on what I hear from teachers and other educators (including administrators, counselors, school psychologists, and social workers), some believe that schools should teach "how to be American." Although nebulous at best, the quote above suggests that to be "American" means that we should not focus on diversity. It is also unclear who the writer is referring to as those who cannot read and write. There is an implicit message in the blog post that diverse students are those who cannot "read are right" (note the incorrect spelling as written in the blog). Such mind-sets and positions suggest that there is still much work to be done to transform mind-sets and belief systems related to the benefits and assets that all students bring to our learning contexts—even when we are not prepared to recognize those assets and teach to the diversity of their brilliance.

GET FIRED UP!

I have decided to use words that I convey to end many of my class sessions and professional development workshops across the United States and beyond: *get fired up!* The goal is to inspire, motivate, and encourage readers to move powerful, transformative, caring, revolutionary, and equitable ideas into action. Books, journal articles, newspaper articles, and a range of other social and professional media are inundated with reports of problems facing preK–12 students and teachers across US society and beyond. The reports often focus on problems of opportunity and diversity, but too rarely center on ways to address, counter, and disrupt the issues. With some concretized ways of thinking about opportunity-centered practices and policies, I am hopeful that readers are now "fired up" about reenvisioning and reimagining possibilities for their curriculum development and instructional practices in various learning contexts.

I am also hopeful that educators will choose to build relationships with students and to treat them like people who are developing rather than people who are prisoners, focusing on rules to the detriment of learning the explicit curriculum (see the important work of Eisner and of McCutcheon regarding the nature and form of the curriculum).[3] Below, I share short story 3, Hallway Example of a School-to-Prison Pipeline Practice, and a final short story 4 in this chapter, Classroom Example of a School-to-Prison Pipeline Practice.

Short Story 3: Hallway Example of a School-to-Prison Pipeline Practice

I recall walking down a hallway in an urban elementary school in the Midwest when a teacher proclaimed: "We are not moving until I see a straight line." I was stunned as I noticed the third graders desperately, attentively trying to figure out how to construct the hallway line straight enough so that they could "move." For six minutes, the teacher stood with a look of disgust on her face because the students apparently could not make the line straight enough. As an observer, I wondered what kinds of learning opportunities the students were supposedly gaining and concurrently missing during her six minutes of "teaching" the students that they would not move until she saw a straight line. This story is not unique. All over the United States but especially in schools that are highly populated with Black and Brown students, those whose first language is not English, those who live below the poverty line, and those who vary in their learning, teachers focus so much on rules that they sometimes forget they are working with human beings who are developing and grappling with a range of life occurrences, not a group of young prisoners whom they believe they must control. Elsewhere, my colleagues and I debunk the idea that students' bodies should be controlled. Although we often hear teachers lament how "out of control" students are, we believe that students *should* be out of control. Our goal should not be to control students but to co-construct the kinds of learning environments with students that allow them to make mistakes and to control their own bodies (and minds).[4]

While I have spent a considerable amount of time visiting urban schools (from elementary to high) where the students are viewed as "problems," I have also observed suburban and independent schools. What I have learned is that despite these different social contexts, student behaviors are similar in many ways: students talk sometimes without raising their hands, they have conflicts with their classmates, they forget to complete their homework, they sometimes use profanity, and they even struggle to stand in a straight line. However, there is a stark difference between how teachers handle students' mistakes in suburban and independent schools. In many urban schools, students are treated like prisoners (see the important work of Noguera for more on this), while in suburban and independent schools, students are treated as individuals who are learning and developing.[5] In communicating with teachers of mostly White, wealthy children, teachers articulate how students will "get there" over time. But in many urban and highly diverse schools, students are seen as incapable of success. Students in urban schools are viewed as those who should already possess what they need to succeed. Because children tend to need support to get better, these students are those who educators often write off as prison-bound. However, educators may fail to understand that the practices they promote (standing in straight lines, not talking, following mundane directions) are the very practices that push students into the criminal justice system.

Indeed, these students are learning how to follow rules but are rarely learning how to develop their own academic, social, and political awareness and positions inside the classroom. These students are demonstrating with their actions that something is wrong with how school is structured, but they may not be able to articulate the issue. And the issue is this: when we push rule following and attempt to control students rather than honoring students and helping them develop, schools are preparing their students for jobs that require these skills—to take orders and to be controlled. Suburban and independent schools as Noguera explains are preparing their students to develop and *give* orders.

It is important to note that I am not suggesting that teachers should not help students understand rules and the consequences for not following them. Indeed, many of our students have only known or experienced the negative consequences of what it means not to follow rules. Still, I understand that we must have rules and laws in society and schools in order to live and function. However, focusing on rules over helping students develop, to be seen as young people who have the capacity to learn and grow over time based on their social world, is problematic. Yet prison-like practices are pervasive in some schools across the United States. But these practices can change. I am hopeful that OCT will assist teachers in shifts in practices that disrupt hallway-school-to-prison practices such as the one described here.

Short Story 4: Classroom Example of a School-to-Prison Pipeline Practice

When I began my career attempting to extend the work of Ladson-Billings documenting successful practices of teachers in urban schools, I was stunned by some of the nominations I received from other educators about what they perceived as "successful" practices.[6] One recommendation I received in my efforts to identify practices I could study was an elementary school classroom in an urban community. Although the teacher's practices were identified as exceptional, she used writing as a form of punishment when students were "out of line." When I visited her classroom, I observed the following written on the board in the left-hand corner:

> *Copy 100 times:* I will not talk while others are talking.
>
> *Copy 50 times:* I will keep my hands to myself when walking to the lunchroom.
>
> *Copy 50 times:* I will raise my hand before answering a question.

It was clear by the way the directions were written on the board that they were a permanent feature of the classroom. According to the purple writing on the board, the words were not to be erased. There was a purple horizontal line that separated the directions from the other space on the board that could be used. It was clear that these directions—a writing assignment—were consistently used as a means to correct behavior among the second-grade students.

There were likely several learning opportunities embedded in this practice. One lesson for sure was that writing was a punishment for them. How can students develop an appreciation and love for writing when it is used to punish or correct them?

But writing can be a vehicle of emancipation. When I was a student, it was writing that made such a powerful impact on me. I was able not only to write about literary elements, as expected in my English arts classes, but also to express my frustration about situations I was experiencing and observing in society. I even recall writing to express my frustration about my teachers' assignments. I also wrote about disagreements I had with my parents and siblings. Although I dared not call it such, I began journaling at an early age, which allowed me to situate myself within a broader social context.

But how can we propel students' writing interest? When helping students see writing as a space and tool of freedom, teachers should consider the following:

1. Stress the *when* and *where* of writing: Students need to be encouraged to write (and read) at any time, not just for school-related work. It was understanding the "when" of writing that helped me express myself and build my identity because I was able to write at times that made sense for me. In other words, writing is an anytime practice that can allow students to deepen their knowledge and ideas about a particular issue. The freedom of writing whenever one desires is a gift from which I benefited immensely.
2. Expand the *what* of writing: When students start to realize that writing is a form of expression that can and should consider a range of topics and themes, they are better able to identify topics and issues that resonate with them as students/human beings. Student freedom on the focus/content of writing rejects prepackaged writing assignments that force them to write only about what they are told. Teachers often pretend students have choice in their selections when making assignments for term papers or short essays. But students know this is rarely the case.
3. Reimagine the *how* of writing: Most teachers have bought into, adopted, and supported a standardized way of communicating. But stressing standardized writing and forms of communication can stifle students' ideas and desire to engage in writing. We have socially constructed standardized ways of being that can counter some students' ways of communicating.
4. Be explicit about the *why* of writing: Teachers have an extraordinary opportunity to help students consider the potential healing nature of writing. Showing students how writing can bring joy and freedom can transform their perception of writing as merely an exercise to meet a classroom assignment or expectation.
5. Write *across* the curriculum: What I have observed is that when the above recommendations are in place, expanding students' opportunities to write across the curriculum can increase their willingness and

interest in writing. To be clear, my point is not that additional writing time (in the traditional sense in which schools tend to increase student writing) will automatically propel student interest in writing for freedom. But when we reimagine what writing can do, for whom, and for what purposes, students can start to imagine writing as far more than an exercise for the sake of it.

Supporting students to write for freedom requires that we make a culture shift in the very ways that we as educators support and co-organize writing opportunities in schools. Students have an opportunity to heal from varying forms of oppression they have experienced inside and outside of school and write for freedom if we as educators get out of their way and get out of our own way. I am hopeful that as teachers adopt OTC worldviews and approaches that they will resist classroom-level school-to-prison pipeline practices.

SCHOOL LEADERSHIP

Although teachers, other educators in the school, students, and community members co-create the ethos of a school, it is the school leader who develops the kind of environment that honors students and that allows students to make mistakes. Moreover, principals help create a learning environment that does not focus on rules over other important aspects of teaching and learning.

Thus, as school leaders co-construct a school climate that promotes development over punishment, I offer the following imperatives:

- *Imperative #1:* Professionals—including superintendents, principals, social workers, school counselors, and teachers—need (and deserve!) opportunities and especially time to develop and improve their practices.
- *Imperative #2:* Principals need support to get better too. We should deliberately support principals/leaders in schools to improve for sustainability. A coaching model from effective leaders could really help

principals think through their curriculum and instructional leadership. Many spend their time on punishment structures in the name of "discipline." But management issues decrease when students are actively engaged in the classroom, school, and community due to effective instruction. Thus, leaders need to focus on good teaching and classroom management challenges will take care of themselves.
- *Imperative #3:* Principals need to hire and/or provide space for the development of teachers who know their content/subject matter well but also understand how to teach the students in front of them. Teachers can learn to build instructional practices that help students build knowledge, but they must have time and opportunities to build the skills. Unfortunately, teachers and principals alike tend to have very little professional development time to get better.
- *Imperative #4:* We need to make sure families and communities are actively involved in the education of their children. How can we build on the many strengths and assets of our communities inside of schools? Educators can learn much from families and communities.
- *Imperative #5:* Our focus should be on helping students develop and, in particular, build a love of learning—the benefits of education (not schooling!).[7]

Indeed, the answers to problems and challenges in schools can be found in the context of the situation.[8] Principals have the potential to demonstrate their leadership by working with all—students, teachers, counselors, social workers, and community members—to co-construct an environment where students take risks, are inquisitive, and love learning. School climates can change when we see students as developing beings—human beings capable of improving. But for students to get better, we, the adults in the school, must improve, too. My challenge for principals is to help create these types of spaces that honor development over punishment.

Even when the practices I describe above are commonplace among teachers, I hope they will *not stay there.* I hope educators will "get fired up" and continue to grow.

IN CONCLUSION

If viewed separately, the individual portraits of these teachers and their practices provide some powerful narratives of teachers working to address the diverse needs of all their students. However, collectively, the narratives in this book provide important broader implications beyond individual classrooms. Educators are invited to assess their current circumstances, draw meaning from these narratives, and transfer the lessons learned that are relevant and appropriate for their practices. I have chosen to share the kinds of practices, mind-sets, strategies, and ideas that I have seen in my own empirical work over the years as well as insights garnered from an established body of educational research, theory, and practice. Thus, it is critical that readers consider the broader implications and recommendations offered in this book both tacitly and overtly.

In a similar vein, I encourage educators to critique the practices and mind-sets of these teachers. There are no perfect practices or people in education. We must do our very best to meet the complex and challenging needs of all students. However, while recognizing the imperfection among policy, practice, and people, it is essential to think about changes necessary to address opportunity gaps that may exist. When teachers transform their individual practices in one school, for instance, their students inevitably have an opportunity to benefit across a grade and age span.

Indeed, I want to pose a set of questions for individual teachers to ponder as they transfer lessons in this book to their particular classrooms: What would happen if a group of teachers transformed their practices to address opportunity gaps as they build opportunity-centered practices? What if an entire school decided to refocus its efforts to build on some of the principles, recommendations, and suggestions discussed here? In what ways might students benefit when teachers collectively transform the very fabric of an entire school or district? The answers to these questions are dynamic. Fundamentally, I believe that individual teachers can make a difference; but I believe that groups of teachers, schools, districts, regions, and entire states can make a *huge* difference in addressing opportunity gaps that exist in preK–12 social contexts. Thus, while I certainly am hopeful that individual teachers will change—significantly improve—their practices, I am even more hopeful that groups of teachers and administrators will come together to change and improve broader institutional, systemic, and structural factors that prevent some students from succeeding.

I am not only optimistic about the possibilities for teachers and students, I am also *hopeful* about what is possible when we all refuse to accept injustice. As philosopher Cornel West wrote in the preface to the important book *Restoring Hope: Conversations on the Future of Black America*:

> Hope is not the same as optimism. Optimism adopts the role of the spectator who surveys the evidence in order to infer that things are going to get better . . . Hope enacts the stance of the participant who *actively struggles* [emphasis added] against the evidence in order to change the deadly tides of wealth inequality, group xenophobia, and personal despair. Only a new wave of vision, courage, and hope can keep us sane—and preserve the decency and dignity requisite to revitalize our organizational energy for the work to be done. To live is to wrestle with despair yet never to allow despair to have the last word.[9]

Thus, I conclude this book with optimism and hope (and perhaps hope more than optimism) that educators will be courageous enough to do what is right on behalf of students, all students, every day, even when no one else is looking and even when no one else will. Opportunity-centered practices, policies, and mind-sets require that we reject neutrality in our work. Indeed, there is absolutely no room for neutral spaces in our journey toward opportunity and diversity. The teachers in this book remain, as do I, critical of current social, historic, economic, and political ills and are concurrently optimistic and *hopeful* about the change that can emerge when we refuse to do business as usual in education. I am optimistic that we all will get better—that every educator who reads this book will START WHERE THEY ARE, BUT WON'T STAY THERE!

Epilogue

IN THIS EPILOGUE, I describe how I came to learn about and share the practices of Mr. Hall, Dr. Johnson, Mr. Jackson, Ms. Shaw, and the six White teachers learning to teach presented in this book. I also briefly discuss important insight to help readers understand *what* I did in collecting these stories, *where* the stories were collected, *why* I made particular decisions in collecting and reporting the narratives, and *how* I collected and analyzed the research. I begin with a brief discussion of my research journey to explain who I am and who I am becoming as a social scientist and how I have come to engage in my work.

A BRIEF GLANCE AT MY RESEARCH JOURNEY

Since 1998 when I began doctoral study at The Ohio State University, I have been interested in the roles teachers play in students' opportunities to learn in a range of sociocultural contexts. While in graduate school, I participated on a research team with educational anthropologist Peter Demerath, who helped me develop my research knowledge and skills as I learned to study real people in real places. Indeed, he taught me to make the familiar strange and the strange familiar as I attempted to understand people, places, policies, and practices. I was able to build and sharpen my research skills on that team because we pushed each other to think more deeply about what we were observing, how we were developing conjectures, what interview questions we would pose, how (and why) we would analyze documents, and how we would represent what we learned to others. I was propelled to deepen my understanding about, construct, and respond to important epistemological questions like how I came to know what I believed I knew and what evidence I was drawing from to make claims. That research team propelled me to examine my ways of knowing as I attempted to build knowledge about practice. Further, being in the field, in a high school, allowed me to implement and practice what I was reading about in my research courses as a student.

While I was collecting data, I was working closely with and learning with my major professors, curriculum theorist Gail McCutcheon and educational psychologist Anita Woolfolk Hoy. Although they approached their research differently—they posed different types of questions and designed their studies in ways that did not seamlessly complement each other—I learned the important lesson that our research designs should in fact be secondary to the kinds of questions we posed. Thus, I learned about qualitative research as well as survey research working with my mentors. I have gained tremendously from the opportunity to learn different methods for studying problems and solutions in education. Importantly, both McCutcheon and Woolfolk Hoy were interested in studying teachers and their practices, and these interests (consistent with my own) intensified as I worked with them.

I also studied with Professor Tyrone Howard, whose research had already interrogated what culturally relevant[1] and culturally responsive[2] teaching looked like in practice. Drawing from his ethnographic studies of teachers' practices, Professor Howard taught me the importance of centering issues of equity not only in my research designs but also in the tools I used to analyze human experience as well as make sense of the data I analyzed. It was through the leadership and guidance of Professor Howard that I read germinal texts about equity, justice, diversity, and culture that would be essential for my own conceptual, empirical, and epistemological journey as a university professor and researcher. Moreover, my knowledge and understanding of theory, centered on race, equity, culture, and diversity, was greatly enhanced under the guidance and support of Professor Cynthia Dillard.

My earliest research as a participant on the research team was conducted in a suburban school, what I have called Stevenson High School in this book. With a colleague and a mentor, I studied student culture and student identity development. For a thorough synopsis of the work we engaged in at that school, see "Decoding Success: A Middle-Class Logic of Individual Advancement in a U.S. Suburb and High School," by Demerath et al.[3] Though my research skills and abilities deepened and my understanding of student culture and identity at Stevenson High elevated, I still wondered about the influence of teachers in the construction of students' perception of culture and student identity development. Thus, my individual research began to take on a different shape and focus. I increasingly became interested in matters of diversity (especially race), and I wanted to know about social interactions between students and between teachers and students.

Moreover, I was interested in the curriculum and the role race played in the classroom. As I attempted to understand and deepen my knowledge about some of these interests more clearly and precisely, I began to study the practices of several teachers at Stevenson High, including Dr. Johnson. Although I studied other teachers, I became intrigued by the ways in which Dr. Johnson talked about her role in the mostly White context and, perhaps more than anything, I was motivated to learn more about her and her practices and interactions because her students seemed so captivated by her, her curriculum development, and her teaching practices.

My interests in race and student learning opportunities did not shift much after I completed my graduate studies. When I moved to Vanderbilt University in Nashville, Tennessee, my first faculty position, I immediately began collecting stories about the teaching, learning, curriculum, and diversity (mostly race) nexus. I first studied this interplay at a local urban high school. Later, I moved my research project to a local urban middle school, what I refer to in this book as Bridge Middle School. Although I worked in a local high school for one academic year, I realized working in a middle school would allow me to more deeply understand a broader range of students and teachers over time. Students in middle school in terms of their development were just beyond elementary school, and they were moving toward high school. Indeed, I work with both elementary and high school educators, and the middle school environment allowed me a window into both. At Bridge Middle School, I studied the practices of six teachers from different subject-matter areas. I showcase three of the teachers' practices I studied in this book: Mr. Hall, Mr. Jackson, and Ms. Shaw.

It is also important to note that I was a teacher volunteer at another local urban middle school in the same city. In this capacity, I served as a language arts teacher for eighth-grade male students. In that space, I intentionally did not collect any data systematically or attempt to write about my experiences and learning. I decided not to publish research articles and books about that volunteer work because I believe it is important for researchers and professors to provide service to local schools and districts as they are able to learn from and with educators and students. My volunteer work at the local middle school taught me a tremendous amount. The principal invited me to work with a group of eighteen students who had not passed the state-mandated test in language arts. Many of them were considered difficult to teach. My experience there was important for many reasons. For instance, it insisted that I test some of the principles, conjectures, and ideas I have come to believe and that I share with teachers in professional development and in my teacher education courses. In addition, it enabled me to stay grounded in real classroom problems and to design instructional practices to support student learning and development. All of these experiences shaped me, helped me analyze and write about the evidence presented through these narratives, and propelled me to write and revise this book.

BRIDGE MIDDLE SCHOOL

The names of all the people and places showcased in this book are pseudonyms to maintain their anonymity. Constructed in 1954, Bridge Middle

School is an urban school in a relatively large city in the southeastern region of the United States. At the time of the study, according to a Bridge County real estate agent, houses in the community then sold for between $120,000 and $175,000. There were also many rental houses zoned to the school. Many of the neighborhood students from higher socioeconomic backgrounds who were zoned to Bridge Middle School attended private and independent schools in the city rather than Bridge. The practice of students' attending private and independent schools rather than their zoned school was very common in the district. A larger number of students from lower socioeconomic backgrounds attended Bridge.

Bridge Middle School was considered a Title I school, which meant that the school received additional federal funds to assist with instructional and related resources and needs. The school accommodated approximately 350 students. While the demographics were constantly evolving because of the transience among students, the most current information available during the study revealed that 59.8 percent of the students at Bridge were African American, 5.6 percent Hispanic American, 31.6 percent White, 0.3 percent American Indian, and 2.8 percent Asian American, a truly racially and ethnically diverse learning environment (note these are the demographic labels shared with me, and I have not altered that labeling here). The free and reduced-price lunch rate was 79 percent. At the time of the study, there were twenty-seven teachers at the school, 45 percent of them African American and 55 percent White. Seven of the teachers were men and twenty were women.

Bridge Middle School was known for competitive basketball, wrestling, track, and football teams. The school building was brick, and windows were usually open during the spring and summer. Although not overly uncomfortable, many of the school spaces did not have air conditioning. There was a buzzer at the main entrance of the school. Visitors rang the bell, were identified by a camera, and allowed to enter the school by one of the administrative associates in the main office. When I visited the school, I signed a logbook in the main office before proceeding to the classrooms, the cafeteria, or the library. During my first month of conducting this research, one of the hall monitors insisted that I go back to the main office to get a red visitor's name badge, so I could be identified as a visitor/researcher. The floors in the hallways were spotless. There was no writing or graffiti on the walls. Especially during the month of February, Black history/heritage/celebration posters and bulletin boards occupied nearly all the wall space in the hallways and classrooms.

Why Bridge Middle School

I selected Bridge Middle School because it was known in the district and community as one of the "better" middle schools in the urban area. For instance, when I asked practicing teachers enrolled in my classes at the university to "community nominate" some of the "strong" and "better" urban schools in the city, Bridge Middle School was consistently nominated.[4] In addition, people in the supermarket would also mention Bridge as one of the "better" schools in the district upon my queries. When I met with a school official at the district office to gain entry into a school, he also suggested Bridge as a place to work. I wanted to learn in a school that was considered urban and highly diverse. Building on the research traditions of Jackie Irvine, Gloria Ladson-Billings, Geneva Gay, Vanessa Siddle Walker, Michelle Foster, Carol Lee, and Tyrone Howard, I also wanted to study successful educational practices of teachers working with students of color and those living below the poverty line.

STEVENSON HIGH SCHOOL

Stevenson High School was an economically affluent midwestern suburban high school. It accommodated approximately 1,650 students, with a mostly racially and ethnically homogeneous population. Specifically, during the time of the study, 86 percent of Stevenson High students were White or European American, 4 percent were Black or African American, and 10 percent were Asian American; 2 percent spoke limited English, 2 percent came from low-income homes, 7 percent received special education, and the turnover rate was 3 percent. At the time of the study, prices for houses on the real estate market in the district ranged from around $150,000 to $930,000, with the majority being on the higher end for most students. It was one of two high schools in the Stevenson County District.

Stevenson High School was known for competitive soccer and lacrosse teams. Constructed in 1992, the school building was brick, and the architecture was modern and sophisticated. A large portion of the common area was carpeted, and parts of it resembled a coffee shop more than a school lunchroom. Students often congregated there before school, during lunch, and after classes. The hallways were light and airy, and artwork was displayed throughout most of the hallways, including original pieces by Stevenson High seniors.

Why Stevenson High School

As mentioned, during my doctoral studies, I was invited to join a research project that was occurring at Stevenson High School. Later, I decided to continue working at Stevenson to collect narratives for my independent research. I chose to work at Stevenson because the space allowed me to understand the interplay between teachers' identities (especially their racial and ethnic identities) and their skills, abilities, and choices in developing and implementing curriculum practices. Also, the context allowed me to study how, whether, and to what extent issues of diversity and multicultural education were incorporated into student learning, by whom, and why in the mostly White and wealthy social context. Finally, the social context allowed me to understand social relationships and interactions between students and teachers, especially in the mostly White context. In particular, my research with Dr. Johnson allowed me to consider what issues of diversity and opportunity really meant in a predominantly White teaching context when a teacher deliberately developed, implemented, and transformed curriculum practices, centering race and culture.

TEACHER EDUCATION PROGRAMS

I have worked with preservice teachers in different teacher education sites over the years. While I have worked with teachers from diverse backgrounds, the majority have been White women. These teacher education programs have varied in terms of size, research emphasis, and commitment to issues of diversity and social justice. I included in this book what I consider representative stories of six White teachers to provide a picture into some of the tensions, challenges, and possibilities that can emerge when teacher educators and teacher education programs attempt to foster and support teachers' learning, thinking, and practices related to diversity and opportunity.

HOW I COLLECTED THE NARRATIVES

In this book, I report on a collection of qualitative studies I have conducted over the years. In qualitative research, researchers systematically design studies to learn, in depth, about people in places and situations. I see qualitative research as an opportunity to study the nouns and verbs of human experience: we study people, places, products, things, and ideas. We also study the action verbs of those nouns: in qualitative research, we observe what people actually do and say.

I invite readers to transfer what they read into their own practices, based on aspects of the research that they find applicable and relevant to their particular situations. Qualitative research allows researchers to construct stories of participants that are grounded in participants' reality; in my study of the teachers showcased in this book, I was able to uncover not only important dimensions of their practices but also their conceptions, beliefs, and thinking about those practices. I learned with, from, and about the teachers through three primary data sources, tools, and techniques: (1) interviews, (2) observations, and (3) document analyses. I have found that being able to study not only what people say but also what they do—their practices and actions—provides for analytic sites that help nuance, complicate, confirm, and clarify what I learn in a study.

Interviews

Interviews played an important role in my ability to generate and convey the narratives of each teacher as well as the collective narrative of the six White teachers learning to teach.[5] In particular, I conducted interviews with each of the teachers to gain their perspectives about what I was learning and observing regarding their curriculum and instructional practices related to diversity and opportunities. I conducted these interviews over time to gauge how their thoughts and positions shifted at different time periods. The interviews typically took place during the teachers' lunch hour or planning block, or after school. Interviews with the participants were audiotaped. I (rather than a transcriptionist) transcribed the tapes for Dr. Johnson to gain a deeper level of intimacy with the data; I hired a transcriptionist to transcribe the interviews with the other teachers due to time restrictions. It is important to note that while I conducted formal interviews with all the teachers showcased in this book, including those learning to teach, I also documented countless informal interviews with these teachers and captured their words and perspectives in my observation notebook.

Social Context Observations

In addition to conducting interviews, I observed the teachers in their teaching practices and other contexts in the school. My opportunity to observe the teachers in their classroom and in the broader school community allowed me to deepen my understanding of the contextual nature of their work. I also attended other school-related activities outside of their classrooms, such as a band concert, a school play, and an honor roll assembly, and I consistently visited and observed in other locations in the school, such as the library and the lunchroom. I wanted to gain as much knowledge and perspective about life at the two schools as I possibly could as I attempted to generate and construct the narratives shared here. It is important to note that I intentionally studied the broader landscape of the schools I describe in this book. As I drove to and from the schools, I observed the greenspace (or lack thereof) available in the communities. I paid special attention to supermarkets, housing structures (including Section VIII housing), and the kinds of parks, recreation centers, and libraries available (or not). I purposely gassed my car in the areas where I conducted research. I drove through unfamiliar neighborhoods. I bought food and ate in the restaurants in the communities. I walked to the local convenience store a few hundred yards away from Bridge Middle School. These experiences allowed me to deepen my knowledge, insights, and understanding of the school contexts and districts themselves.

I was typically in the schools for the entire day, one day a week. Most mornings, I was in the school before the bell rang, talking to students and teachers as well as reviewing my field notes or documents, which were recorded or collected, respectively, throughout the study. I observed students as they exited the school bus or their parents' cars. Although I participated in some of the classroom tasks, I was more observer than participant in the study. In some cases, I took part in group discussions or, as a former high school English teacher, I commented on themes as they emerged in a particular reading, especially in the language arts classes. However, most of the time, I simply observed the classroom and related contexts and recorded detailed and careful notes.

Document Analyses

In addition to participating in interviews and allowing me to observe their classroom practices, the teachers also shared their plan books and/or other documents that shaped their thinking about what they would teach, how, and why. Teachers and students allowed me to review their assignments as well, such as work sheets, novels they would read, lab assignments, and other materials, to help me gain a deeper understanding and knowledge base relative to the thought processes and goals that guided their decisions.

Moreover, the opportunity to analyze documents enabled me to draw connections between what I learned in interviews and what I observed.

I also read the local newspaper and paid special attention to stories about the districts and/or schools. I watched the local news, too, and was always listening for stories about Bridge Middle School and Stevenson High. Also, because the six White teachers learning to teach were in different schools, I listened for insight about their particular school sites as well. Although I conducted field research in a middle and high school, the six White teachers in this book taught in elementary schools, too, which allowed me to learn about the full range of students: elementary, middle, and high.

ANALYZING THE DATA

Data from interviews, observations, and documents I analyzed were hand coded. Essentially, my analysis followed a recursive, thematic process; as interviews and observations progressed, I used analytic induction and reasoning to develop thematic categories. The patterns of these thematic findings emerged from multiple data sources—observations, interviews, and document analyses—resulting in triangulation. For instance, when a teacher repeated a point several times throughout the study, I called this a "pattern." When what teachers articulated during interviews also became evident in their practices and actions, in documents, or in others' actions, I called this a "triangulational pattern." In my analyses, I attempted to uncover what urban educational researcher and dean Marvin Lynn expressed as the teachers' "thoughts, ideas, and histories" to understand and construct their stories.[6]

SITUATING MYSELF WITHIN THE STUDY AND THE STORIES

Throughout the representation of the stories and discussion, I deliberately use first person because, in a sense, I am telling my own narrative as much as I am telling the stories of the participants. I was living a story line myself as I spent so much time in these schools learning with these educators. As an African American male researcher and a former English teacher in a predominantly Black US secondary school, I attempted to understand the stories of these teachers while I reflected on my own practices, thoughts, and interactions. Thus, as I tell the stories of these educators, I share my own interactions, analyses, and interpretations to enhance their narratives. In addition, I use first person to distinguish my own experiences from those of the participants.

WHY NARRATIVES

We all live storied lives, and researchers—whether quantitative or qualitative—report their findings in a story format. Accordingly, we represent lived experiences through narrative. Thus, I have chosen to share what I learned about these teachers and their relationship to opportunity and diversity through stories or narratives. As a researcher, I constructed the stories based on what I observed, the documents I analyzed, and the interviews I conducted as well as my best attempts to make sense of what was happening based on my own experiences (including what I read, taught, and observed elsewhere). The idea is that teachers' (and others') stories provide an entry into the real human condition. Researchers study narratives that research participants tell and then shape broader narratives to convey results to consumers of research. In qualitative research, we have come to understand that "lived experiences can be translated into rich narrative stories useful for *both* teaching and research" [emphasis added].[7] Many narrative researchers believe that people come to see themselves situated within various story lines of events, situations, and experiences. Narratives provide people an opportunity to enter into the experiences of people they may not have access to otherwise. Thus, the narrative can be described as the study of the stories that people come to experience, live, represent, and tell in the world and in education.[8]

A BRIEF LOOK AT MY CURRENT RESEARCH

My colleagues Lori Delale-O'Connor, Ira Murray, and Adam Alvarez and I developed a survey, the Teachers and Race Talk Survey, one of the first survey instruments focused on teachers' beliefs about the roles and importance of race.[9] Among other factors, the survey attempts to capture teachers' reported beliefs about the role and importance of race in classroom discourse and learning, teachers' reported beliefs about their preparedness to discuss race in their work, and teachers' reported beliefs about whether they should discuss police violence against unarmed Black people. Researchers interested in capturing relationships between race and classroom talk have found the survey useful as it is being adapted for studies across the field of education. Implications from this research are outlined in my book *Rac(e)ing to Class: Confronting Poverty and Race in Schools and Classrooms*.[10] I have also begun studying the insights of people who are experiencing and have formerly experienced the juvenile justice system. This research attempts to more deeply understand how schools contribute to incarceration. What practices and policies propel a school-to-prison pipeline according to people who have experienced the juvenile justice system? How can we learn from those who have experienced the juvenile justice system to improve policies and practices in schools?

Overall, my research continues in the tradition to uncover more about how we build classroom ecologies and systems that promote racial justice and equity. Indeed, I believe knowing more about race, education, and opportunity structures can help us all fight for a better world that our young people deserve.

Notes

Introduction

1. G. Ladson-Billings, "From the Achievement Gap to the Education Debt: Understanding Achievement in U.S. Schools," *Educational Researcher* 35, no. 7 (2006): 3–12.
2. J. J. Irvine, foreword to *Culture, Curriculum, and Identity in Education*, ed. H. R. Milner (New York: Palgrave Macmillan, 2010), 12.
3. Irvine, xii.
4. T. C. Howard, *Why Race and Culture Matter in Schools: Closing the Achievement Gap in America's Classrooms* (New York: Teachers College Press, 2010).
5. M. W. Apple, "Understanding and Interrupting Neoliberalism and Neoconservatism in Education," *Pedagogies: An International Journal* 1, no. 1 (2006): 21–26.
6. P. L. Carter, *Keepin' It Real: School Success Beyond Black and White* (New York: Oxford University Press, 2005).
7. G. A. Duncan, "Critical Race Ethnography in Education Narrative, Inequality and the Problem of Epistemology," *Race, Ethnicity and Education* 8, no. 1 (2005): 93–114; M. A. Gooden and T. Y. Nowlin, "The Achievement Gap and No Child Left Behind: Is There a Connection?" in *No Child Left Behind and Other Federal Programs for Urban School Districts, 2006*, Advances in Educational Administration, vol. 9, ed. F. Brown and R. Hunter (Oxford: Elsevier, 2006), 231–48; C. Lewis, "African American Male Teachers in Public Schools: An Examination of Three Urban School Districts," *Teachers College Record* 108, no. 2 (2006): 224–45; D. B. Martin, "Researching Race in Mathematics Education," *Teachers College Record* 111, no. 2 (2009): 295–338; H. R. Milner, "Critical Race Theory and Interest Convergence as Analytic Tools in

Teacher Education Policies and Practices," *Journal of Teacher Education* 59, no. 4 (2008): 332–46.

8. K. Gutierrez and B. Rogoff, "Cultural Ways of Learning: Individual Traits or Repertoires of Practice," *Educational Researcher* 32, no. 5 (2002): 19–25; J. J. Irvine, *Educating Teachers for Diversity: Seeing with a Cultural Eye* (New York: Teachers College Press, 2003); C. D. Lee, *Culture, Literacy, and Learning: Blooming in the Midst of the Whirlwind* (New York: Teachers College Press, 2007); S. Nieto, *The Light in Their Eyes: Creating Multicultural Learning Communities* (New York: Teachers College Press, 1999); R. H. Sheets, "From Remedial to Gifted: Effects of Culturally Centered Pedagogy," *Theory into Practice* 34, no. 3 (1995): 186–93.
9. J. A. Banks, *Cultural Diversity and Education: Foundations, Curriculum, and Teaching* (Boston: Pearson, 2006); C. A. Grant and C. E. Sleeter, *Doing Multicultural Education for Achievement and Equity* (New York: Routledge, 2007).
10. P. Freire, *Pedagogy of the Oppressed* (New York: Continuum, 1998).
11. G. Gay, *Culturally Responsive Teaching: Theory, Research, and Practice* (New York: Teachers College Press, 2000), 116.
12. Sport management researchers John Singer and Kwame Agyemang, building on the important work of African American studies scholar and educational researcher Mwalimu Shuja, stress the important distinction between "schooling" and education. Singer and Shuja encourage those of us in education to shift our emphasis from schooling practices to educational practices. Understanding the distinct differences between the two (schooling and education) has compelling implications. See J. N. Singer and K. Agyemang, "Understanding the (Mis)education of African American Male College Athletes: Toward a Multilevel Framework" (presentation, College Sport Research Institute annual conference, University of North Carolina, Chapel Hill, NC, April 22, 2010); and M. J. Shuja, ed., *Too Much Schooling, Too Little Education: A Paradox of Black Life in White Societies* (Trenton, NJ: Africa World Press, 1994).
13. J. Sheurich and M. Young, "Coloring Epistemologies: Are Our Research Epistemologies Racially Biased?" *Educational Researcher* 26, no. 4 (1997): 4–16; M. Foster, "Race, Class, and Gender in Education Research: Surveying the Political Terrain," *Educational Policy* 13, no. 1 (1999): 77–85; G. Ladson-Billings, "Preparing Teachers for Diverse Student Populations: A Critical Race Theory Perspective," *Review of Research in Education* 24 (1999): 211–47; H. R. Milner, "Race, Culture, and Researcher Positionality: Working Through Dangers Seen, Unseen, and Unforeseen," *Educational Researcher* 36, no. 7 (2007): 388–400.

14. D. Y. Ford, *Reversing Underachievement Among Gifted Black Students: Promising Practices and Programs* (New York: Teachers College Press, 1996); H. R. Milner, "What Does Teacher Education Have to Do with Teaching? Implications for Diversity Studies," *Journal of Teacher Education* 61, nos. 1/2 (2010): 118–31; J. E. Morris, "Can Anything Good Come from Nazareth? Race, Class, and African American Schooling and Community in the Urban South and Midwest," *American Educational Research Journal* 41, no. 1 (2004): 69–112.
15. C. B. Dillard, "The Substance of Things Hoped for, the Evidence of Things Not Seen: Examining an Endarkened Feminist Epistemology in Educational Research and Leadership," *International Journal of Qualitative Studies in Education* 13, no. 6 (2000): 661–81.
16. E. W. Eisner, *The Educational Imagination: On the Design and Evaluation of School Programs* (New York: Macmillan College Publishing, 1994).

Chapter 1

1. It is well accepted and understood that race is socially constructed. In addition, race is constructed phenotypically and physically. See C. R. Monroe, "Coloring Educational Research: African American Life and Schooling as an Exemplar," *Educational Researcher* 42 (2013): 9–19; and J. N. Singer, "African American Male College Athletes' Narratives on Education and Racism," *Urban Education* 51, no. 9 (2016): 1065–95. People examine and interpret the physicality and outside markers of individuals in constructing race. Race is also contextually, geographically, and spatially constructed. See J. E. Morris and C. R. Monroe, "Why Study the U.S. South? The Nexus of Race and Place in Investigating Black Student Achievement," *Educational Researcher* 38 (2009): 21–36; W. F. Tate, "'Geography of Opportunity': Poverty, Place, and Educational Outcomes," *Educational Researcher* 37 no. 7 (2008): 397–411; and S. M. Williams, "African American Education in Rural Communities in the Deep South: 'Making the Impossible Possible,'" in *No Longer Forgotten: The Triumphs and Struggles of Rural Education in America*, ed. M. McShane and A. Smarick (Lanham, MD: Rowman and Littlefield, 2018), 29–44.

   For instance, race is conceptualized differently across continents and space. Race is also legally constructed as laws and policies influence what we know and do in society. See D. Bell, *Silent Covenants: Brown v. Board of Education and the Unfulfilled Hopes for Racial Reform* (Oxford: Oxford University Press, 2004).

   And race is historically constructed as historical moments and movements such as slavery, eugenics, Reconstruction, Jim Crow, redlining, desegregation, and busing influence policy and practice. See J. D. Anderson, *The Education of Blacks in the South* (Chapel Hill: University of North Carolina Press, 1988); and V. Siddle-Walker, *Their Highest Potential: An African American School Community in the Segregated South* (Chapel Hill: University of North Carolina Press, 1996).

Racism can be defined as "that which maintains or exacerbates inequality of opportunity among . . . groups. Racism can be expressed through stereotypes (racist beliefs), prejudice (racist emotions/affect) or discrimination (racist behaviours and practices)." G. Berman and Y. Paradies, "Racism, Disadvantage and Multiculturalism: Towards Effective Anti-Racist Praxis," *Ethnic and Racial Studies* 33, no. 2 (2010): 217.

Moreover, racism is a practice of injustice and discrimination that intentionally or unintentionally maintains the White status quo. It is important to note that racist acts may emerge deliberately or unintentionally. Carter defines racism as "the transformation of racial prejudice into . . . racism through the use of power directed against racial group(s) and their members, who are defined as inferior by individuals, institutional members, and leaders, which is reflected in policy and procedures with the *intentional* and *unintentional* [italics added] support and participation of the entire race and dominant culture." R. T. Carter, "Racism and Psychological and Emotional Injury: Recognizing and Assessing Race-Based Traumatic Stress," *Counseling Psychologist* 35, no. 1 (2007): 24–25. The practice of racism is a vicious move that can leave people of color in their workplace or in society marginalized while White people are assumed to be the norm by which others should be compared or measured.

2. K. D. Gutiérrez and B. Rogoff, "Cultural Ways of Learning: Individual Traits or Repertoires of Practice," *Educational Researcher* 32, no. 5 (2003): 19–25.
3. L. Johnson, "'My Eyes Have Been Opened': White Teachers and Racial Awareness," *Journal of Teacher Education* 53, no. 2 (2002): 153–67; A. E. Lewis, "There Is No 'Race' in the Schoolyard: Colorblind Ideology in an (Almost) All White School," *American Educational Research Journal* 38, no. 4 (2001): 781–811.
4. A. Lorde, *Zami: A New Spelling of My Name* (Trumansburg, NY: Crossing Press, 1981), 81.
5. J. A. Banks, "Citizenship Education and Diversity: Implications for Teacher Education," *Journal of Teacher Education* 52, no. 1 (2001): 12.
6. The curriculum can be defined as what students have the opportunity to learn in schools. See E. W. Eisner, *The Educational Imagination: On the Design and Evaluation of School Programs* (New York: MacMillan College Publishing,

1994); G. McCutcheon, *Developing the Curriculum: Solo and Group Deliberation* (Troy, NY: Educators' Press International, 2002). In *The Educational Imagination*, curriculum theorist Elliot Eisner postulates several important forms of the curriculum: the explicit curriculum, the implicit curriculum, and the null curriculum. See the introduction for a discussion of Eisner's perspective.

7. G. Gay and T. Howard, "Multicultural Teacher Education for the 21st Century," *Teacher Educator* 36, no. 1 (2000): 1–16; K. Zumwalt and E. Craig, "Teachers' Characteristics: Research on the Demographic Profile," in *Studying Teacher Education: The Report of the AERA Panel on Research and Teacher Education,* ed. M. C. Smith and K. M. Zeichner (Mahwah, NJ: Lawrence Erlbaum Associates, 2005), 111–56.
8. Adam Alvarez, "'Seeing Their Eyes in the Rearview Mirror': Identifying and Responding to Students' Challenging Experiences," *Equity & Excellence in Education* 50, no. 1 (2017): 53–67.
9. J. J. Irvine, *Educating Teachers for Diversity: Seeing with a Cultural Eye* (New York: Teachers College Press, 2003).
10. J. S. Bennett, "A Privileged Perspective: How a Racially Conscious White Male Teacher Interacts with His Students," *Whiteness and Education* 3, no. 1 (2018): 56–75.
11. D. Easton-Brooks, *Ethnic Matching: Academic Success of Students of Color* (Lanham, MD: Rowman & Littlefield), 2019).
12. E. O. McGee, "Devalued Black and Latino Racial Identities: A By-Product of STEM College Culture?" *American Educational Research Journal* 53, no. 6 (2016): 1626–62.
13. G. Gay, *Culturally Responsive Teaching: Theory, Research, and Practice* (New York: Teachers College Press, 2000), 205.
14. G. Ladson-Billings, "Toward a Theory of Culturally Relevant Pedagogy," *American Education Research Journal* 35 (1995): 465–91.
15. Irvine, *Educating Teachers for Diversity*; S. Nieto, "Lessons from Students on Creating a Chance to Dream," *Harvard Educational Review* 64, no. 4 (1994): 392–426; V. Siddle Walker, "Valued Segregated Schools for African American Children in the South, 1935–1969: A Review of Common Themes and Characteristics," *Review of Educational Research* 70, no. 3 (2000): 253–85.
16. C. E. Sleeter and H. R. Milner, "Researching Successful Efforts in Teacher Education to Diversify Teachers," in *Studying Diversity in Teacher Education*, ed. A. F. Ball and C. Tyson (Washington, DC: American Educational Research Association, 2011).

17. M. Foster, *Black Teachers on Teaching* (New York: New Press, 1997); Irvine, *Educating Teachers for Diversity*; H. R. Milner, "Developing a Multicultural Curriculum in a Predominantly White Teaching Context: Lessons from an African American Teacher in a Suburban English Classroom," *Curriculum Inquiry* 35, no. 4 (2005): 391–428.
18. Lewis, "There Is No 'Race' in the Schoolyard."
19. D. A. Bell, "Serving Two Masters: Integration Ideals and Client Interests in School Desegregation Litigation," *Yale Law Journal* 85, no. 4 (1976): 470–516.
20. H. R. Milner, "What Does Teacher Education Have to Do with Teaching? Implications for Diversity Studies," *Journal of Teacher Education* 61, nos. 1/2 (2010): 118–31.
21. Milner, 2012.
22. Milner, 2015.
23. Milner & Laughter, 2015.
24. Winn & Souto-Manning, 2017; Harris & Leonardo, 2018.
25. Culture can be defined as a group of people who possess and share deep-rooted connections such as values, beliefs, languages, customs, and norms. Yet culture is not a static concept, "a category for conveniently sorting people according to expected values, beliefs, and behaviors" (A. H. Dyson and C. Genishi, *The Need for Story: Cultural Diversity in Classroom and Community* [Boston: Harvard University Press, 1994], 3). Rather, culture is dynamic and encompasses other concepts that relate to its central meaning. The supplemental categories that make up culture include, but are not limited to, identity (race and ethnicity), socioeconomic status, class, economic status, sexual orientation, geography, and gender.
26. M. Foster, *Black Teachers on Teaching* (New York: New Press, 1997); T. C. Howard, "Telling Their Side of the Story: African American Students' Perceptions of Culturally Relevant Pedagogy," *Urban Review* 33, no. 2 (2001): 131–49; Irvine, *Educating Teachers for Diversity*.
27. J. A. Banks, *An Introduction to Multicultural Education*, 2nd ed. (Boston: Allyn and Bacon, 1998), 22–23.
28. L. Delpit, *Other People's Children: Cultural Conflict in the Classroom* (New York: New Press, 1995).
29. H. R. Milner, H. B. Cunningham, L. Delale-O'Connor, and E. G. Kestenberg, *"These Kids Are Out of Control": Why We Must Reimagine "Classroom Management" for Equity* (Thousand Oaks, CA: Corwin, 2018).
30. K. D. Gutiérrez and B. Rogoff, "Cultural Ways of Learning: Individual Traits or Repertoires of Practice," *Educational Researcher* 32, no. 5 (2003): 19–25.

31. Gutiérrez and Rogoff, 24.
32. Classroom management continues to be a serious concern for most educators, especially new educators (see S. A. Melnick and D. G. Meister, "A Comparison of Beginning and Experienced Teachers' Concerns," *Educational Research Quarterly* 31, no. 3 [2008]: 39–56). Educators' concerns are sometimes exacerbated when considering classroom management in urban and highly diverse settings. In the thirty-ninth Annual Gallup Poll, Rose and Gallup found that the public consistently ranked "discipline" as one of the top five problems that schools face (L. C. Rose and A. M. Gallup, "The 39th Annual Phi Delta Kappa/Gallup Poll of the Public's Attitude Toward the Public Schools," *Phi Delta Kappan* 89, no. 1 [2007]: 33–45), and White educators, in particular, consistently point to classroom management with culturally diverse students as one of their weakest areas of preparation (H. R. Milner, "Disrupting Deficit Notions of Difference: Counter-Narratives of Teachers and Community in Urban Education," *Teaching and Teacher Education* 24, no. 6 [2008]: 1573–98).
33. Delpit, *Other People's Children.*
34. P. A. Noguera, "Schools, Prisons, and Social Implications of Punishment: Rethinking Disciplinary Practices," *Theory into Practice* 42, no. 4 (2003): 341–50.
35. Milner et al., "*These Kids Are Out of Control.*"
36. M. Haberman, "Pedagogy of Poverty Versus Good Teaching," *Phi Delta Kappan* 73, no. 4 (1991): 290–93.
37. J. Anyon, "Social Class and the Hidden Curriculum of Work," *Journal of Education* 162, no. 1 (1980): 366–91; Haberman, "Pedagogy of Poverty Versus Good Teaching"; J. Kozol, *The Shame on a Nation* (New York: Crown Books, 2005).
38. R. J. Skiba, R. S. Michael, A. D. Nardo, and R. L. Peterson, "The Color of Discipline: Sources of Racial and Gender Disproportionality in School Punishment," *Urban Review* 34, no. 4 (2002): 317.
39. Skiba et al., "The Color of Discipline."
40. H. R. Milner, *Rac(e)ing to Class: Confronting Poverty and Race in Schools and Classrooms* (Cambridge, MA: Harvard Education Press, 2015).
41. P. McIntosh, "White Privilege: Unpacking the Invisible Knapsack," *Independent School* 90, no. 49 (1990): 31–36.
42. J. M. Henslin, *Essentials of Sociology: A Down-to-Earth Approach*, 5th ed. (Boston: Pearson, 2004), 174.

43. I. Randolph-McCree and E. Pristoop, "The Funding Gap 2005: Low-Income and Minority Students Shortchanged by Most States," Special Report by the Education Trust (Washington, DC: Education Trust, 2005), 2.
44. M. Cochran-Smith, "Uncertain Allies: Understanding the Boundaries of Race and Teaching," *Harvard Educational Review* 65, no. 4 (1995): 547.
45. G. Ladson-Billings and B. Tate, "Toward a Critical Race Theory of Education," *Teachers College Record* 97, no. 1 (1995): 47–67.
46. M. W. Apple, "Understanding and Interrupting Neoliberalism and Neoconservatism in Education," *Pedagogies: An International Journal* 1, no. 1 (2006): 22.
47. G. Ladson-Billings, "From the Achievement Gap to the Education Debt: Understanding Achievement in U.S. Schools," *Educational Researcher* 35, no. 7 (2006): 3–12.
48. J. MacLeod, *Ain't No Makin' It: Aspirations and Attainment in a Low-Income Neighborhood* (San Francisco: Westview Press, 1995), 11.
49. B. M. Gordon, "The Necessity of African-American Epistemology for Educational Theory and Practice," *Journal of Education* 172, no. 3 (1990): 88–106.
50. D. Y. Ford, *Reversing Underachievement Among Gifted Black Students: Promising Practices and Programs* (New York: Teachers College Press, 1996), 84.
51. Milner, "Disrupting Deficit Notions of Difference."
52. M. Haberman, "The Pedagogy of Poverty Versus Good Teaching," *Phi Delta Kappan*, December 1991, 290–94.
53. M. Winn, *Justice on Both Sides: Transforming Education Through Restorative Justice* (Cambridge, MA: Harvard Education Press, 2018).
54. C. M. Steele, "A Threat in the Air: How Stereotypes Shape Intellectual Identity and Performance," *American Psychologist* 52 (1997): 613–29.
55. S. M. Williams and A. A. Grooms, *Educational Opportunity in Rural Contexts: The Politics of Place* (Charlotte, NC: Information Age, 2015).
56. F. Rios, ed., *Teacher Thinking in Cultural Contexts* (Albany: State University of New York Press, 1996).
57. W. F. Tate IV, "'Geography of Opportunity': Poverty, Place, and Educational Outcomes," *Educational Researcher* 37, no. 7 (2008): 397–411.
58. J. E. Morris and C. R. Monroe, "Why Study the U.S. South? The Nexus of Race and Place in Investigating Black Student Achievement," *Educational Researcher* 38 (2009): 21–36.
59. P. E. Barton, *Parsing the Achievement Gap: Baseline for Tracking Progress* (Princeton, NJ: Educational Testing Services, 2003).
60. Tate, "'Geography of Opportunity.'"

61. M. Roza, *How Districts Shortchange Low-Income and Minority Students* (Washington, DC: Education Trust, 2006), 11.
62. H. R. Milner, "Beyond a Test Score: Explaining Opportunity Gaps in Educational Practice," *Journal of Black Studies* 43, no. 6 (2012): 693–718.
63. J. A. Banks, *Cultural Diversity and Education: Foundations, Curriculum, and Teaching* (Boston: Pearson, 2006); T. C. Howard, *Why Race and Culture Matter in Schools: Closing the Achievement Gap in America's Classrooms* (New York: Teachers College Press, 2010); Milner, "Developing a Multicultural Curriculum."
64. Banks, *An Introduction to Multicultural Education*, 23.
65. C. Jenks, J. O. Lee, and B. Kanpol, "Approaches to Multicultural Education in Preservice Teacher Education: Philosophical Frameworks and Models for Teaching," *Urban Review* 33, no. 2 (2001): 87.
66. J. C. Laughter, "Rethinking Assumptions of Demographic Privilege: Diversity Among White Preservice Teachers," *Teaching and Teacher Education* 27 (2011): 43–50.
67. P. Freire, *Pedagogy of the Oppressed* (New York: Continuum, 1998).
68. McCutcheon, *Developing the Curriculum*.

Chapter 2

1. I am grateful to Vincent Windrow for helping me understand the importance of a learner's assuming the proper posture to learn. Teachers can teach when students are ready to learn.
2. P. Freire, *Pedagogy of the Oppressed* (New York: Continuum, 1998).
3. C. R. Monroe and J. E. Obidah, "The Influence of Cultural Synchronization on a Teacher's Perceptions of Disruption: A Case Study of an African American Middle School Classroom," *Journal of Teacher Education* 55, no. 3 (2004): 256–68.
4. L. Delpit, *Other People's Children: Cultural Conflict in the Classroom* (New York: New Press, 1995).
5. G. Ladson-Billings, "Fighting for Our Lives: Preparing Teachers to Teach African American Students," *Journal of Teacher Education* 51, no. 3 (2000): 206–14.
6. H. R. Milner, *Rac(e)ing to Class: Confronting Poverty and Race in Schools and Classrooms* (Cambridge, MA: Harvard Education Press, 2015); H. R. Milner, "Race, Talk, Opportunity Gaps, and Curriculum Shifts in (Teacher) Education," *Literacy Research: Theory, Method, and Practice* 66, no. 1 (2017): 73–94; H. R. Milner, "Where's the Race in Culturally Relevant Pedagogy?" *Teachers College Record* 119, no. 1 (2017): 1–32.

Chapter 3

1. J. A. Banks, "Multicultural Education and Curriculum Transformation," *Journal of Negro Education* 64, no. 4 (1995): 392.
2. J. A. Banks, "Teaching Literacy for Social Justice and Global Citizenship," *Language Arts* 81, no. 1 (2003): 18.
3. b. hooks, *Teaching to Transgress: Education as the Practice of Freedom* (New York: Routledge, 1994).
4. C. West, *Race Matters* (Boston: Beacon Press, 1993).
5. W. E. B. DuBois, *The Souls of Black Folk* (New York: Fawcett, 1903).
6. P. McIntosh, "White Privilege: Unpacking the Invisible Knapsack," *Independent School* 90, no. 49 (1990): 31–36.
7. A. E. Lewis, "There is No 'Race' in the Schoolyard: Colorblind Ideology in an (Almost) All White School," *American Educational Research Journal* 38, no. 4 (2001): 781–811.
8. E. Buendia, A. Gitlin, and F. Doumbia, "Working the Pedagogical Borderlands: An African Critical Pedagogue Teaching Within an ESL Context," *Curriculum Inquiry* 3, no. 3 (2003): 291–320.
9. C. A. Banks and J. A. Banks, "Equity Pedagogy: An Essential Component of Multicultural Education," *Theory into Practice* 34 (1995): 153.
10. P. Freire, *Pedagogy of the Oppressed* (New York: Continuum, 1998).
11. Buendia et al., "Working."
12. Banks, "Teaching Literacy," 18.

Chapter 4

1. To substantiate this point, see the important work of Ladson-Billings, which showcases successful teachers from different racial backgrounds of African American students: G. Ladson-Billings, "Toward a Theory of Culturally Relevant Pedagogy," *American Education Research Journal* 35 (1995): 465–91.
2. For a thorough overview of this line of thinking, see S. Fordham and J. A. Ogbu, "Black Students' School Success: Coping with the Burden of 'Acting White,'" *Urban Review* 18, no. 3 (1986): 176–206.
3. For good examples of counternarratives, see J. E. Morris, "Can Anything Good Come from Nazareth? Race, Class, and African American Schooling and Community in the Urban South and Midwest," *American Educational Research Journal* 41, no. 1 (2004): 69–112; and H. R. Milner, "Disrupting Deficit Notions of Difference: Counter-Narratives of Teachers and Community in Urban Education," *Teaching and Teacher Education* 24, no. 6 (2008): 1573–98.

4. R. Suskind, *A Hope in the Unseen: An American Odyssey from the Inner City to the Ivy League* (New York: Broadway, 1998).
5. V. Siddle Walker, "Valued Segregated Schools for African American Children in the South, 1935–1969: A Review of Common Themes and Characteristics," *Review of Educational Research* 70, no. 3 (2000): 253–85.
6. Hip-hop, some would argue, is a culture that supports youth to engage in customs and experiences that allow them to express themselves through music, film, art, and other forms of expression that can run counter to more mainstream and dominant forms of living and being in society. Hill explains that educators have successfully incorporated features of hip-hop culture into the preK–12 classroom to make teaching and learning more relevant, responsive, and accessible to youth (M. L. Hill, *Beats, Rhymes, and Classroom Life: Hip-Hop Pedagogy and the Politics of Identity* [New York: Teachers College Press, 2009]). From his empirical perspective, hip-hop can be used to "improve student motivation, teach critical media literacy, foster critical consciousness, and transmit disciplinary knowledge" (2).
7. J. G. Irizarry, "Representin': Drawing from Hip-Hop and Urban Youth Culture to Inform Teacher Education," *Education and Urban Society* 41, no. 4 (2009): 490.
8. M. Haberman, "Pedagogy of Poverty Versus Good Teaching," *Phi Delta Kappan* 73, no. 4 (1991): 290–93.
9. American Society for the Positive Care of Children, http://americanspcc.org/bullying/statistics-and-information/.
10. Edudemic, "This Is How Teens Are Using Social Media," www.edudemic.com/2013/07/this-is-how-teens-are-using-social-media.
11. J. P. Gee, "The Classroom of Popular Culture: What Video Games Can Teach Us About Making Students Want to Learn," *Harvard Education Letter* 21, no. 6 (2005).
12. J. Duncan-Andrade and E. Morrell, "Turn Up That Radio, Teacher: Popular Cultural Pedagogy in New Century Urban Schools," *Journal of School Leadership* 15 (2005): 284–304.
13. P. Freire, *Pedagogy of the Oppressed* (New York: Continuum, 1998).
14. Freire, *Pedagogy of the Oppressed*, 53.
15. G. McCutcheon, *Developing the Curriculum: Solo and Group Deliberation* (Troy, NY: Educators' Press International, 2002).
16. Duncan-Andrade and Morrell, "Turn Up That Radio, Teacher," 284.
17. Duncan-Andrade and Morrell, "Turn Up That Radio, Teacher."

18. M. Foster, *Black Teachers on Teaching* (New York: New Press, 1997); J. J. Irvine, *Educating Teachers for Diversity: Seeing with a Cultural Eye* (New York: Teachers College Press, 2003).
19. Foster, *Black Teachers on Teaching*; M. Foster, "The Politics of Race: Through the Eyes of African-American Teachers," *Journal of Education* 172 (1990): 123–41; R. W. Irvine and J. J. Irvine, "The Impact of the Desegregation Process on the Education of Black Students: Key Variables," *Journal of Negro Education* 52 (1983): 410–22; S. King, "The Limited Presence of African-American Teachers," *Review of Educational Research* 63, no. 2 (1993): 115–49.
20. Siddle Walker, "Valued Segregated Schools," 265–66.
21. V. Siddle Walker, *Their Highest Potential: An African American School Community in the Segregated South* (Chapel Hill: University of North Carolina Press, 1996).
22. L. C. Tillman, "(Un)Intended Consequences? The Impact of the *Brown v. Board of Education* Decision on the Employment Status of Black Educators," *Education and Urban Society* 36, no. 3 (2004): 282.
23. V. O. Pang and R. Gibson, "Concepts of Democracy and Citizenship: Views of African American Teachers," *The Social Studies* 92, no. 6 (2001): 260–61.
24. Freire, *Pedagogy of the Oppressed*, 23.
25. Anya Kamenetz, "Study Finds Students of All Races Prefer Teachers of Color," NPR Ed, October 7, 2016, https://www.npr.org/sections/ed/2016/10/07/496717541/study-finds-students-of-all-races-prefer-teachers-of-color; H. Y. S. Cherng and P. F. Halpin, "The Importance of Minority Teachers: Student Perceptions of Minority Versus White Teachers," *Educational Researcher* 45, no. 7 (2016): 407–20.
26. Cherng and Halpin, 407.
27. Siddle Walker, *Their Highest Potential.*
28. G. McAllister and J. J. Irvine, "The Role of Empathy in Teaching Culturally Diverse Students: A Qualitative Study of Teachers' Beliefs," *Journal of Teacher Education* 53, no. 5 (2002): 433–43.
29. P. H. Collins, *Black Feminist Thought: Knowledge, Consciousness, and the Politics of Empowerment: Perspectives on Gender*, vol. 2 (New York: Routledge, 1991); Irvine, *Educating Teachers for Diversity.*
30. H. R. Milner, "A Black Male Teacher's Culturally Responsive Practices," *Journal of Negro Education* 85, no. 4 (2016): 417–32; H. R. Milner, "Culturally Relevant, Purpose-Driven Teaching and Learning in a Middle School Social Studies Classroom," *Multicultural Education* 21, no. 2 (2014): 9–17; H. R. Milner, "Culturally Relevant Pedagogy in a Diverse Urban Classroom," *Urban Review* 43, no. 1 (2011): 66–89; H. R. Milner and F. B. Tenore, "Classroom

Management in Diverse Classrooms," *Urban Education* 45, no. 5 (2010): 560–603; H. R. Milner, "Disrupting Deficit Notions of Difference: Counter-Narratives of Teachers and Community in Urban Education," *Teaching and Teacher Education* 24, no. 6 (2008): 1573–98; H. R. Milner, "The Promise of Black Teachers' Success with Black Students," *Educational Foundations* 20, no. 3–4 (2006): 89–104.

Chapter 5

1. C. E. Sleeter, "Epistemological Diversity in Research on Preservice Teacher Preparation for Historically Underserved Children," *Review of Research in Education* 25 (2001): 209–50.
2. H. R. Milner, "Reflection, Racial Competence, and Critical Pedagogy: How Do We Prepare Preservice Teachers to Pose Tough Questions?" *Race, Ethnicity, and Education* 6, no. 2 (2003): 193–208.
3. F. B. Tenore, "An Analysis of the Subject Positions Offered and Denied in Three Conceptions of Teacher Development" (major area paper, Department of Teaching and Learning, Vanderbilt University, 2009); P. Grossman et al., "Teaching Practice: A Cross-Professional Perspective," *Teachers College Record* 111, no. 9 (2009): 2055–2100.
4. L. Darling-Hammond, R. Chung, and F. Frelow, "Variation in Teacher Preparation: How Well Do Different Pathways Prepare Teachers to Teach?" *Journal of Teacher Education* 53, no. 4 (2002): 286–302.
5. H. R. Milner and M. Smithey, "How Teacher Educators Created a Course Curriculum to Challenge and Enhance Preservice Teachers' Thinking and Experience with Diversity," *Teaching Education* 14, no. 3 (2003): 293–305.
6. J. C. Laughter, "Change Agents: Empowering White Female Preservice Teachers Through Dialogue and Counter-Narrative" (PhD diss., Vanderbilt University, 2009), http://etd.library.vanderbilt.edu/available/ etd-06302009-150423/.
7. I realize that there is no such thing as a homogeneous school.
8. H. R. Milner, H. B. Cunningham, L. Delale-O'Connor, and E. G. Kestenberg, *"These Kids Are Out of Control": Why We Must Reimagine "Classroom Management" for Equity* (Thousand Oaks, CA: Corwin, 2018).
9. B. D. Tatum, *"Why Are All the Black Kids Sitting Together in the Cafeteria?" and Other Conversations About Race* (New York: Basic Books, 1997).
10. H. R. Milner, "But Good Intentions Are Not Enough: Theoretical and Philosophical Relevance in Teaching Students of Color," in *White Teachers/ Diverse Classrooms: A Guide to Building Inclusive Schools, Promoting High*

Expectations and Eliminating Racism*, ed. J. Landsman and C. W. Lewis (Sterling, VA: Stylus Publishers, 2006), 79–90.

11. M. Cochran-Smith, "Learning and Unlearning: The Education of Teacher Educators," *Teaching and Teacher Education* 19 (2003): 5–28.
12. M. Cochran-Smith, "Uncertain Allies: Understanding the Boundaries of Race and Teaching," *Harvard Educational Review* 65, no. 4 (1995): 546.
13. E. L. Brown, "What Precipitates Change in Cultural Diversity Awareness During a Multicultural Course: The Message or the Method?" *Journal of Teacher Education* 55, no. 4 (2004): 326. Also see B. D. Tatum, "Talking About Race, Learning About Racism: The Application of Racial Identity Development Theory in the Classroom," *Harvard Educational Review* 62, no. 1 (1992): 1–24.
14. E. Ellsworth, "'Why Doesn't This Feel Empowering?' Working Through the Repressive Myths of Critical Pedagogy," *Harvard Educational Review* 59, no. 3 (1989): 297–324.
15. G. Ladson-Billings, "Preparing Teachers for Diverse Student Populations: A Critical Race Theory Perspective," *Review of Research in Education* 24 (1999): 211–47.
16. M. M. Merryfield, "Why Aren't Teachers Being Prepared to Teach for Diversity, Equity, and Global Interconnectedness? A Study of Lived Experiences in the Making of Multicultural and Global Educators," *Teaching and Teacher Education* 16 (2000): 430.
17. H. R. Milner, "Preservice Teachers' Learning About Cultural and Racial Diversity: Implications for Urban Education," *Urban Education* 41, no. 4 (2006): 343–75; H. R. Milner, "Race, Narrative Inquiry, and Self-Study in Curriculum and Teacher Education," *Education and Urban Society* 39, no. 4 (2007): 584–609; H. R. Milner, "Critical Race Theory and Interest Convergence as Analytic Tools in Teacher Education Policies and Practices," *Journal of Teacher Education* 59, no. 4 (2008): 332–46.
18. K. S. Cockrell et al., "Coming to Terms with 'Diversity' and 'Multiculturalism' in Teacher Education: Learning About Our Students, Changing Our Practice," *Teaching and Teacher Education* 5 (1999): 363.
19. Ladson-Billings, "Preparing Teachers for Diverse Student Populations," 221.
20. K. Zeichner, "Reflections of a University-Based Teacher Educator on the Future of College and University-Based Teacher Education," *Journal of Teacher Education* 57, no. 3 (2006): 328.
21. Here, I am referring to the course syllabus, and the goals and objectives outlined on it as policy. See J. Agee, "Negotiating a Teaching Identity: An African

American Teacher's Struggle to Teach in Test-Driven Contexts," *Teachers College Record* 106, no. 4 (2004): 747–74; A. D. Dixson, "What's Race Got to Do with It? Race, Racial Identity Development, and Teacher Preparation," in *Race, Ethnicity, and Education: The Influences of Racial and Ethnic Identity in Education*, ed. H. R. Milner and E. W. Ross (Westport, CT: Greenwood/Praeger, 2006), 19–36; G. Gay, *Culturally Responsive Teaching: Theory, Research, and Practice* (New York: Teachers College Press, 2000).

22. B. D. Tatum, "Professional Development: An Important Partner for Antiracist Teacher Education," in *Racism and Racial Inequality: Implications for Teacher Education,* ed. S. H. King and L. A. Castenell (Washington, DC: AACTA Publications, 2001), 53.
23. Dixson, "What's Race Got to Do with It?" 24; Agee, "Negotiating a Teaching Identity," 749.
24. G. Ladson-Billings, "Silences as Weapons: Challenges of a Black Professor Teaching White Students," *Theory into Practice* 35 (1996): 79.
25. Cochran-Smith, "Uncertain Allies."
26. L. Delpit, *Other People's Children: Cultural Conflict in the Classroom* (New York: W.W. Norton, 1995).
27. B. D. Tatum, "Teaching White Students About Racism: The Search for White Allies and the Restoration of Hope," *Teachers College Record* 95, no. 4 (1994): 462–76.

Chapter 6

1. b. hooks, *Teaching to Transgress: Education as the Practice of Freedom* (New York: Routledge, 1994).
2. L. Delpit, "The Silenced Dialogue: Power and Pedagogy in Educating Other People's Children," *Harvard Educational Review* 58, no. 3 (1988): 280–99.
3. M. Morris, *Pushout: The Criminalization of Black Girls in Schools* (New York: New Press, 2016).
4. I am grateful to William Moseley, then head of school at the Ensworth School in Nashville, Tennessee, for sharing this idea with me.
5. For an excellent discussion of this issue, see M. A. Gooden, "What Does Racism Have to Do with Leadership? Countering the Idea of Color-Blind Leadership: A Reflection on Race and Growing Pressures of Principalship," *Education Foundations*, Winter/Spring 2012.
6. M. J. Shujaa, ed., *Too Much Schooling, Too Little Education: A Paradox of Black Life in White Societies* (Trenton, NJ: Africa World Press, 1994).

7. J. A. Banks, *Cultural Diversity and Education: Foundations, Curriculum and Teaching*, 6th ed. (Boston: Pearson, 2015); L. Shulman, "Knowledge and Teaching: Foundations of the New Reform," *Harvard Educational Review* 57 (1987): 1–22.
8. L. C. Tillman, "(Un)Intended Consequences? The Impact of the *Brown v. Board of Education* Decision on the Employment Status of Black Educators," *Education and Urban Society* 36, no. 3 (2004): 280–303; V. Siddle Walker, *Their Highest Potential: An African American School Community in the Segregated South* (Chapel Hill: University of North Carolina Press, 1996).
9. H. R. Milner, *Rac(e)ing to Class: Confronting Poverty and Race in Schools and Classrooms* (Cambridge, MA: Harvard Education Press, 2015).
10. Milner, *Rac(e)ing to Class*; E. O. McGee and D. Stovall, "Reimagining Critical Race Theory in Education: Mental Health, Healing, and the Pathway to Liberatory Praxis," *Educational Theory* 65, no. 5 (2015): 491–511; T. C. Howard, *Why Race and Culture Matter: Closing the Achievement Gap in American Classrooms* (New York: Teachers College Press, 2010).
11. McGee and Stovall, "Reimagining Critical Race Theory."
12. Milner, *Rac(e)ing to Class.*
13. C. R. Monroe, "Colorizing Educational Research: African American Life and Schooling as an Exemplar," *Educational Researcher* 42, no. 1 (2013): 9–19.
14. Monroe, "Colorizing Educational Research."
15. G. Ladson-Billings and W. F. Tate, "Toward a Critical Race Theory of Education," *Teachers College Record* 97, no. 1 (1995): 47.
16. C. I. Harris, "Whiteness as Property," *Harvard Law Review 106* (1992): 1707.
17. J. D. Anderson, *The Education of Blacks in the South, 1860–1935* (Chapel Hill, NC: University of North Carolina Press, 1988).
18. H. R. Milner, *Start Where You Are, but Don't Stay There* (Cambridge, MA: Harvard Education Press, 2010); Milner, *Rac(e)ing to Class.*
19. D. W. Sue et al., "Racial Microaggressions in Everyday Life: Implications for Clinical Practice," *American Psychologist* 62, no. 4 (2007): 271.
20. McGee and Stovall, "Reimagining Critical Race Theory."
21. Milner, *Rac(e)ing to Class.*
22. Milner, *Rac(e)ing to Class*; Milner, *Start Where You Are.*
23. Milner, *Rac(e)ing to Class.*
24. McGee and Stovall, "Reimagining Critical Race Theory."
25. W. A. Smith, M. Hung, and J. D. Franklin, "Racial Battle Fatigue and the Miseducation of Black Men: Racial Microaggressions, Societal Problems, and Environmental Stress," *Journal of Negro Education* 80, no. 1 (2011): 63–82.

26. G. Ladson-Billings, *The Dreamkeepers: Successful Teachers of African American Children* (San Francisco: Jossey-Bass, 2009); Milner, *Start Where You Are.*
27. M. Rowe, "Micro-affirmations and Micro-inequities," *Journal of the International Ombudsman Association* 1, no. 1 (2008): 45–48.
28. R. Kohli and D. G. Solórzano, "Teachers, Please Learn Our Names!: Racial Microaggressions and the K–12 Classroom," *Race Ethnicity and Education* 15, no. 4 (2012): 441–62.
29. T. C. Howard, "Why Race, Culture and Trauma Matter: Addressing Real Equity for Marginalized Populations" (lecture presented at the University of Pittsburgh Center for Urban Education, Pittsburgh, PA, October 2017).
30. Howard, "Race, Culture, and Trauma."
31. Morris, *Pushout.*
32. P. Freire, *Pedagogy of the Oppressed* (New York: Continuum, 1998).

Conclusions and Recommendations for Practice

1. D. A. Bell, "*Brown v. Board of Education* and the Interest-Convergence Dilemma," *Harvard* Law Review 93, no. 3 (1980): 518–33.
2. A. G. Hilliard, "Behavioral Style, Culture, and Teaching and Learning," *Journal of Negro Education* 61, no. 3 (1992): 375.
3. E. W. Eisner, *The Educational Imagination: On the Design and Evaluation of School Programs* (New York: Macmillan College Publishing, 1994); G. McCutcheon, *Developing the Curriculum: Solo and Group Deliberation* (Troy, NY: Educators' Press International, 2002).
4. H. R. Milner, H. B. Cunningham, L. Delale-O'Connor, and E. G. Kestenberg, *"These Kids Are Out of Control": Why We Must Reimagine "Classroom Management" for Equity* (Thousand Oaks, CA: Corwin, 2018).
5. P. A. Noguera, "Schools, Prisons, and Social Implications of Punishment: Rethinking Disciplinary Practices," *Theory into Practice* 42, no. 4 (2003): 341–50.
6. G. Ladson-Billings, *The Dreamkeepers: Successful Teachers of African American Children* (San Francisco: Jossey-Bass, 2009); H. R. Milner, *Start Where You Are but Don't Stay There: Understanding Diversity, Opportunity Gaps, and Teaching in Today's Classrooms* (Cambridge, MA: Harvard Education Press, 2010).
7. M. W. Shujaa, ed., *Too Much Schooling, Too Little Education: A Paradox of Black Life in White Societies* (Trenton, NJ: Africa World Press, 1994).
8. P. Freire, *Pedagogy of the Oppressed* (New York: Continuum, 1998).

9. C. West, *Restoring Hope: Conversations on the Future of Black America*, ed. K. S. Sealey (Boston: Beacon Press, 1997), xii.

Epilogue

1. T. C. Howard, *Why Race and Culture Matter in Schools: Closing the Achievement Gap in America's Classrooms* (New York: Teachers College Press, 2010); G. Ladson-Billings, *The Dreamkeepers: Successful Teachers of African American Children*, 2nd ed. (San Francisco: Jossey-Bass, 2009).
2. G. Gay, *Culturally Responsive Teaching: Theory, Research, and Practice*, 3rd ed. (New York: Teachers College Press, 2018); Howard, *Why Race and Culture Matter in Schools.*
3. P. Demerath et al., "Decoding Success: A Middle-Class Logic of Individual Advancement in a U.S. Suburb and High School," *Teachers College Record* 112, no. 12 (2010).
4. Ladson-Billings, *The Dreamkeepers*, 147.
5. I. Seidman, *Interviewing as Qualitative Research: A Guide for Researchers in Education and the Social Sciences* (New York: Teachers College Press, 1998).
6. M. Lynn, "Education for the Community: Exploring the Culturally Relevant Practices of Black Male Teachers," *Teachers College Record* 108, no. 12 (2006): 2501.
7. S. P. Rushton, "Using Narrative Inquiry to Understand a Student-Teacher's Practical Knowledge While Teaching in an Inner-City School," *Urban Review* 3, no. 1 (2004): 61–79.
8. M. He, "A Narrative Inquiry of Cross-Cultural Lives: Lives in the North American Academy," *Journal of Curriculum Studies* 34, no. 5 (2002): 513–33; J. Phillion, "Becoming a Narrative Inquirer in a Multicultural Landscape," *Journal of Curriculum Studies* 34, no. 5 (2002): 535–56.
9. H. R. Milner, L. A. Delale-O'Connor, I. E. Murray, and A. J. Alvarez, Teachers and Race Talk Survey, 2016, https://pitt.co1.qualtrics.com/jfe/form/SV_cIsNBHIZlAfqx6t.
10. H. R. Milner, *Rac(e)ing to Class: Confronting Poverty and Race in Schools and Classrooms* (Cambridge, MA: Harvard Education Press, 2015).

About the Author

H. RICHARD MILNER IV is Cornelius Vanderbilt Distinguished Professor of Education and Professor of Education in the Department of Teaching and Learning at Peabody College of Vanderbilt University in Nashville, Tennessee. He holds courtesy professorships in the Department of Sociology and the Department of Leadership, Policy, and Organizations at Vanderbilt. His research, teaching, and policy interests concern urban education, teacher education, African American literature, and the social context of education. Professor Milner's research and scholarly contributions have been recognized by the American Educational Research Association (AERA) with an Early Career Award and an Innovations in Research on Diversity in Teacher Education Award. In 2018, he was selected as the youngest ever to give the prestigious AERA *Brown vs. Board of Education* lecture to a record number of attendees in Washington, DC. He is also a Fellow of AERA and has received the Carl A. Grant Multicultural Award from the National Association for Multicultural Education as well as the John Dewey Society Outstanding Achievement Award for efforts to relate research to practice. He is editor-in-chief of the journal *Urban Education* and has published seven books, including *Rac(e)ing to Class: Confronting Poverty and Race in Schools and Classrooms* (Harvard Education Press, 2015), *"These Kids Are Out of Control": Why We Must Reimagine "Classroom Management" for Equity* (Corwin Press, 2018), and the *Handbook of*

Urban Education (Routledge Press, 2014). Professor Milner consults with schools, districts, and universities. He can be reached at h.richardmilner@gmail.com.

Index